RATIONAL DECISION

NOMOS:

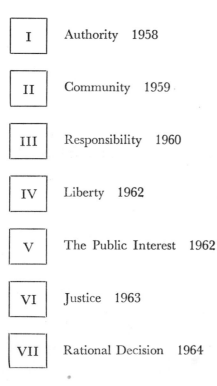

Yearbook of the American Society for Political and Legal Philosophy

NOMOS
VII

RATIONAL
DECISION

Edited by CARL J. FRIEDRICH

THERTON PRESS   70 FIFTH AVENUE, NEW YORK   1967

NOMOS VII: RATIONAL DECISION

Carl J. Friedrich, editor

Copyright © 1964 by Atherton Press

Copyright under International, Pan American, and Universal Copyright Conventions

Atherton Press
70 Fifth Avenue, New York, New York 10011

Library of Congress Catalog Card Number 64-19823

Printed in the United States of America

SECOND PRINTING: JANUARY 1967

PREFACE

Rational Decision, like its predecessors, was the choice of the membership of the American Society for Political and Legal Philosophy for its annual meeting of 1962, held in conjunction with the American Philosophical Association (Eastern Division). It will be followed by *Revolution* and, hopefully, *Equality.* The treatment is somewhat independent of the actual program, since one basic paper presented, that of Judith Shklar, was considerably altered, and an important dimension added by the inclusion of Heinz Eulau's behavorial study. Unfortunately, Ernest Nagel and Harry Kalven, Jr., were unable to complete papers dealing with their comments at the session, Sheldon Wolin was prevented from attending by illness, and Charles E. Lindblom was called to India and thereby prevented from adding his remarks. I decided to include his summary comments, as well as remarks by Felix E. Oppenheim and Sir Isaiah Berlin, in the brief chapters at the end. I was fortunately able to enrich the volume through the paper contributed by Harvey Mansfield, Jr., who significantly broadened the historical perspectives which I myself undertook to open up. The papers by Gottfried Dietze, A. A. Mavrinac, and Margaret Spahr were developed from contributions to the discussion.

The topic of rational decision presents the student of philosophical politics with the vast and inexhaustible problem of rationality in its relation to decision-making. The present interest in decision-making among social scientists has tended to apply inadequate attention to the problem of rationality. It is hoped that the *Nomos* volume will help in filling this gap, and the editor hopes that it will be understood as such; for he is well aware of the fact that many other aspects of the analysis of decision-making deserve attention and have been treated more fully elsewhere. The interdependence of institution, decision, and policy, often placed in opposition, is perhaps most clearly seen in considering the question of rationality. Or was the poet right when he claimed that in the end "chance governs all"?

CARL J. FRIEDRICH

CONTENTS

CONTRIBUTORS

SIR ISAIAH BERLIN
Political Science, Oxford University

GOTTFRIED DIETZE
Political Science, Johns Hopkins University

HEINZ EULAU
Political Science, Stanford University

WILLIAM K. FRANKENA
Philosophy, University of Michigan

PAUL A. FREUND
Law, Harvard University

CARL J. FRIEDRICH
Political Science, Harvard University

ABRAHAM KAPLAN
Philosophy, University of Michigan

JOHN LADD
Philosophy, Brown University

CHARLES E. LINDBLOM
Economics, Yale University

HARVEY C. MANSFIELD, JR.
Political Science, Harvard University

A. A. MAVRINAC
Political Science, Colby College

FELIX E. OPPENHEIM
Political Science, University of Massachusetts

J. ROLAND PENNOCK
Political Science, Swarthmore College

MURRAY L. SCHWARTZ
Law, University of California, Los Angeles

JUDITH N. SHKLAR
Political Science, Harvard University

MARGARET SPAHR
Political Science, Hunter College

GENERAL ISSUES
OF RATIONAL DECISION

1

DECISIONISM

JUDITH N. SHKLAR

To a historian the most interesting thing about decisions is the fact that everyone is talking about them. No one interested in social ideas can fail to notice how large a part the word "decision" has, of late, come to play in the vocabulary of moral and political discourse. It meets one on every page. Inevitably one asks, "Why?" Why is there so much talk of decisions and of those who are said to make them? Are there any ideological reasons for it? The following pages are an effort to answer this question in a tentative way.

By ideology, nothing complex or pejorative is implied here. The term is used to refer merely to personal responses to what is regarded as a prevalent social situation and to the efforts to critically explain and evaluate that situation, whether the latter be real, imagined, or a bit of both. An investigation of the ideological aspects of political concepts is, clearly, not the only way to explain them, but this and similar genetic explorations can show us how and why large numbers of people at any given time come to concentrate on specific intellectual issues. If they can tell us little about the validity or rationality of political ideas, they can provide a degree of self-understanding without which political thought is apt to become complacent, irrelevant, and excessively abstract. To be sure, the effort to "uncover" ideology, to reduce all political thought to a common emotive level, can be a mere exercise in debunking, but it need not be. Indeed there is nothing denigrating in recognizing the ideological perimeter within which political ideas move. It will seem so to only those of us who identify the worth and rationality of our thinking with its remoteness from our own experiences, and especially from those that we share with our less reflective neighbors.

Although it is obvious that a concern with decisions and decision-making is prevalent, it does not simply follow that one can speak of "decisionism" as an identifiable, single ideology. On the contrary, at first sight it would seem that the term "decision" is used in such a variety of contexts and to such different ends that there is no common element to be found here. Nevertheless, it is possible to recognize certain kinds of political thinking in which decisions play a central part and, in comparing them, to discern common features. There are at least three types of political theory which illustrate what one could term a decisionist temper. The oldest of these is romantic and existentialist thinking. In legal theory there is the movement known in America as "legal realism" and its European counterpart, the "free-law" school. Lastly, there are those theories, especially of international relations, that think of power and power manipulation as *the* essential concepts of politics. All these theories have at least one thing in common, a revolt against legalism. It is a rejection of the notion that stable rules of conduct are "there" and that these are binding upon all those to whom they are addressed, under all circumstances. Against "legalism" it is said that either there really are no rules—that these are figments of a misguided imagination—or that there are rules, but that they should not be followed. Usually both these apparently contradictory assertions appear together. This is not surprising, because both correspond to the experience that gives rise to the decisionist temper. The general feeling here is that rules are inefficacious because they do not, in fact, yield the security that they are alleged to provide, that the search for security is in itself a mistake, and that to look for rules is simply a childish way of evading personal responsibilities and the inevitability of having to choose. In short, whether one says one is following a rule or not, one is still making a personal decision, and the decision to follow a rule is a bad one, because it is an effort to hide behind some impersonal screen. Thus these so-called rules are not at all binding, and a rule that is not binding is, clearly, not a rule. What is usually called a rule is therefore just a poor excuse for evasiveness, irresponsibility, and deceptions practiced upon ourselves and each other.

One perennial source of these attitudes is the individualism of those who feel that they have no place to go, of those who are self-conscious "outsiders." They need not, by any means, be irrationalists of the sort that glory in their ineffable individuality and uniqueness. On the contrary, they may be thinkers who find traditional rationalism and the rules that identify rationality unacceptable, but who do not reject the possibility or desirability of a new form of rationality. In the nineteenth century there is perhaps no figure more representative of this attitude than Alexander Herzen. In our own time that "Descartes of the Absurd," Albert Camus, provides another perfect example.[1] As a Russian exile and a revolutionary in politics, Herzen was so much an outsider that he was able to remain aloof even from his own situation and to analyze it coolly. In this he was far removed from the romanticism of the professional Bohemians. Thus he wrote of himself, "I am a spectator, but that is not my role and is not my nature."[2] This condition he recognized to be due to his rejection of the old, dying "official Europe," or what is now called the Establishment, and his equally intense distaste for the coming age of enslaving "isms" and total ideologies. From this vantage point he was bound to proclaim, "You want a book of rules, while I think that when one reaches a certain age one ought to be ashamed of having to use one."[3] And "the truly free man *creates* his own morality."[4] However, he seems not to have regarded this as a declaration of moral anarchy. For one thing, the rules of logic were not to be suspended; for "logic, when it comes of age, detests canonized truths."[5] In this, Herzen, again, showed himself to be remote from that poetic romanticism that scorned the confines of

---

[1] This is Sartre's description of Camus, "Tribute to Albert Camus," in *Camus,* ed. Germaine Brée (1962), p. 174.
[2] Alexander Herzen, *From the Other Shore,* ed. I. Berlin (1956), p. 92.
[3] *Ibid.,* p. 28.
[4] *Ibid.,* p. 141.
[5] *Ibid.,* p. 51.

coherence. In any case, like modern existentialists, he seems to have believed that, somehow, any moral choice must necessarily be universal and unifying, even if there are no immutable or eternal rules.[6] The important point here is Herzen's vision of the moral chooser and of morality as a matter of personal decisions made by people doomed to self-reliance, because they are caught between an ocean-like, fearful future and a repulsive and decadent past. Far from rejoicing in a sense of liberation, this duty of deciding is shouldered as a burden. Its main end is to de-ideologize morality and to free it from the rules of conventional, as well as of revolutionary, officialdom. As such it avoids fraud and error, but it promises nothing.

To some extent this morality of the chooser is a form of compensatory megalomania. Expressing, as it usually does, a sense of victimization, it tries to raise an image of moral man as completely aloof, solitary, and morally, at least, omnicompetent. Hence, too, the hatred—strident in France, but present in attenuated form in English-speaking literature and "little-magazine" culture—against every form of institutionalized life. The present attack on criminal law thus is often not a bit concerned with the reform of that eminently reformable institution, but with the fundamental wrongness of trying to govern with rules, especially punitively. It is generally true that most great reformers of the criminal law since the eighteenth century have not been concerned solely with rationalizing and humanizing its administration. Almost all have also challenged the values, religious and social, that the criminal law has at various times tried to promote. Indeed, it is questionable whether "substantive" and "procedural" values can really ever be separated in any serious attempt to judge legal institutions, especially when reform is at stake. However, even if one remembers all this, it is still fairly startling to find objections to the criminal law that aim at its institutionalized regularity. Considering the many other grounds on which one can reject capital punishment, it is certainly interesting to see it abhorred because it is an *official* act. The immense sympathy shown for criminal offenders, many of whom have very little claim to it, would seem to show that many perfectly respectable

---

[6] See R. Wollheim, "The Political Philosophy of Existentialism," *The Cambridge Journal,* VII (1953), 3–19, for an incisive criticism of the assumption that the universality of one's defiance entails altruism and moral unity.

people feel a deep affinity for anyone who defies the legal standards of their society, simply because he is defiant, not because his acts are anything other than reprehensible. People who would never commit a crime themselves are drawn to criminals and not to their victims because the latter do not symbolize anything. Their fate can be chalked up to the failings of society and its laws. For it is society that is always to blame for everything. Thus it was Camus, with all his reputation for reasonableness and moderation, the very conscience of a generation, who insisted that "every society has the criminals that it deserves."[7] Therefore, he concluded that these acts of "administrative assassination" disturbed his conscience more than the spectacle, which we all have shared, of an entire innocent generation destroyed in war.[8] His reason for this sense of outrage was that the state today is more dangerous to the individual than other killers are.[9] And he meant *any* criminal, not just "political offenders." He also meant *any* state, not just regimes in the grip of total ideologies, which he so eloquently denounced in the name of "rebellion." For rebellion meant for him essentially what it meant to Herzen—throwing all the rulebooks out of the window: the conventional book, the ideological book, and, indeed, any institutionalized book. Only the lone decider has the right to judge. Decisions replace rules.

A great distance, both emotional and intellectual, separates the world of those who adhere to moral decisionism from any conceivable legal theory. Lawyers are not romantic as a rule. It is therefore a different sort of decisionism that one finds among those radicals who, during the years of the New Deal, became the leading spokesmen of legal realism. Before one can understand their peculiar character it should be noted that the word "decision" in legal parlance is used for any judicial verdict and the opinions supporting it, but mostly these acts of judicial choice are described in terms of the rules which condition them. Clearly, in these traditional usages of the word "decision" there is no element of decisionism as an ideology. The peculiarity of American legal thinking for many years has been the gap between academic realism and a legalistic ideology to which the public and many lawyers adhere. The accepted ideology amounts to the belief that judges do not legislate or even choose. They are priests of the law, oracles whose mouths merely

[7] A. Camus, "Reflections on the Guillotine," *Evergreen Review,* I, No. 3 (1957), 31.
[8] *Ibid.,* p. 16.
[9] *Ibid.,* p. 48.

give voice to rules. For decades academic lawyers have, with relatively little impact, denounced this cherished belief in the name of
realism. The sources of this realism and its main spokesmen are
not necessarily radical. Indeed, many realists have been entirely
conservative. They have merely responded to some fairly obvious
facts of American judicial life. Some species of rule skepticism is
bound to appear here, and the judge- or court-centeredness of
American jurisprudence is no accident, when one considers a legal
system of fifty-one jurisdictions, in which the lower judiciary is often
elective and poorly trained, where academic legal education is a
relative novelty, where the bar is anything but integrated and, above
all, when one considers the character and functions of the Supreme
Court.[10] However, the realism of the age of Roosevelt went far beyond this mere recognition of the obvious characteristics of judicial
activity in America. In a sense it offered a truly amazing spectacle
of antilegalistic lawyers. For it did not stop at exposing the unreality
of the lawyer's central credo that rules are "there." It suggested an
alternative. Jerome Frank not only ridiculed the "basic myth,"
though clearly its use by the Supreme Court to strike down every
attempt at social reform was what gave his ideas their momentum.
What he suggested in his most radical moods was that the end
which law is ideally meant to achieve, the security of expectations,
is itself wrong. In this he and his fellow social experimenters departed from the deepest traditions of Anglo-American law reform,
whose greatest inspirer was Bentham. And no one has cared more
for security, and for law as a rationalized means to it, than Bentham
and his followers. Indeed, English analytical jurisprudence to our
own day is incomprehensible as an enterprise if this major preoccupation of legal thinkers, even the radical reformers among them, is
forgotten. Only in the European free-law movement and in Frank's
type of realism has it been abandoned.[11] The basic myth, the faith
in rules that are there, Frank argued, was only an expression of an
infantile craving for security, a sort of father substitute. Since it

[10] R. W. M. Dias and G. B. J. Hughes, *Jurisprudence* (1957), pp. 468–
478, for an excellent English discussion of realism in these terms.

[11] This has led to some misunderstanding. Thus Professor H. L. A. Hart
suggested that Frank's problems would disappear if he stopped asking "What
is law?" and asked instead "What sort of statement is a statement of law?"
It appears that he does not realize that Frank's unlawyerly aim was not to
analyze law, but to promote social change. H. L. A. Hart, review of *Law
and the Modern Mind,* in *Mind,* LX (1950), 268–270.

interfered with social reforms, it was to be replaced by the "fully mature" judge, who, perfected by psychoanalysis, would make decisions based not on rules, but on his own estimate of the real needs of the persons appearing before him and of society as a whole. This judge would *really* make decisions, and without recourse to myths. One might well wonder if the image of this fully mature judge, resembling in Frank's description Justice Holmes to a remarkable degree, was not a father figure too.[12] This impression is strengthened when one looks at the views of some of Frank's most radical associates, Thurmond Arnold and Frank Rodell. For here the judge-as-decider is entirely rejected in favor of the expert. The expert has no need for rules at all, since his judgment is believed to be based solely on facts. The assumption was, apparently, that a sufficient number of facts yield decisions. The model here is the doctor, the healer of social ills. What America needed was "a competent ruling class," "practical and benevolent," and even "opportunistic."[13] What was needed was not law or even judges to make it. There were even no concrete proposals for reform. The only things suggested were social experiments and experts to make disconnected social decisions. Since, according to Professor Rodell, law is but a "high-class racket," "a hoax," "streamlined voodoo," and "word magic," the rule of social workers and psychologists would certainly be a preferable alternative.[14] For rules are "unreal" symbols, whereas a social engineer or doctor experimenting is "real."

What is significant in this sort of realism is the notion that legalism and decisiveness, the rule-follower and the fully mature arbiter, are treated as opposing, contrasting entities. It is this that seemed to give the medical analogy, the ruler-as-doctor, its curious appeal and reality, in stark contrast to the immobility of the Supreme Court and a legal ideology that seemed incapable of saying anything but "no" to every effort to cope with the social crisis of the thirties. The medical analogy is, moreover, also an outsider's image. It is a patient's view of the doctor as an omnicompetent figure. It is not the average physician's view of his own powers. As such, it is a common enough, but thoroughly unhistorical, resort to a com-

---

[12] Jerome Frank, *Law and the Modern Mind* (1949), pp. 170–185, 222–228, 243–252, 253–260.

[13] T. Arnold, *The Symbols of Government* (1935), pp. 21, 46, 271.

[14] F. Rodell, *Woe Unto You, Lawyers!* (1957), pp. 14, 16–17, 121.

forting figure who stands not only outside the governmental establishment, but, in fact, is remote from any actuality. Somehow *he*
can cope.

The most questionable aspect of radical realism is whether *any*
legal system can survive without some form of the basic myth.
Since most of the realists were not quite as radical as they sounded,
they were soon absorbed by the established order, and their objections to the legal system as a means of government lost its intensity.
Some like Frank became judges, and fact skepticism was added to
rule skepticism. That is, the improvement of the judicial process,
the traditional object of law reformers, rather than the abolition of
rules, became his end too. It was the probability of judicial error,
especially in cases where capital punishment was involved, that
occupied him in the years following the war. However, decisionism,
the faith in the mature decider, lived on. Indeed, the courts have
become the idols of the ex-radicals. Disillusioned with the ways
of administrative boards and discouraged by Congressional inaction
in such fields as civil rights, the ex-critics of the law have come to
venerate the nine, no longer old, men.[15] The yearning for decisiveness has, however, not abated. The image of the mature decider
has returned to the courts among those who feel that the major
agencies of government have become deadlocked in pettiness and
formalism. Today there is more concreteness in the demands made
upon the courts. More is asked of them than just accepting social
legislation, especially where civil rights are involved, though this
itself is due in a large measure to Congressional and Presidential
inactivity. This, however, only contributes to a general frustration
about the absence of a "national purpose" and of decisiveness in
government. What was significant about the earlier radical realists
was often their extreme vagueness. What was needed were mature
deciders of some kind, but who these were and what they were to
do were not specified. What they were *not* was, on the other hand,
very clear. They were not the members of the American Bar Association, not legalistic, and not bound by precedents and traditional
ideologies. Above all, they were not given to the inertia that afflicts
the process of government in a pluralistic society. The assumptions

---

[15] See especially the recantations of Walter Gellhorn, *Individual Freedom
and Governmental Restraint* (1956), and James Landis, "The Administrative
Process: The Third Decade," *American Bar Association Journal,* XLVII
(1961), 135–139.

were that myths, illusions, and clichés were the sources of all our failures and that, if one had a government liberated from these, all would go well. With these comes the continuing call for decisiveness, leadership, clear-cut policy, and someone who is "in charge" in Washington.[16]

The most prevalent form of decisionism today is not concerned with domestic politics. It is rather centered on the all-important realm of foreign policy. The realism of the moment is no longer legal, but political. This realism has as its main theme the notion that power is, or at any rate ought to be, the central concept of politics, especially of international politics. Without this notion, it is argued, intellectual disorder and practical failure are bound to occur.[17] Considering the vagueness of such favorite realist conceptions as "power" and the "national interest," the great professional and popular appeal of this neo-Machiavellian doctrine might seem astonishing. It is only when its negative impulses are understood that realism, as an ideological reaction, becomes comprehensible. For power as the central concept of political thought makes sense, even as an ordering device, only if it is understood as a negation. Power politics is the antithesis of legalistic and moralistic politics. Political realism is saved from utter vagueness only by its opposition to that still-lingering legalism, the "Hague fantasy," that regards international adjudication as both a substitute for foreign policy and a means to end conflict. Even more noxious, in realist eyes, is the tendency to ideology, especially in America, where it takes the form of treating international rivals as if they were criminals upon whom the righteous are executing a judgment. The argument is not just that, *in fact,* politics is a series of power calculations made by governments. Realism is not a descriptive approach to international relations. It is extremely didactic. Politics should be a matter of decisions, taken by those who have the power to make them stick. The greatest danger to success in politics is not just indecisiveness, but a faith in legalism, in the belief that rules of international law, or of personal morality, have any application to power relations. In some cases it appears that the sheer hypocrisy, not only the impracticality, of using moral and legal arguments in foreign affairs is

[16] For a most detailed account of the sources and character of this sort of discontent today, see S. P. Huntington, "Strategic Planning and the Political Process," *Foreign Affairs,* XXXVIII (1960), 285–299.

[17] For the best brief statement of the position, see H. J. Morgenthau, *Dilemmas of Politics* (1958), pp. 54–87.

what the realist finds intolerable. This is, I think, very evident in
the writings of George Kennan. In truth, however, it is far from
clear that hypocrisy does not work. Quite the contrary, one would
think. More to the point is that political realism is a rejection of a
certain kind of hypocrisy, that is, that of the great "isms" which,
it is argued, prevent power-manipulators from coming to a rational,
calculated decision which would enhance their power. Especially
the traditional moralistic and legalist ideology of America has led
to delusion, hysteria, and collective bungling. This, too, is a response
to frustration, to feelings that America's traditional institutions and
attitudes have become a liability in its relations with other world
powers and that the old rules are deceiving us, as indeed *all* rules
that limit our faculty for making calculated power decisions must.[18]
Here too the note of compensatory megalomania enters. For all realists persist in blaming every setback or failure on Americans, and
on the liberals especially. The villain of the modern world is less
Hitler or Stalin than Woodrow Wilson. The assumptions, of course,
are that America is omnipotent and that, if its leaders followed the
advice of these artists in the use of power, we would have it our
own way all the time. Like the individual of romantic morality, this
nation is alone in the world, completely free to decide and succeed
in its own interests. This, too, is an outsider's view, not that of the
actual politician, who is apt to be more aware of his limitations.
It is also a sum of frustrations put forth as an explanation. As such,
it is in some respects a comforting theory. In the past, democratic
thinkers dreaded "secret covenants" and diplomatic negotiations
carried on by professionals as conspiratorial enterprises in which
the destinies of entire peoples were ruthlessly manipulated. Today,
on the contrary, people are frightened by the absence of caretakers,
of individual figures in corporate, bureaucratically structured governments where no one appears to be in control of an intolerably
complex international scene. Realism at least holds out the hope
that statesmanship, as de-ideologized power-planning, may yet bring
to government men with orderly minds, who will succeed in re-
establishing the international world of the nineteenth century, which
in retrospect has acquired all the attractions of reasonable, comprehensible dimensions.

Unlike romanticism and legal realism, political realism is radical

18 G. Kennan, *American Diplomacy: 1900–1950* (1952), especially pp.
49–50, 65, 82–89.

only in its rebellion against American traditions. In European terms it is conservative and backward-looking. Far from looking to such typically American social saviors as the experts, the social engineers, and adventurous experimenters, it looks to a vaguely Metternich-like image. When we are told that what is needed is true statesmanship, not law, a very traditional sort of politician is resurrected. The man who has a grasp of the "eternal verities of politics" has no use for scientific gimmicks.[19] His knowledge of the proper rules of the "political art" is drawn from history, where lessons are still to be learned. That too, of course, is a comforting thought. To the question, who exactly today corresponds to this kind of statesman, who is prudent in the sense of Machiavellian rationalism, there are few clear answers. One author of the realist persuasion suggests the British official classes as a model of traditional wisdom in the conduct of diplomacy.[20] To a student of international affairs in the decade preceding the Second World War this model may not be quite convincing. The only conclusion to be drawn is that this modern, like the oldest, "mirror of princes" is just a piece of polished glass. The new decider is only an artifact, the sum of all the virtues that contemporary politicians appear to lack. It is evident enough what he is *not;* it is not clear what he, in fact, does.

A theory of statesmen pursuing something as vague as the national interest has not proven acceptable to theorists of a more systematic turn of mind. Decisionism, however, has a vast appeal, precisely because the vision of a limited number of political actors engaged in making calculated choices among clearly conceived alternatives is an essential basis for any theory that wishes to reduce international complexities to systematic, diagrammatic form. This impulse may be the same as that which inspires neo-Machiavellian statecraft, but it is certainly a rejection of the intuitive, historically oriented, "unscientific" character of the latter. Instead, we are offered highly abstract paradigms of game-playing by actors who make rational decisions according to rules that both sides observe. Others, most notably Professor Richard Snyder and his associates, have devised very elaborate models for decision-making which do not exclude any conceivable element in the process of politics. As such, they escape the artificial pseudorationality of game theory, but many

---

[19] H. J. Morgenthau, *op. cit.,* pp. 1–2, and *Scientific Man vs. Power Politics* (1946), pp. 108–121 *et passim.*
[20] K. W. Thompson, *Political Realism* (1960), pp. 113–127.

observers have found them too cumbersome.[21] If every possible factor leading to an action by a government is taken into account,
then the word "decision" means only that at a given time certain
actions were performed. To understand what led up to this action,
everything relevant that preceded it must be investigated. If this be
the object of decision-making models, old-fashioned narrative history
has been at it for a long time, without the benefit of a new vocabulary. This, however, does not appear to be the aim of those who
have devised decision-making models. Their general belief is that
"the acts of nation states result from more or less deliberate and
conscious choices by someone at some time."[22] The emphasis thus
is upon decisiveness, upon choosing. This impression is reinforced
by the one example offered to illustrate the uses of the decision-
making model, President Truman's decision to enter the Korean
War. Here we do, in fact, have an occasion on which a great deal
of decisiveness was displayed by a limited and identifiable number
of persons. It was also a highly exceptional event. Declarations of
war are, after all, relatively rare incidents in international relations.
A model of international relations based on such examples could
hardly cover the routine conduct of foreign affairs, least of all that
part which concerns the relations between allied states or states that
do not have the remotest expectation of engaging in war with each
other. Indeed, a model, whether structured in terms of game theory
or decision-making "boxes," that assimilates foreign policy to strategic calculations is apt to have little relevance to situations which
are not crises, in which no spectacular acts of choice are expected,
and which are characterized by the slow, grinding routine processes
of politics-as-accommodation. That, however, is not the purpose of
decisionism in international affairs. It, too, is a surrogate rationalism. Its main end is to impose a pattern of calculable and predictable moves upon an international scene that looks chaotic. If the
moral and legal rationalism of the past, that suited an age when
Americans could afford to ignore foreign affairs totally or to think
of them in domestic, familiar ideological terms, is gone, it has been
replaced by the technical rationalism of those who want to reduce

[21] H. McCloskey, "Concerning Strategies for a Science of International
Politics," in *Foreign Policy Decision-Making,* ed. R. C. Snyder *et al.* (1962),
pp. 186–205, for this criticism of R. C. Snyder *et al.*, "Decision Making as
an Approach to the Study of International Politics," *ibid.,* pp. 14–185.

[22] R. C. Snyder *et al.*, "U.S. Decision to Resist Aggression in Korea,"
op. cit., p. 211.

sudden complexity to manageable proportions and to a formal vocabulary.

The demand that prudent decision-makers remove themselves from the hurly-burly of democratic political processes and ideology in order to conduct foreign policy in a statesmanlike manner or to make rational strategic choices has an elitist air about it. This should not be taken too seriously, however. Traditional elitism was an ideology with a specific content. The decisionist is out to de-ideologize politics entirely. Who is to make the decisions is not really determined. If there is explicitly or implicitly a call for decisiveness, there is no concern with finding a new group to bring it to government, nor is the content of decisions prescribed. To do so would, at once, lead to an ideological stance, which decisionism, as a method or a program, is designed to avoid. This is especially clear in those instances when "decision-makers" is a phrase used in evident preference to the older word "elites." In the highly technical literature on decisions, this is not the case, but there is a relatively simple, descriptive approach to decision-making and -makers that is recognized as the methodological heir of the old elite theories. Since these theories are not normatively elitist, the use of "decision-makers" is to provide a neutral, antiseptic, and ideology-free substitute for the comparatively controversial word "elites." The intention here is to pay due attention to those who happen to occupy the seats of power. As such it is a conscious reaction against the group-interest approach to domestic politics. It is meant to examine the behavior of the most active and professional participants in politics, who are often neglected by those who concern themselves exclusively with the social groups whose interests the politicians are said to represent.[23] This is surely a needed corrective, as long as one does not go on to attribute too high a degree of conscious power-manipulation and premeditated choice to the agents of government. This, however, is something that seems likely to occur in decision-oriented studies of domestic politics no less than of international affairs. There is simply an ideological, though not logical, affinity between the notions of "politics as power operations" and "politics as decision-making."[24]

[23] For an example of all these trends, see D. Marvick, "Introduction: Political Decision-Makers in Contrasting Milieus" in the collaborative volume, *Political Decision Makers, International Yearbook of Political Behavior Research* (1961), II, 13–28.

[24] B. Leoni, "The Meaning of 'Political' in Political Decisions," *Political Studies,* V (1957), 225–239.

Both cling to a rather simple faith in the technical rationality of political actors. Concentrating on those who are conspicuously in the seats of power appears to involve the view that power is an entity that is managed purposefully. Whether this is really the way the professional officials of modern governments behave is, nevertheless, an open question. Do they really choose policies, or is it a more complex series of minute interactions? Thus, an academic study of the British Treasury asserted that its highest permanent officials wield great power because they can get their decisions accepted by other agencies of government. To this an insider replied that one does not make decisions out of the blue in Whitehall. One accepts *idées reçus,* being surrounded by the opinions of other men, inside and outside. Far from imposing decisions, the official spends his day listening to others.[25] In short, the decision-makers are not decisive and the crisis view of government as perpetual choice and change is artificial. Its attractions may lie precisely in the emotionally intolerable realities of big government as an undirected, faceless, infinitely complex series of numberless little human actions and reactions.

This brief review of some types of decision-oriented political thinking is by no means exhaustive. It is merely intended to illuminate some of the attitudes which appear to condition it. It seems to be a way of thinking congenial to people who, having rejected the substantive moral and legal rationalism of the past, try to reconstruct for themselves new images of a world upon which they can impose their own order. Since, however, his personal rationality is so deeply identified with the rejection of any of the conventional ideologies, be they radical or conservative "isms," it is difficult for the decisionist to establish anything but a formal framework for his ideal of rational deciding. He is clear as to what it is not, he is clear about the *conditions* under which choice is made, and clear too as to the necessity of making decisions, but nothing is said about the content, the purpose, or the validity of these choices. One rebels in order to rebel, one decides in order to decide, one chooses because one simply ought. It is an ideology without any substance, the resort of those who are perennially on the periphery. It is the outsider's view of moral unity, the political patient's view of social health, the academic's tidy little picture of the corridors of power.

[25] C. H. Sisson, *The Spirit of British Administration* (1959), pp. 129–130.

It epitomizes every sort of malaise in an overinstitutionalized social world.

In view of the many doubts about decisionism raised so far, one might well suppose that the purpose of this paper has been simply to criticize. This is not, in fact, the case. If decisionism is not a self-evident necessity in morals and politics, it is at least an effort to cope with the most difficult issues. At least it is better than its alternatives, the conventional lament and call to a return to the ancestral pieties and academic systems, and the total apathy of those who are crushed entirely by the difficulties of not being able to live either with, or without, ideological sustenance. At least, it is a sign of wanting to create order, moral and intellectual, and of wanting to break through the more hoary walls of clichés surrounding the Establishment. It is one thing to note that decisionism has not succeeded in de-ideologizing morals and politics, except at the cost of allowing poses, stances, methods, and unspecified experiments to replace substantive ideas; it is quite another to say that it ought not to have been tried. The latter is certainly not the aim of this paper. On the contrary, fortified by a heavy dose of skepticism, decisionism may yet prove the most practical way of dealing with morals and political history. For at its core lies a perception of a fundamental historical reality: that the formal concepts of traditional thought no longer serve any descriptive or prescriptive purpose in a social world that has for decades defied the inherited categories of political theory.

2

DECISIONISM AND SEPARATISM IN SOCIAL PHILOSOPHY

WILLIAM K. FRANKENA

One Harvard philosopher has characterized our time as the age of decision and another has proclaimed that decision is king, even though neither of them is an existentialist (nor an essentialist either!). On all sides of them, from Sartrians, from social scientists, from theologians, we hear about decision and decision-making, and about their possible rationality or inevitable and ultimate irrationality. Central in all this talk Mrs. Shklar has found two notions: (a) one which she labels "decisionism," that decision is somehow basic in the human condition, and (b) the notion that we must separate legal, moral, and political decisions. She raises two corresponding questions: (a) "Why all this talk about decisions?" (b) "Why distinguish legal, moral, and political decisions?" Then she offers an interesting and debunking sociopsychological explanation of the rise of the two notions in question. But she also seems to be

thinking that the two notions are incompatible and mistaken. Here
I partly agree and partly disagree. I agree that the two notions are
incompatible and that the first is mistaken, at least if it is held without qualification, but I think that the second is in a sense essentially
correct. In what follows I propose, with her discussion as a background, to sketch out my reasons for my positions.

Let us take the second notion first. To establish it one might argue
that all decisions are essentially of the same nature—they involve
inner conflict and are inescapably personal choices; it is always one
indivisible man making up *his* mind. Now I have no inclination to
deny this; it seems obviously true in a sense that all human decisions
have this general character. One cannot infer, however, that all
decisions are therefore "moral" and, hence, not to be distinguished
into moral, legal, and political ones. If saying that they are all moral
here is just another way of saying that they all involve conflict and
are personal, we need not object. But then it may still be that there
is another sense of "moral" in which decisions are not all moral and
may be divided into legal, political, and moral ones. It may also be
that our second thesis is to be construed as saying that all decisions
are subject to moral judgment and ought to be consistent with moral
principles. Then again, except for the political realists, we may
agree. But we may still insist that actual decisions can be distinguished by the grounds on which they are made or the reasons which
are decisive in making them. Decisions are not always made on
moral grounds; the grounds on which they are made may be legal,
political, prudential, aesthetic, or what have you. Even if we say
they ought all to be moral in the sense of being consistent with
moral requirements, we need not argue that they ought all to be
made *on moral grounds*. It may still be that some decisions are
legitimately made on other grounds, or at least partly on other
grounds—for example, a decision about one's career or vocation or
about the decoration of one's living room. Hence it seems to me
that we may, and even must, distinguish between kinds of decisions
or at least between kinds of grounds or reasons for decisions, namely,
between moral, legal, and political decisions or grounds for decision.

To see the importance of this one has only to look at the discussion
of some complex social problem, for instance, that of the place of
religion in our public schools. Clarity and rationality in this matter
require us to distinguish between the Constitutional, moral, and

political aspects of this question. Otherwise, we cannot tell what is a reason for what. In fact, it is partly a failure to make such distinctions that introduces so much confusion today even into the thinking of those who have not yet succumbed to decisionism or to their emotions. It may be true that any final decision must take into account all of these different kinds of considerations and that it must ultimately rest on moral grounds, but this is no reason for not making any distinctions at any point in our deliberations. Sometimes we are deciding only whether a certain practice is Constitutional. Sometimes we are trying to decide whether it is morally right or wrong even when we admit it is Constitutional. And this is as it should be.

Against any attempt thus to distinguish between different kinds of considerations, rationales, and rules, it might be argued as follows. If one is to distinguish moral rules and reasons from others, one must know which rules and reasons are moral ones and which are not. This would mean either making an exhaustive list of all moral rules and reasons and looking to see what is common and peculiar to them, or choosing some moral criterion and saying that the rules and reasons conforming to it are moral and the rest are immoral. The former procedure, however, is unworkable and has not even been tried by would-be classifiers, and the latter is clearly not classification, but persuasion and taking sides.

There are, it seems to me, two things wrong with this reasoning. First, distinguishing moral rules from others, for example, legal ones, does not necessarily involve constructing an exhaustive list of every conceivable moral rule; it only involves finding a set of criteria such as those offered, for example, by H. L. A. Hart, John Ladd, Kurt Baier, A. E. Duncan-Jones, and others. Second, finding such a set of criteria does not necessarily involve choosing one morality and saying that what conforms to it is moral and everything else is immoral. For the criteria in question do not purport to distinguish the moral from the immoral but the moral from the *non*moral, that is, from the legal, the aesthetic, and so on. In other words, the procedure involved *is* classification of a sort, not mere persuasion.

Of course, what I have been saying about the second notion involved in recent talk about decision implies that decisions may and should be based on reasons, rules, and the like, and this, I take it, is just what "decisionism" denies. That is why I agree with Mrs. Shklar in thinking that the two notions we are talking about are incompatible. At any rate, there seems to be little sense and no point in holding that legal, moral, and political reasons are to be distinguished, if reasons cannot and should not influence our decisions at all. In fact, it seems to me that the decisionists who accept the first notion are precisely those who are least concerned to maintain the second. It may even be that a failure to separate legal, moral, and political considerations is partly responsible for their conclusion that decisions are basically irrational.

We come thus to the first of the two notions in question, and I wish now to indicate why I regard it as mistaken, whatever its socio-psychological explanation may be. A mild form of decisionism would hold that decisions cannot be mere deductions from or applications of rules or reasons via some kind of practical syllogism or logical inference. This we may grant. Whenever two or more divergent reasons or rules operate in a situation, in other words, whenever "decision" is called for, then such a deductive procedure cannot suffice. Such an admission is, however, compatible with the view that reasons, rules, and so on may and should *guide*, if not constrain, our decisions. A more drastic kind of decisionism, then, would deny that reasons, rules, and so on do, can, or should even so much as guide our decisions. It is about this kind of decisionism that I wish to say something. (About legal realism and rule skepticism in law I shall be content with what H. L. A. Hart has said in *The Concept of Law*.) This kind of decisionism proposes, among other things, to give up completely the appeal to rules and reasons as a snare and a delusion, a childish search for security, a self-deceiving effort to hide behind some impersonal screen. For it, we are and of right ever ought to be free and independent agents—lone, mature, if anxious, deciders, as Mrs. Shklar very nicely puts it—and are simply mistaken or dishonest if we try to claim that our decisions are justified in some intersubjectively valid way by any rules, reasons, ideologies, or the like.

I should like now to point out what such a view involves. Some 200 years ago David Hume argued that, apart from the language in which we assert or describe matters of fact and relations of ideas, we speak at least two other languages. One is the language of self-love and of other sentiments peculiar to oneself and arising from one's particular circumstances and situation, as "when a man denominates another his *enemy*, his *rival*, his *antagonist*, his *adversary*." Here what one says is a direct function either of one's self-interest or of what Joseph Butler called one's primary appetites. The other language, Hume says, involves a "peculiar set of terms" invented in order to express universal sentiments of approbation or censure and general ideas of human conduct and behavior, as "when [one] bestows on any man the epithets of *vicious* or *odious* or *depraved*." In describing the latter Hume was thinking specifically of moral terms, but he might have included also many others, such as "beautiful," "true," "desirable," "probable," "entails," "valid," "real," and their opposites. In using all such terms, as he says of ethical ones, one

> speaks another language, and expresses sentiments, in which he expects all his audience are to concur with him. He must here, therefore, depart from his private and particular situation, and must choose a point of view, common to him and others; he must move some universal principle of the human frame, and touch a string to which all mankind have an accord and symphony.[1]

Now, as I see it, decisionism of the more drastic kind represents a repudiation of this last sort of discourse and all that goes with it. For decisionism, to glorify such discourse is to be hopelessly eighteenth century, as Hume was, and even to use it sincerely (and for it one ought not to use it insincerely) is self-deception, escapism, and other-directedness. We should, it implies, talk only the language of matters of fact and relations of ideas (and it does not seem to prize this very highly, *vide* its views about science and mathematics and its neglect of logic) or the language of self-love, private sentiments, and lone mature decision. We should not talk at all the "peculiar" language in which we purport to put our decisions, thoughts, and reactions out into a public arena with the claim that they will hold their own there, not by virtue of any force or weapon they may enlist, but by virtue of their viability under discussion. I myself, however, see in the confident though careful use of this peculiar language the chief source of such humanity as man may have, as do Cassirer, Hart, Bernard Mayo, and so many other of us eighteenth-century minds born 200 years too late. We may not become gods if we thus eat of "the tree of the knowledge of good and evil" of which Genesis speaks, but we must eat of it if we are to be men and not the happy innocents of the Garden of Eden or the beasts of a state of nature—or even the rhinoceroses of a recent Broadway play. Aristotle sensed this long ago when he wrote:

---

[1] David Hume, *An Enquiry concerning the Principles of Morals,* Section IX, Part I.

The mere making of sounds serves to indicate pleasure and pain, and is thus a faculty that belongs to animals in general. . . . But language serves to declare what is advantageous and what is the reverse, and it therefore serves to declare what is just and what is unjust. It is the peculiarity of man . . . that he alone possesses a perception of good and evil, of the just and the unjust, and of other similar qualities; and it is association in [a common perception of] these things which makes a family and a polis.[2]

Of course, there are familiar arguments against the credulous use of words like "good," "right," "justified," "valid," "true," "real," and "rational," with their implicit claims to a hypothetical consensus with others—for example, the argument that all such claims are false and illusory. But this contention has not been established beyond the peradventure of a considerable doubt, as far as I can see, though I cannot try to show this now. It must suffice here to point out that radical decisionism cannot assert itself in the public arena, as it has and does, unless it inconsistently talks in just the manner it condemns. For if it speaks there at all, as it willy-nilly must, it must contend that claims to intersubjective validity are *mistaken* or *dishonest,* that it is *true* that the appeal to reason and rules is just *pretense* and *self-deception,* that pretense and self-deception and escapism are *reprehensible,* and so on. But for it thus to use words like "mistaken," "dishonest," "true," "pretense," "self-deception," and "reprehensible"—not to mention "authentic"—is illegitimate. If it is to be consistent, which it cannot be, it must construe even its own theses and pronouncements as mere externalizations of private beliefs, wishes, decisions, commitments, and the like, that is, as purely autobiographical self-revelations or self-creations. Perhaps this explains at once why it must resort to writing such novels as Camus' *The Stranger* and why this novel, or rather its hero (if one may use this term here), is so baffling to us eighteenth-century readers.

The "compleat" decisionist will, of course, reply that all uses of such terms as "right," "justified," "valid," "rational," and so on depend (a) on a prior decision to espouse some criterion, standard, method, point of view, or way of life, and (b) on a yet more basic decision to claim a kind of public justifiability for one's opinions, decisions, and way of life. And he will claim, further, that such prior

[2] *The Politics of Aristotle,* ed. and trans. Ernest Barker (1962), p. 6.

decisions are and must be arbitrary and irrational. Now, I agree that these basic decisions (if they are decisions at all) cannot be justified by logical deduction or inference from premises known to be true, if only because they are decisions, not propositions. It does not follow, however, that they are arbitrary or irrational—as John Dewey, P. W. Taylor, J. W. Smith, and many others have recently been trying to show, sometimes in reply to certain other passages of David Hume. For example, my decision to use screws instead of nails to hold up a bookcase does not follow logically from the premise that screws hold more firmly than nails (or any other such premises). However, it is rational for all that. Of course, it does involve a prior desire to have a stable and upstanding bookcase. But this desire may also be perfectly rational in the sense of being based on empirical data about the consequences of instability in bookcases (though not in the sense of following inductively or deductively from such data). Again, of course, this desire depends on a still more basic desire (decision?) to avoid the consequences attendant upon the ownership of unstable bookcases. And now, it will be argued, this desire is and must be arbitrary and irrational. In reply I suggest that such a desire is almost a paradigm of rationality—what could be more rational than a desire to avoid dangers, difficulties, inconveniences, pains, and frustrations? Decisionists (and many others) forget this, I think, because they conceive of rationality too much on the model of deductive or inductive inferability. A decision is not irrational merely because it is a decision or because it cannot be a conclusion of a logical inference, simple or complex.

I wish also to remark that the basic desire in question here can hardly be said to be or rest on a "decision" and that to aver that it involves a "decision" is to suggest, misleadingly and unjustifiably, that it involves a wholly free and unguided choice. I know, of course, that radical decisionists contend at this point that we somehow have a freedom of choice even about our most basic desires, native endowments, and so on, but, if they must resort to such unintelligible claims to maintain their position, then I regard my point as made. Enough is enough. A commitment to the kind of public rational enterprises that are involved in the use of the "peculiar" form of discourse identified by Hume (though he himself underplayed its rationality) may likewise not rest on any "decision" which we can make or unmake, but whether it does or not, it can hardly be called "irrational" or "arbitrary" (except perhaps in certain senses).[3] For these words themselves can be consistently used only by one who is already committed to such enterprises.

One of the Harvard philosophers referred to earlier, in proclaiming that decision is king, argues that the fundamental human problem is "Why should I do anything?" and that this question is "beyond reason" though it is not "senseless."[4] Perhaps so, but it does not follow that the answer to this question is irrational; indeed, there remains a sense in which the question itself is irrational, since one can always reply that we cannot fail to do something and that the only sensible question to ask is "What should I do?" Neither does it follow that decision is king, for, if we cannot fail to do something, then we can hardly be said to *decide* to do something. Even if we agree that ultimately decision is king, however, we need not conclude that it has driven out Zeus. In whatever sense of "decision" that may be involved, we may still decide to use the peculiar art that Zeus is supposed to have given mankind after Epimetheus' terrible failure. To say in reply that this decision is "gratuitous" and "without reason" will hardly do; it is too much like saying that what has all the virtues is without virtue. It does make sense to say that what cannot fail to have all the virtues is not virtuous, but then, like Kant, we must add that it is holy and what is this but another use of the peculiar language signalized by Hume? One may, of course, ask, "Why should I use this peculiar language?" But then one's very question is parasitic; it borrows a term from the vocabulary it pretends it can reject.

> When me they fly, I am the wings;
> I am the doubter and the doubt,
> And I the hymn the Brahmin sings.[5]

[3] I am not happy with all that R. M. Hare says in a much discussed passage, but I find a good deal of sense in the following part of it:
> To describe such ultimate decisions as arbitrary, because *ex hypothesi* everything which could be used to justify them has already been included in the decision, would be like saying that a complete description of the universe was utterly unfounded, because no further fact could be called upon in corroboration of it. . . . Far from being arbitrary, such a decision would be the most well-founded of decisions, because it would be based upon a consideration of everything upon which it could possibly be founded. *The Language of Morals* (1952), p. 69.

[4] H. D. Aiken, *Reason and Conduct* (1962), p. 87.
[5] Ralph Waldo Emerson, "Brahma."

3

LOGICS OF RATIONALITY
IN UNANIMOUS DECISION-MAKING

HEINZ EULAU*

My starting point is an empirical observation: the tendency of much democratic decision-making to terminate in unanimous or near-unanimous voting.[1] My problem is elusive: Does unanimity in

* I am grateful to my colleagues, Professor Martin Shapiro and Professor Richard A. Brody, as well as to Dr. Kenneth Prewitt and Dr. John D. Sprague, for comment that cleared up several confusions. Needless to say, perhaps, they are absolved from any responsibility for what I have written.

[1] "Democratic" here simply means that there must not be in the decision-making situation external structural constraints which make free choice impossible, as in dictatorship (where only the dictator has free choice). There may be, of course, other constraints—and I shall mention some of them later on. But whatever other conditions may be specified for democratic decision-making, I only require of the situation that it contain a *potential* for free choice. I shall leave the adjective "near-unanimous" operationally undefined and, subsequently, absorb it into the unanimous category. For, conceptually, it makes little difference whether unanimity is fully achieved or not. Where

26

democratic decision-making satisfy criteria of rationality?[2]

In order to deal with the problem, I shall first try to show that the frequency with which unanimity occurs in democratic decision-making does, indeed, represent a "problematic situation" that deserves serious inquiry (Section I). I shall then briefly review the institutional arrangement where unanimity is a formal rule of decision-making, and I shall touch upon the principle of rationality involved in constitutional unanimity (Section II). Then, in order to develop a typology of unanimity that can be used to order empirical situations, I shall introduce two dimensions of unanimity—first, what I shall call "ways of decision-handling" (Section III), and second, what I shall call "ways of interest articulation" (Section IV). Once the typology has been elaborated and illustrated by reference to empirical examples (Section V), I shall examine each type of unanimity in terms of whatever criterion of rationality would seem to be useful (Section VI). I shall conclude that certain types of unanimity are not necessarily dysfunctional or symptomatic of a breakdown of the democratic decision-making process (Section VII).

I

Democratic decision-making is most readily observable in

---

unanimity is not a constitutional decision rule, there is always the bitter-end intransigent or the unpredictable maverick whose behavior defies the tendency towards unanimity. This may be an empirically interesting phenomenon. But the quantitative deviations from the norm that are permissible in order to speak of "near-unanimous" decisions need not be defined for the theoretical purposes of this paper.

[2] There are numerous models of rational behavior. Most prominent are the "means-ends" model often encountered in theories of formal organization, the "maximization" model of economic theories, the "minimax" model of game theory, and the "adaptive behavior" models found in psychology. All of these models make behavioral assumptions that present advantages and difficulties. My discussion of rationality in unanimous decision-making does not require that I systematically explicate various models or choose between them. I shall invoke one or the other as the discussion of one or another type of unanimity may suggest. For my purposes the only requirements of rationality that must be met, whatever assumptions are made or whatever other conditions are specified, are that there be a free choice among alternatives and that the choice be consciously made. Nevertheless, I should acknowledge that my thinking in the matter has been greatly influenced by Herbert A. Simon's discussions of rationality. See his *Administrative Behavior* (2nd ed.; 1957), pp. 61–78. Also "A Behavioral Model of Rational Choice," in *Models of Man* (1957), pp. 241–260; and "Some Strategic Considerations in the Construction of Social Science Models," in *Mathematical Thinking in the Social Sciences*, ed. Paul F. Lazarsfeld (1954), pp. 388–415.

legislative bodies.[3] The great amount of unanimous or near-unanimous decision-making in the final stage of the legislative process is a matter of record.[4] Many of these decisions are made, of course, by the formal rule of "unanimous consent" or on private-bill calendars which prohibit passage if a single member objects or requests that the bill be delayed for further consideration.[5] Most of these actions lie outside the arena of political warfare or any other lines of cleavage. But others involve subjects of real importance for individuals or groups.[6] Some of these have the endorsement of all interested parties, thus making for unanimity or near-unanimity, but others do not. This set of decisions—where one should expect division on substantive grounds of divided interests, but where it does not occur— makes unanimity a puzzling affair. For there is no overt evidence as to why it should occur—no logrolling, no leadership instructions, no purposive "engineering of consent." There has been, as I shall point out in Section V, some empirical speculation about the possible dynamics of the legislative process when it culminates in this kind of unanticipated unanimity, but real empirical evidence is scarce.[7]

[3] The emphasis here is on "observable." Although, for certain theoretical purposes, the electorate can be conceived as a "committee," the secrecy of the electoral process and its aggregate character make observation impossible. Similarly, the decision-making process in juries escapes direct observation. It is for this reason that I shall deal, at least initially, with decision-making in legislative bodies, though here, too, much of what occurs remains hidden.

[4] See V. O. Key, Jr., *Politics, Parties, and Pressure Groups* (1958), pp. 727–731; and Avery Leiserson, *Parties and Politics* (1958), pp. 339–344.

[5] These constraints are external to the decision-making process, as are dictatorial constraints, and therefore not within the purview of this discussion, which assumes the potential for free choice among alternatives.

[6] William J. Keefe, in a study of the 1951 Pennsylvania legislature, for instance, found many unanimous or near-unanimous votes on such matters as mental health, the training of the physically handicapped, increased aid to the blind, the local department of health operations, stream clearance, control over narcotics, absentee voting for military electors, sabotage control, retirement systems, school-district and school-board elections, merit-system extensions, and improvement of state institutions. See "Comparative Study of the Role of Political Parties in State Legislatures," in *Political Behavior*, ed. Heinz Eulau, Samuel J. Eldersveld, and Morris Janowitz (1956), p. 315; and "Parties, Partisanship, and Public Policy in the Pennsylvania Legislature," *American Political Science Review*, XLVIII (1954), 452, 461–462.

[7] In part, this lack of evidence is probably due to prevailing research strategies. Studies of legislative decision-making by way of roll-call votes are usually limited to the relatively few situations in which legislatures are divided. The criteria used to determine whether a roll call is to be considered controversial vary, and different research methods employed by different

Unanimity or near-unanimity may occur, then, in vital as well as minor policy matters. However, in democratic political systems differences over issues of public policy between political actors and conflicts between them are generally expected. The democratic system is, by definition, a contrivance designed to institutionalize conflicts and facilitate the clarification, crystallization, and resolution of political differences. A democratic legislature is an institution composed of opposed sides, and, the more the lines of division follow predictable lines, the more rational would the legislative process seem to be. If predicted divisions do not occur, the rationality of legislative decision-making becomes problematical. Regardless, therefore, of whether issues of high policy significance are involved or not, the fact that many legislative actions where controversy might be expected are consummated by unanimity poses a problem for political theory. This is not to imply that in every case of legislative action division is thought desirable. In crisis situations, notably war and economic emergencies threatening community survival, unanimity rather than division is the preferred decision norm and celebrated as a political achievement.[8]

II

In order to come to grips with the problem, I shall briefly turn to the institutional arrangements, where unanimity is a formal, constitutional requirement of decision-making, for two reasons—one theoretical, the other methodological. In the first place, there has been a good deal of explicit theoretical concern with the constitutional unanimity rule from the standpoint of its rationality. And second, it would seem that constitutional unanimity, with its imputed rationality, may serve as a kind of "ideal type."[9] Treated as an ideal-type model, rational constitutional unanimity provides a criterion for appraising the rationality of the several situations where unanimity emerges as an empirical phenomenon. As Weber put it,

---

students have led to divergent findings about the importance of one or another factor that is assumed to make for division.

[8] In other words, crisis situations may be considered as introducing constraints of an environmental character which make for self-imposed structural constraints. Again, the potential for free choice is severely restricted. Actually, the choice in these situations has already been made elsewhere, and the final decision is not really a matter of choice but rather of promulgation.

[9] See Talcott Parsons' interpretation in *The Structure of Social Action* (2nd ed.; 1949), pp. 604–605.

by comparison with this [ideal type] it is possible to understand the ways in which actual action is influenced by irrational factors of all sorts, such as affects and errors, in that they account for the deviation from the line of conduct which would be expected on the hypothesis that the action were purely rational.[10]

The most familiar case of constitutional unanimity is found today in an international decision-making body such as the Security Council of the United Nations. Here unanimity among the permanent members is a requirement for any substantive decision to be made. The empirical reasons for the rule are well known: On the one hand, the area of potential disagreement between nations is so large, and, on the other hand, its "interests" are considered so "vital" by each participating nation, that, in order to win support for and acceptance of a decision, unanimity rather than another voting rule is made the formal and effective requirement.[11]

Unanimity as a voting requirement is a rule of long standing. Indeed, unanimity did not give way to majority voting until certain conditions—as just those characteristic of international decision-making today—had given way to other conditions. Gierke reports that in the political life of the early Germanic tribes unanimous consent was sought for decisions precisely because a strong feeling of individuality made for the recognition that what could not be done unanimously would not be done at all.[12] In other words, unanimity appeared as the only decision rule which, if each participant was to be guaranteed membership in the decisive group, facilitated the replacement of private by collective action.

On the other hand, unanimity may serve to prevent collective action. Simmel discusses the dysfunctional consequences of the unanimity rule in the Polish Diet and the Aragonese Cortes, but of interest here are the conditions which made for maintaining the rule —among them the inequality in status and power of the participants, insufficient rules for deliberation, resistance of the constituent members to a feeble executive authority, and others.[13] If, in the case of

10 Max Weber, *The Theory of Social and Economic Organization* (1947), p. 92.

11 For a mathematical formulation of the constitutional unanimity rule in international bodies, see Duncan Black, *The Theory of Committees and Elections* (1958), pp. 140–155.

12 Otto von Gierke, "Ueber die Geschichte des Majoritaetsprinzips," in *Essays in Legal History*, ed. Sir Paul Vinogradoff (1913), pp. 312–335.

13 Georg Simmel, "The Phenomenon of Outvoting," in *The Sociology of Georg Simmel*, ed. and trans. Kurt H. Wolff (1950), pp. 240–241.

the Germanic tribes, each participant was to be guaranteed membership in the decisive group because all participants were deemed equal, in the cases described by Simmel, membership in the decisive group was to be guaranteed because the participants were unequal in status and power.

Unanimity, it seems, can be the preferred decision rule in two quite different, indeed polar, situations. On the one hand, it may facilitate the transition from private to collective action among equals who recognize that the advantages to be gained from collective action for each participant will be greater than the advantages to be gained from private action. The unanimity rule, then, is the only decision rule capable of resolving deadlock—which means that neither collective nor private action is possible.[14] For under any other rule—majority voting or dictatorship, for instance—each partner would not have a guarantee of being in the decisive group and, therefore, would prefer deadlock. But precisely because each participant is thought to be equal to every other participant and because the advantages to be derived from collective action are greater than those from private action, unanimity must be considered the rational decision rule in this situation.

This explication does not take account, of course, of the costs of decision-making that may be involved in unanimity. It is concerned only with the utilities for each actor that he may anticipate from collective as against private action. But as, in this case of collective action by equals, the costs of unanimity can be assumed to be less than the costs of deadlock, rational actors who are equal will be willing to pay the costs of unanimity.[15]

On the other hand, unanimity may be preferred as the constitu-

[14] This definition of deadlock differs from that of Robert A. Dahl when he writes that "if the deadlock solution is followed, then no governmental action is taken; but if no governmental action is taken, then in fact x is government policy." See *A Preface to Democratic Theory* (1956), p. 41. The situation to which Dahl's statement refers, and quite accurately, is one where the choice is between one collective action as against another, not, as is the situation here, where the choice is between collective action and private action, but where private action will also not be taken.

[15] It seems to me that this aspect of the cost problem involved in unanimous decision-making has been neglected by those who only compare the decision costs of unanimity with the decision costs of majority voting or dictatorship. That, among equals, deadlock in a situation which calls for collective action (because private action is not the alternative) may be more expensive than unanimity that makes collective action possible has been neglected. See, for instance, James M. Buchanan and Gordon Tullock, *The*

tional decision rule in situations where it is the objective of unequal participants to block collective action, not because private action is preferred, but because deadlock is preferred to both private and collective action. Again, unanimity alone guarantees each participant to be in the decisive group, but unanimity is the chosen decision rule not because it resolves deadlock, but because it institutionalizes it. The costs involved may be considerable and, in the long run, as has often been pointed out, dysfunctional for the individual participants as well as for the collectivity because it makes for constitutional anarchy. Unanimity rational in the short run may contain, therefore, the seeds of irrationality in the long run.

The discussion suggests that, under specified conditions, unanimity may be more rational than other formal decision rules. This may come as a startling conclusion, for common sense and experience would seem to prove otherwise. But it is startling only if one fails to specify the conditions. Let me repeat them as a paradigm:

1. Each participant in the decisional situation is equal in status and power to every other participant.
2. Each participant in the decisional situation is guaranteed membership in the decisive group.
3. Each participant expects greater advantages for himself from collective than from private action.
4. The costs of unanimous decision-making for collective action are less than the costs of deadlock.

The explication suggests that, under the conditions specified, the constitutional unanimity rule appears as the "ideal-rational" decision rule, whereas other decision rules appear as variants which become relevant only if the conditions for unanimity are not met.[16] The conditions are, of course, extremely strict and not likely to be found in the real world of politics. This is precisely the reason why the constitutional unanimity rule, however rational it may be, has to yield to behaviorally more viable rules like majority voting or dictatorship.

Implicit in the model of constitutional unanimity is the assumption that unanimity is rational if, upon their merits, all possible alternatives among decision rules—such as exceptional majority voting,

---

Calculus of Consent: Logical Foundations of Constitutional Democracy (1962), pp. 85–116.

[16] *Ibid.*, p. 96, comes to the same conclusion, if by a very different theoretical route.

bare majority voting, plurality voting, decisional dictatorship (arbitration), or even anarchy—have been considered. The availability of alternate rules, then, is a necessary condition of rationality in the choice of a rule, but it is not a sufficient condition. A second condition is that the decision of how to make decisions involve conscious selection of the rule to be followed in preference to other rules. In other words, if unanimity occurs in a voting situation without alternate decisional possibilities having been consciously contemplated, the unanimous decision cannot be considered as prima facie rational. Now, it is evident that the rationality criterion, so interpreted, pertains to constitutional unanimity, for it is the only situation in which unanimity as a decision rule is consciously selected and institutionalized as against other rules.

But what of situations where unanimity occurs, but where it is not a constitutional rule of decision-making? For instance, if a city council unanimously adopts a measure, even though individual members may be reluctant at first to support it, because it believes that a split decision would undermine its authority in the community, and if the alternatives of unanimous versus split decision have been consciously considered, the decision is rational, given the group's values. On the other hand, if the relationship between the group's perception of its authority in the community and its voting pattern is not consciously invoked, and if it has consequences that were not consciously anticipated, then the unanimous decision must be explained on another than its rational basis. Consciousness, then, has to be postulated as an important ingredient of rationality, for otherwise the behavior involved in a unanimous decision where unanimity is not a formal rule would have to be accepted, ex post facto, as rational.

Whether unanimity in situations where it is not a formal voting requirement is rational or not is, therefore, a matter of empirical determination. I shall come back to various possibilities in Section VI.

III

As already mentioned, the defense of the formal, constitutional unanimity rule must be predicated on certain behavioral assumptions which, however, are not empirically tenable. The rule seems to assume that human beings are invariably rationally calculating, in the sense that they seek to maximize personal benefits by some hedonistic calculus and make choices, including the decision of how to make decisions, in terms of least cost. And it seems to be assumed that men live in some kind of state of nature, very much as that of the social-contract theories. In these theories one individual is related to any other individual in some private way that is assumed to be prior to social bonds of family, friendship, or any other interpersonal link, and which the individual only enters if it suits his own interests.

These assumptions cannot be made if one wishes to develop an empirically relevant typology of situations in the real world, where unanimity is not a formal decision rule but an existential phenomenon. In the first place, decisions in the real world are not made as if they were the decisions of an individual alone. An individual may take the initiative in seeking to achieve his own interests through collective action. But a great deal of collective decision-making is designed to achieve public as well as individual interests. The behavioral assumption must be made that man is, indeed, a social animal, that he always lives in a group and is part of a group. The notion implicit in the individualistic model of rationally calculating man that only individual but not public interests are "natural" cannot be maintained as behaviorally adequate. The conception of the solitary, individual man unrelated to others but by ties of self-interested calculation does not provide a viable model.

It would seem that when unanimity occurs spontaneously in democratic decision-making, it stems from a confluence of two behavioral dimensions—the ways in which decisions are generally handled and the ways in which interests are articulated. I shall deal with the latter in the next section.

Constitutional unanimity has been called a formal decision rule. Taking this as a clue, I would like to suggest that decisions, whatever the constitutional rule for decision-making, may be handled informally as well as formally and that both informal and formal patterns may characterize decisional behavior. In fact, the combination of formal and informal processes seems to be characteristic of the kind of behavior conventionally called "political." Though the range from informal to formal patterns is best thought of as a continuum of decision-handling, I shall, for conceptual brevity, present a trichotomous classification.

Informal-Consensual Decision-Handling. Here the emphasis is on the spontaneously consensual and informal character of the decision process. Because there is much customary consensus on the prerogatives of the actors, decision-making is likely to be characterized by little conflict. Decisions are handled through traditional, interpersonal arrangements that are only weakly institutionalized in the governmental sense, but they are highly stable nevertheless. Not only are the relations of the members of the collectivity easygoing, face to face, and permanent, but the group itself is likely to be held together by strong bonds of solidarity. Conflict, if it occurs, is likely to be settled through the intervention of mediators. The situation here stylized is probably characteristic of primary groups, but it can probably be extended both to modern committees in a generic sense and to larger communal groups which are fairly homogeneous in composition, culturally isolated, and relatively static in development.

Formal-Ministerial Decision-Handling. At the opposite pole of the decision-handling continuum, behavior is thought to be formal-ministerial. As the concept "ministerial" conveys, decisions are handled ex officio, that is, by persons who do what they do by virtue of the official position they occupy in the group. Rather than being spontaneous, decision-handling is routinized and bureaucratized. There is relatively little room for personal intervention. Decisions are made by rules which are highly institutionalized, either by constitution or convention. Maximum value is placed on consistency in decision-handling. Decisions are likely to be functionally specialized, with great attention being paid to impersonal authority rather than to personal opinions. Favoritism is improper. The participants in the decision process are not held together by ties of friendship, but rather by formal arrangements that, if removed, would spell the end of the relationship. Conflicts will be resolved by appeal to higher jurisdiction. The formal-ministerial pattern would seem to be characteristic of courts of law or administrative organizations where the personal attributes of the decision-makers are considered irrelevant, and where the group is likely to be heterogeneous in background and pluralistic in composition.

Political Decision-Handling. This type of decision-handling may be located somewhere in the middle between consensual and ministerial ways of making decisions. In other words, it partakes of both formal and informal, personal and impersonal patterns. On the one hand, there is likely to be some agreement, more or less, on the "rules of the game" that is as deeply ingrained as are the norms of consensual decision-handling.[17] On the other hand, the relations among decision-makers are also regulated by formal constraints as in the ministerial pattern. On the one hand, a good deal of the behavior involved in political decision-handling is personal—there is room for bargaining and trades which, unlike the ministerial process, give the actor fair latitude in negotiations before the decision is made. On the other hand, limits are set to decision-handling, not only by formal rules, but by the whole network of interpersonal relations outside of the decision-making group itself (the political environment). The political decision-handling pattern seeks to cope with conflict not through mediation or other pacifying techniques, as the informal-consensual pattern, or through appeal to jurisdictional authority, routine, or precedent, as the formal-ministerial pattern, but through clarifying and crystallizing the conflict in debate or negotiation in order to arrive at a point where the decision will represent a compromise which is acceptable to both sides. Unlike the consensual pattern, the composition of the group is more heterogeneous, though it is held together by some shared characteristics, such as language, historical background, or common fate.

Although I have referred, for illustrative purposes, to some particular types of human group, such as the primary group or the administrative organization, as being representative of one or another way of decision-handling, the three patterns should be clearly understood as analytic categories and not as concrete processes which can be identified in crystalline purity with particular decision-making structures.[18] Any one pattern of decision-handling can probably be found, with more or less impact, in any one concrete decision-making structure. Whether it will or not is an empirical research question, not a conceptual or definitional problem.[19]

[17] For an enlightening discussion of the slippery concept of consensus and the extent of consensus on decision rules in American politics, see James W. Prothro and Charles M. Grigg, "Fundamental Principles of Democracy: Bases of Agreement and Disagreement," *Journal of Politics,* XXII (1960), 276–294.

[18] For the distinction between analytic and concrete structures, see Marion J. Levy, Jr., "Some Aspects of 'Structural-Functional' Analysis and Political Science," in *Approaches to the Study of Politics,* ed. Roland Young (1958), pp. 52–65.

[19] See below, footnote 30, where I point out that the Supreme Court's ways of decision-handling have been quite different from time to time. It seems that all three ways of decision-handling here described have been variously employed.

IV

It seems reasonable to assume, for the purposes of this discussion, that men engage in collective political action to advance both their individual interests and those of the group to which they belong. If the group's decision is unanimous, furthermore, it may be assumed that different types of unanimity will result, depending on the ways in which individual and group interests are articulated within the group, as well as depending on the ways of decision-handling that are practiced. These assumptions would seem to be more tenable than individualistic assumptions, for they derive directly from the social nature of man. We can assume that, precisely because every man is inevitably and invariably a member of a group, he will want to realize his group's as well as his own individual interests.[20] It is in the interchange of individual and group articulation of interests that the particular format of decision-making emerges.

It is necessary to explain here why I am using, in a discussion which is to deal with the rationality of unanimous decision-making, the concept of "interest" rather than the concepts of "goal" and "utility" that are usually employed in connection with treatments of rational action. I do so partly in order to disengage the discussion from models of rationality that make individualistic assumptions, as those of economic choice, or from models that make assumptions about the relationship between means and ends, as those of organizational behavior. But there is a positive reason as well for introducing the notion of "interest" as a critical dimension. It is a term more appropriate in models of *political* decision-making. Unlike organizational or economic behavior, political behavior rarely centers in the search for or the achievement of a single goal or a single value. The multi-valued "ends" and the equally diverse "means" of politics are often difficult to disentangle. The objects of political activity are more or less coherent complexes of individual and group demands and their supporting expectations. To these complexes we give the name of "interests."[21] Any particular decision, even though

[20] This is not to deny that, in reality, there will occur pathological deviations from the norm. Criminals, certainly, seek to maximize their personal utilities without regard to the utilities of others or the public costs that are involved. But even within the criminal community there are "public interests" which the individual criminal can disregard only at great risk for himself.

[21] This definition is indebted to Harold D. Lasswell: "An interest is a pattern of demands and its supporting expectations." See Harold D. Lass-

it may relate to a particular end or means of collective action, is invariably embedded in a more-or-less well-articulated configuration of propinquitous demands, expectations, and evaluations that influences not only the content of decisions but also their format. The ways in which interests, so defined, are articulated may help to account for particular voting patterns—whether unanimous, majoritarian, or plural.

Moreover, speaking of interests is advantageous in a discussion of political decision-making for another reason. Interests are likely to be characterized by an intrinsic reciprocity precisely because they refer to both public and private spheres. Academic excellence, for instance, is an interest of the university (the group) as a whole because it concerns the university's standing among all universities. But the university's academic excellence is also an interest that affects every individual member of the university—students, faculty, and administration alike. The more specifically academic excellence as an interest is articulated by the group as a whole as well as by its individual members, the more agreement can undoubtedly be achieved in connection with any particular decision that may have to be made.

I have spoken of "interest articulation" without defining it. I mean by it the ways in which individual or group interests are structured in the perceptions and verbalizations of the decision-makers. In order to deal with this structuring most efficiently, I shall dichotomize interests into those which are "specific" and those that are "diffuse." These articulations represent forms of orientations to action which decision-makers bring into the choice situation.[22] From

---

well and Abraham Kaplan, *Power and Society* (1950), p. 23. "Interest" is admittedly an ambiguous term. Though it is so widely used in political science, it has not been really explicated or operationalized. David B. Truman's definition—"The shared attitudes . . . constitute the interests"— does not seem useful for my purposes. See his *The Governmental Process* (1951), p. 34.

[22] The notion that interest articulation may be specific or diffuse is indebted to Talcott Parsons' conception of "pattern variables," defined as "a dichotomy one side of which must be chosen by an actor before the meaning of a situation is determinate for him, and thus before he can act with respect to that situation." See *Toward a General Theory of Action,* ed. Talcott Parsons and Edward A. Shils (1951), p. 77. However, my own usage, it should be noted, deviates somewhat from the Parsonian explication of the specificity-diffuseness "dilemma." Similar formulations are in *The Politics of the Developing Areas,* ed. Gabriel A. Almond and James S. Coleman (1960), pp. 33–38.

this perspective, both individual interests and group or public interests may be described as being specifically or diffusely articulated.

Interest Diffuseness. Interests may be said to be diffusely articulated if the demands that are made, either by an individual or a group, do not constitute a hierarchy of preferences which would give priority in decision-making to one demand over another. In other words, the decision-maker will promote any demand that is compatible with other demands, whether public or private, without, at least initially, ordering these demands in terms of the values which may be involved. By not committing himself to one demand over another in advance, the decision-maker is likely to be guided in the choices he makes by the exigencies of the decisional situation, and he is likely to respond to the situation in terms of his predispositions at the time of decision-making and the nature of the problem at hand. For instance, a city council is intent on making the city "a better place to live in." It does not quite know what it means by this or how to achieve it. Its interest is diffusely articulated. A proposal to build a community ball park is made, seconded, and, in due time, voted on, without much attention being given to alternatives.

Interest Specificity. Interests may be said to be specifically articulated if the different demands that are made, either by an individual or a group, can be readily located within some hierarchy of preferences so that the relevance of a demand in regard to other demands, and to the choice problem at hand, can be specifically determined. In other words, the decision-maker will give priority to that one of his demands over all other demands that is immediately relevant to the problematic situation. To put this somewhat differently, the decision-maker confronts the problematic situation in terms of specifically articulated interests and the requirements for their achievement, but this behavior will be compatible with the exclusion, temporary or permanent, of other interests. For instance, a political group decides to support X, who is running for office. The group proceeds to collect money, distribute leaflets, and arrange coffee hours for the candidate. The group's interest in seeing X win is specifically articulated, for in ordering its preferences it presumably concluded that support of this candidate will not preclude advancing and attaining other interests.

It is possible now to suggest ways of collective interest articulation that result when individual and group interests are either specifically or diffusely articulated. The following matrix shows the possibilities:

		Articulation of Member	
		Specific	*Diffuse*
	Specific	(1)	(2)
Articulation of Group		Pluralism	Monism
	Diffuse	(3)	(4)
		Dictatorship	Anarchy

In cell one of the matrix, as the interests of every individual in the group as well as of the group itself are specifically articulated, the decisional problem is one of dealing with specific demands of a rather plural character by setting priorities through bargaining. Because of the probably very great number of specific demands that are made, the setting of priorities is never likely to be completed. Decisions are likely to be made through majority voting by shifting coalitions. Collective articulation is essentially plural and democratic.

In cell four, on the other hand, inaction is the likely result, for the diffuseness of interest articulation, by all the members as individuals and by the group as a whole, prevents collective articulation. In fact, the situation has so little empirical viability that the group is likely to disintegrate in view of its inability to articulate individual or group interests. Insofar as there is articulation, it is best conceptualized as anarchic.

The outcome of cell-two articulation is quite different. In a situation in which the group's interest articulation is specific, but the individual's articulation is diffuse, there is likely to be strong pressure to accede to group demands. Unlike the situation in cell one, the individual with diffuse interest articulation will not order his own individual preferences in view of the group's specifically articulated interests. The situation points towards a monistic articulation of group interests with unanimous decision-making as a strong possibility.

Finally, the situation that emerges in cell three suggests dictatorship as the form of interest articulation in decision-making. Because the interest articulation of the group as a whole is diffuse, so that there is no predecisional ordering of group preferences, and because at least some individuals have specifically articulated interests, there is a strong strain, initially, towards conflict. But because, unlike in the plural order, group articulation is diffuse, the conflict is likely to be resolved through dictatorship—that is, one person (or a subgroup like a triumvirate) comes to dictate the terms of collective interest articulation. In some respects, this situation, if reinforced by structural constraints of coercion, points to the kind of pseudounanimity which, as Friedrich and Brzezinski suggest, "makes the totalitarians insist on the complete agreement of the entire population under their control to the measures the regime is launching."[23] But even without coercion, group-diffuse, individual-specific interest articulation is likely to make for some form of dictatorial collective articulation.[24]

My concern in the following will be only with the articulation outcomes suggested by cells two and three, for in these situations some form of unanimity appears as a likely decisional result. The process represented by cell one is of no further interest because, if a unanimous decision emerges at all, we can assume that we are dealing with the genuine article that is eminently rational. Presumably, there has been free choice among alternatives and conscious selection, after specific individual or group demands have been deliberated upon and negotiated. But unanimity is not likely in a situation in which individual and group articulation is specific. Majority voting is sufficient to reach decisions. The process represented by cell four will also be ignored in the following discussion. It refers to a situation in which deadlock seems to be preferred. Neither private nor collective action would be possible.

V

A typology of unanimity has the immediate purpose of locating empirical situations of or hypotheses concerning unanimous decision-making in a consistent schema. A typology of this kind can be constructed out of the two dimensions that have been discussed— ways of decision-handling and ways of interest articulation.

The behavioral assumption is made, to repeat, that the relationship between individual and group is such that individual and group interests need not conflict, but are both attainable simultaneously through collective action. Unanimity in decisional patterns would then be evidence of the validity of the behavioral assumption. This does not mean that unanimity is the inevitable decisional outcome whenever a certain way of decision-handling and a certain constellation of interest articulation intersect. However, there is a strong

23 Carl J. Friedrich and Zbigniew K. Brzezinski, *Totalitarian Dictatorship* (1956), p. 132.
24 We may well speak of the "arbitrator" as a dictator in the sense that his decision in a dispute is unanimously accepted, by prearrangement, by both sides to a dispute, as in labor-management relations.

presumption that one or another type of unanimity, when it occurs, is ascertainable in terms of the intersection or confluence of the two dimensions.

We can construct a six-cell unanimity matrix. In interpreting the types represented by the cells, it will be assumed that the three ways of decision-handling will intersect with the two critical ways of interest articulation (group-specific/individual-diffuse and group-diffuse/individual-specific) in characteristic fashion. The tendency towards unanimity is assumed to be present, then, when group and individual ways of interest articulation are asymmetrical, and when they are molded by the prevailing ways of decision-handling so that the particular type of unanimity is clearly distinct from every other type. The following matrix represents the typology:

Ways of Decision-Handling

Ways of interest Articulation	*Consensual*	*Political*	*Ministerial*
Group-specific	(1)	(3)	(5)
Individual-diffuse	Ancestral	Bargained	Functional
Group-diffuse	(2)	(4)	(6)
Individual-specific	False	Projected	Injunctive

Ancestral Unanimity. If the group's interests are specific, but individual interests are diffuse, and if, at the same time, decisions are handled consensually, there is likely to be a very strong commitment to make unanimous decisions, partly because there is long-standing agreement on what, under certain circumstances, should be done, and partly because the maintenance of group solidarity requires that it should be done unanimously. Individual interests, being diffuse, are submerged in group interests, and there is, therefore, little opportunity for individual interests to be sufficiently crystallized to affect the decisional situation and to occasion division. Alternatives facing the group are decided by traditionally ordered priorities, with little likelihood that group agreement will be disturbed by the intrusion of specific individual interests. Whatever private interests an individual may have are fulfilled in the achievement of the group's interests. Unanimity may be said to be ancestral.

This type of ancestral unanimity seems to be implicit in Keefe's hypothesis concerning unanimous decisions in American state legislatures:

The area of agreement on legislative questions is so large in some two-party states that significant divisions along discernible lines (e.g., party, rural-urban, sectional, conservative-liberal, etc.) must necessarily be something less than frequent. It may not be so much a matter of "leadership" as simply a case of like-minded legislators moving from bill to bill in the broad fields of state public policy where consensus rather than conflict obtains.[25]

The hypothesis implies that even in modern, functionally highly differentiated political systems there remain vestiges of traditional, customary understandings of what things should or should not be done by the polity. These group preferences are so firmly established and so widely shared that they preclude the emergence of specific individual interests that might be at odds with group interests.

False Unanimity. An altogether different configuration characterizes the decisional situation in which the interests of the group are diffuse, but those of the individual members are specific, yet where decision-handling is essentially consensual. The group's inability to order its interests preferentially, but the existence of specific individual interests, creates a situation that is potentially full of tension and conflict. Yet, the habit of handling decisions consensually and the need to maintain group solidarity, though group interest articulation is diffuse, makes for superficial agreement that prohibits the airing of individual interests inimical to group solidarity. As a result, individual interests, though specific, are suppressed or concealed in the name of the group. Mediators or conciliators cannot function because they have no way of identifying the sources and parties of conflicts. As group interest articulation is diffuse, decisions, even though unanimous, are not genuine expressions of group consensus. Unanimity may be said to be false.

An illustration of false unanimity is the detailed description of the "politics of unanimity" by Vidich and Bensman in their study of the village and school boards of a small, rural community. The school board, for instance,

> reaches its decisions through a process of discussion which results in an inchoately arrived-at unanimous decision in which no vote, or only a perfunctory one, is taken. . . . It becomes central to the psychology of the members of the board to attempt to minimize or avoid crises, and this leads to further demands for unanimity and concealment.[26]

[25] Keefe, *op. cit.,* p. 311.
[26] Arthur J. Vidich and Joseph Bensman, *Small Town in Mass Society* (1960), p. 176.

As a hypothesis, the notion of concealment or "false unanimity" is probably more viable in small legislative bodies such as city councils or committees than in large institutionalized groups like state legislatures or the Congress, where a façade of unity is practically impossible in normal conflictual situations, and where partisanship rather than friendly agreement is the public expectation.

Bargained Unanimity. Where the task of decision-making is to integrate diffuse individual interests in terms of specific group interests in a decision-handling structure that is "political," unanimity, if it occurs, probably stems from successful trading and bargaining among the individual members. The bargaining process is facilitated, on the one hand, by the diffuseness of the individual interests: No intransigent positions are likely to be taken, and the spirit of compromise prevails. Moreover, the specificity of group interests sets limits to the bargaining process—not everything goes, for, if everything goes, bargaining will not lead to compromise. In this situation, then, conflicts are resolved through compromise in terms of specific group interests. Unanimity may be said to be bargained.

Bargained unanimity is implicit in Truman's explanation of unanimous decisions in larger legislative bodies. He suggests that

> even where virtual unanimity prevails in the legislature, the process of reconciling conflicting interests must have taken place—though perhaps at an earlier stage wholly or partly outside the legislature and the formal institutions of government. When this happens, the legislature merely registers the decision.[27]

There is the assumption, then, first, that conflict has in fact occurred, but second, that the conflict has been so successfully resolved that it culminates in unanimity.

Projected Unanimity. If, on the other hand, group interests are diffuse, yet individual interests are specific, the political bargaining process encounters difficulties. The absence of an articulated group

---

[27] Truman, *op.cit.*, p. 392. Unfortunately, Truman then gives what seems to me a rather dubious example. The last sentence quoted here continues: ". . . as the Congress did in its declaration of war after Pearl Harbor." I am not clear what conflict Truman had in mind that was resolved prior to the declaration of war. If he means the battle between internationalists or interventionists and isolationists, it is inaccurate to say that it had been solved prior to Pearl Harbor. It would be more appropriate to say that it was "tabled." Moreover, as I suggested in footnote 8, the unanimity accompanying the declaration of war is not likely to be one that can be considered due to a process of free choice.

interest makes the political game appear to be fragmented and kaleidoscopic. Conflict is not suppressed as it is in the case of false unanimity, and the game is played as in the case of bargained unanimity. But as political decision-handling is not altogether formal and contains informal patterns, there is likely to be a tendency to go along with a somewhat fictitious group consensus. The consensus is fictitious because the group interest is not really articulated. How can unanimity be explained in this situation? I shall suggest a hypothesis.

Because group interests are poorly articulated and diffuse, the decisional situation will appear ambiguous to the decision-makers. Yet, as there is a pressure for decision—individual specific interests are promoted—some perceptual structuring of the ambiguous situation is needed. Therefore, the individual decision-maker will tend to project his own preferred interests on the group as a whole. Not knowing where others stand, such projection provides the individual with a perceptual anchorage point. He expects others to decide in the way in which he himself decides. This psychological ordering of the ambiguous situation involves a great deal of perceptual distortion.[28] But it may have the effect of creating a cognitive environment in which psychological pressure towards a unanimous decision becomes very great. If it is believed that everybody agrees with everybody else, the image of unanimity can serve as a kind of protective screen from responsibility for failure to resolve an issue in those terms in which it was originally defined by the individual with specific interests himself. Unanimity may be said to be projected.

Projected unanimity seems to be implicit in an interesting finding by Crane concerning party cohesion in the Wisconsin legislature. One might surmise that the absence of division in a legislative party is simply a function of legislators' indifference concerning a piece of legislation. Party cohesion, for instance, should occur only in policy matters where the group's interest is specific enough for legislators to feel strongly about the stakes at issue. Yet, Crane reports, "party

[28] For other examples of the projection hypothesis in politics and some proof, especially in electoral voting, see A. Thomsen, "Psychological Projection and Election," *Journal of Psychology*, II (1941), 115–117; Paul F. Lazarsfeld, Bernard Berelson, and Hazel Gaudet, *The People's Choice* (1948), p. 168; and Heinz Eulau, "Class Identification and Projection in Voting Behavior," *Western Political Quarterly*, VIII (1955), 441–452.

cohesion was most easily maintained on those issues about which legislators were least concerned and apparently regarded as least important."[29] In other words, cohesion within the parties occurred on unimportant rather than, as one might expect, on important issues. Though we are dealing here with a subgroup rather than the full group, it would seem that in the situation described by Crane we encounter a case of projected unanimity for the subgroups in question. Individually specific interests seem to be surrendered in favor of a psychologically satisfying, if unreal, unanimity.

Functional Unanimity. The impact of ministerial decision-handling on a situation in which individual interests are diffuse, but group interests are specific, is likely to produce a kind of unanimity that is compelling because alternatives are drastically reduced. Decision-makers, whether themselves in a ministerial position, as judges are, or whether acting on the advice of persons in ministerial positions, as legislators do on recommendations from administrative experts, appeal to and accept "authority" precisely because individual interests, being diffuse, do not intrude strongly on the decision process. At the same time, the specificity of group interests provides an evaluative reference point for what action must be taken. This does not mean that disagreements over group interests do not exist. But they are clarified and resolved in terms of rather impersonal criteria, such as routine, precedent or specialized knowledge. Unanimity may be said to be functional.

To illustrate functional unanimity, let us shift to judicial decision-making. For instance, speaking of the "powerful factors normally operating to achieve unanimity in the decisions of the Supreme Court," Pritchett attributes unanimous decisions, among other reasons, to "the generally settled character of the American legal system, fairly strict adherence to the principle of stare decisis, and the broad similarities in training and background which tend to characterize Supreme Court justices. . . ." Pritchett also points out that "the influence of a strong and skillful Chief Justice is of great importance in leading to the discovery of solutions satisfactory to all members of the Court."[30] In other words, an issue is resolved by appeal to the authority of precedent.

[29] Wilder Crane, Jr., "A Caveat on Roll-Call Studies of Party Voting," *Midwest Journal of Political Science,* IV (1960), 246–247.

[30] C. Herman Pritchett, *The Roosevelt Court* (1948), p. 24. Pritchett names other factors as well, such as "the discussion which goes on around

Analogous to the authority of precedent in judicial decision-making is probably the authority of routine in legislative action. In city councils, for instance, routine handling of issues serves as an impersonal criterion for deciding what should or should not be done. Or a legislative group may accept the recommendations of an administrative specialist—an engineer who advises on the location of a bridge, or a city manager. Acceptance of an expert's judgment is presumably based on his professional disinterestedness that stems from his specialized know-how rather than from his personal relations with his clients.

Injunctive Unanimity. This is, of course, the behavioral situation which underlies the constitutional unanimity rule. The constitution itself becomes a ministerial-like reference point. Individual interests are so specific and group interests so diffuse that unanimity is the only way of protecting individual interests from each other or preventing the emergence of a collective decision to which individual members cannot subscribe. As suggested earlier, unanimity in this situation may either create deadlock or serve to resolve it. The formal rule of unanimity enjoins the individual members from imposing their specific interests upon each other. Unanimity may be said to be injunctive.

But unanimity of this kind can be present without being constitutionally required. The consensus of the Quaker meeting seems to be of this order. Although formal voting is eschewed, an issue is discussed until a solution emerges to which all individuals can agree or, at least, from which any one individual will not dissent.[31] In the case of the Quaker meeting, the appeal to "conscience" serves as the impersonal criterion for giving or withholding consent. This procedure is functionally equivalent to the constitutional unanimity rule.

---

the judicial conference table, out of which consensus can often be achieved." This suggests that judicial unanimity can also be explained as "bargained unanimity." And "false unanimity" through concealment seems to be relevant in explaining the Court's behavior under Chief Justice Marshall. See John R. Schmidhauser, *The Supreme Court* (1960), p. 114: "The price of maintaining the fiction of judicial certainty, decisiveness, and unity was the camouflaging of real doubt, and occasionally, the acceptance by individual justices of positions which they personally knew to be erroneous. Justice Story was, without doubt, the most careful legal scholar on the Supreme Court during this period. Yet he was persuaded, on several occasions, to accept erroneous decisions silently for the sake of the Court's reputation and unity." In other words, one should not confuse a given type of unanimity with a particular institution.

[31] See Francis Pollard, *Democracy and the Quaker Method* (1949).

It is because the process involved is costly and time consuming that democracy is willing to deviate from the unanimity rule and accept that degree of coercion which majority voting, in the Quaker view, implies.

The typology of unanimity here outlined is probably not exhaustive, for it is necessarily an artifact of the dimensions that were used in constructing it. However, it suggests that unanimity is a multifaceted behavioral phenomenon that cannot be treated as a monomorphic structure. Moreover, the typology seems to be sufficiently comprehensive to accommodate various empirical descriptions of or hypotheses about unanimous voting. We are now in a position to examine the kind of rationality that may be involved in the various types of unanimous decision-making.

VI

As mentioned earlier, one need not start off from the behavioral assumptions of the individualistic theory of rationality in order to use the conditions of constitutional unanimity as criteria in appraising the rationality of unanimous decisions in real-life situations that are not controlled by the formal rule. Let me restate both the assumptions and the conditions for "spontaneous unanimity" (unanimity not constitutionally required) as they have emerged from the discussion, so that they can be referred to in the following appraisal.

Behavioral assumption: There is no necessary conflict between individual and group interests (though there may be), and both individual and group interests can be attained through collective action. Because each participant decision-maker expects to attain his individual interests and the interests of the group through collective action, he will accept the costs of unanimity as being less than the costs of deadlock. Unanimity has the effect of making each participant in the decision equal in status and power to every other participant, and it assures him membership in the decisive group.

First condition: A unanimous decision is rational if it is made in a situation that has the potential for free choice among alternate decisional patterns (such as majority voting or dictatorship). This condition states essentially a requirement made of the environment of choice.

Second condition: A unanimous decision is rational if it is consciously chosen from among alternate decisional patterns. This condition states essentially a requirement made of the individual actor.

To what extent, then, do the types of unanimity developed in the previous section conform to the behavioral assumptions and meet the conditions of rationality here specified?

Ancestral Unanimity: Prerationality. Ancestral unanimity does not seem to invalidate the behavioral assumptions, but it does not satisfy the first condition. The decision-handling structure is such that alternate decisional patterns are not contemplated. The behavioral style of ancestral unanimity seems to be prerational, in the sense that long-standing agreement on unanimity as a way of making collective decisions precludes the availability of alternatives. The consensus is genuine enough, but as there is no potential for free choice among alternate patterns of decision-making, it is prerational rather than rational.

False Unanimity: Counterrationality. In the case of false unanimity, the behavioral assumptions seem to be falsified. There is no guarantee in this situation that individual interests can be achieved through collective action, for they are suppressed in the name of group solidarity. On the other hand, unanimity is chosen as a preferred decisional pattern over alternate patterns, and consciously so. The rationality involved, if it can so be called, is a kind of counterrationality of fear which deters individuals from pursuing certain of their interests and which leads them to act counter to these interests in order to achieve a group interest that is poorly articulated. The consensus of false unanimity is counterrational rather than prerational, as is the consensus of ancestral unanimity.

Bargained Unanimity: Satisfying Rationality. The process that culminates in bargained unanimity seems to meet all the behavioral assumptions as well as the conditions of rationality. However, as the ways of decision-handling call for trading, bargaining, and compromise among diffuse individual interests in terms of group-specific interests, the latter are themselves subject to negotiation. The rationality involved is more likely to be of the kind which Simon calls "satisficing." Therefore, unanimity is by no means the "best" decisional pattern under the circumstances, but it is "good enough" for the attainment of the individual interests at stake. Majority voting might well be a better alternative, but it seems to be consciously ruled out if the participants in the decision-making situation can arrive at a satisfying solution through unanimity. This kind of bargained unanimity, then, is satisficingly rational.

Projected Unanimity: Irrationality. Projected unanimity fails to meet both conditions of rationality. It gives the participants the impression of being able to attain individual and group interests through collective action without really doing so. The decisional process of projected unanimity seems to stymie the ways of decision-handling that one should expect. Because group interests are diffusely articulated, the individual decision-maker is left without a stable point of reference for trading, bargaining, and compromising—a situation in which alternate decision patterns cannot be consciously chosen. The decisional impasse is resolved through unconscious projection of individual upon group interests—a process that violates the behavioral assumptions and is unlikely to attain individual or group interests. Insofar as a decision is unanimously reached in this way, it is irrational in the sense of being accidental or essentially random. Any other decisional pattern is equally plausible.

Functional Unanimity: Procedural Rationality. In situations where the group's interests are specifically articulated and decision-handling is largely ministerial, reliance on authority or precedent would seem to make for a kind of rationality that is procedural in appraising the relevance of alternate decisional patterns, given the group's specific and individuals' diffuse interests. Though the process of cumulatively procedural-rational decision-making might ultimately tend to reduce alternatives in contravention of the first condition, there is little probability that decisional alternatives in the final stages of decision-making will ever be exhausted. Unanimity itself is almost self-evident proof of the procedural rationality involved in the process, for it is likely to occur only after alternate decisional patterns have been consciously eliminated as a result of convincing argument that the choice to be made cannot be anything but unanimous.

Injunctive Unanimity: Maximizing Rationality. Injunctive unanimity presents the situation in which the individual participant with his specifically articulated interests uses his dissent whenever collective action seems to threaten his interests. The rationality involved is essentially maximizing from the individual's point of view. However, injunctive unanimity would seem to falsify our behavioral assumptions. If carried to its ultimate logical conclusion, the attempt to maximize one's individual interests at the expense of the group's interests through unanimity would be self-defeating by creating deadlock, a situation which the rationally maximizing actor does not prefer. Insofar as he prefers some action to deadlock, he will continue to debate an issue until unanimity is reached. Insistence on unanimity in this sense meets both conditions of rationality, for alternate decisional patterns are consciously rejected.

What general observations can be made about the logic of rationality in different unanimous decision-making situations? First of all, only one type—injunctive unanimity—meets the requirements of rationality derived from the classical individualistic conception of the maximizing individual. Because the requirements of maximizing rationality are severe, we should expect that only very few of the spontaneous unanimous decisions reached in the real world of politics would be of the injunctive type. Indeed, the sparse use of the formal unanimity rule in modern circumstances suggests that injunctive unanimity does not recommend itself to rational men except in the most extreme cases where they feel their "vital interests" to be at stake.

Second, only one type of unanimity—projected unanimity—is clearly irrational. It is irrational because unanimity emerges as the outcome of unconscious psychological mechanisms in a situation where one should expect division. Little is known about this type of irrationally projected unanimity, but it should be of considerable empirical research interest. For there is reason to believe that this type of unanimity is not uncommon in large political systems where neither consensual nor ministerial ways of decision-handling provide feasible behavioral alternatives.

Third, a distinction must be made between the irrational behavior involved in projected unanimity and the counterrational behavior of false unanimity. The difference is largely due to the two different ways of decision-handling, but whereas in projected unanimity the process of decision-making remains altogether obscure, in false unanimity it is all too evident. Here decisions are made in self-conscious, if not widely shared, awareness of the consequences that would ensue if the decision-makers were to promote their specifically articulated interests. Yet, they act purposefully counter to their individual interests in the name of a unity that is largely fictitious. Counterrationality might be thought of as a kind of mixture of pre-rationality and irrationality, perhaps as a kind of pseudorationality. It approximates both kinds, but is precluded from being completely prerational or irrational by virtue of its consciousness of alternatives of decisional patterns.

Fourth, the notion that decisions can be made unanimously in the sense of prerationality, as the concept is used here, should not strike one as particularly novel. That a group's consensually validated ways of doing things have an influence on current behavioral patterns has been widely observed in simple societies, and it has been hypostatized into principle by conservative ideologues who distrust the maxims of utilitarian rationality. That this type of prerational, ancestral unanimity is also found in modern decision-making situations should surprise only those who write off as irrelevant the pertinacity of informal, personal ways of decision-handling in complex collectivities.

Fifth, the typology certainly supports the notion that there is a point where the achievement of group interests is halted and circumscribed by the free play of individual interest-seeking through trading, bargaining, and compromise. This point is not likely to be the optimal point for either the attainment of group interests or the attainment of individual interests. But it is likely to satisfy the requirements of rational men. The point is reached not through maximizing but through "satisficing" rational conduct. The extent to which the "satisficing"-rational type of bargained unanimity is characteristic of unanimous decision-making in real-life politics is unknown. In all probability it is rather rare, for "satisficing" rationality does not require unanimity as a decisional pattern that is preferable to others. Satisfaction of interests can be more readily achieved through plurality or majority decisions.

Finally, the typology identifies procedural rationality as a companion of the kind of unanimity that has been called functional. A great deal of unanimity found in modern legislative bodies, as in judicial and administrative institutions, is procedurally rational. It is a kind of rationality that is "built in," so to speak, the kind of situations where the attainment of interests is sought by reliance on available resources. This has long been recognized in judicial and administrative settings, but the presence of procedural-rational unanimity in more immediately political situations, as those of legislative bodies, would seem to defy the conventional categories of institutional analysis. However, recent research on legislative processes and legislative behavior shows that specialization and reliance on expertise are not alien to primarily political decision-making.[32] The notion of

[32] See John C. Wahlke, Heinz Eulau, William Buchanan, and LeRoy C. Ferguson, *The Legislative System: Explorations in Legislative Behavior* (1962), pp. 193–215.

procedural-rational unanimity is likely to be fruitful in explaining much of the unanimous decisional outcomes in democratic institutions such as legislatures and other deliberative bodies where, in general, majority voting is the norm.

VII

We may return now to the starting point of this inquiry: Why unanimity in democratic decision-making? Is such unanimity rational? The typology of unanimity suggests that unanimous decisions may be stimulated by the confluence of diverse types of interest articulation and decision-handling. From the perspective of interest articulation, the typology intimates that there may be some pressure towards unanimity whenever either group interests are specifically articulated, yet individual interests are diffusely articulated, or vice versa. The incidence of these occurrences is an empirical research question. At the same time, different ways of decision-handling give unanimity, when it occurs under one or another condition of interest articulation, a characteristic style or format. The task of research is to locate and classify unanimous decisions in terms of the critical ways in which decisions are generally handled in choice-making situations.

What of the rational character of unanimity? Quite clearly, great caution is called for in assessing the kind of rational conduct involved in the various types of unanimity that have been identified. One result of the argument is beyond doubt: The assumption that unanimity in democratic decision-making is necessarily irrational does not seem to be warranted. Only one type—projected unanimity —could be called irrational. Other types of unanimity seem to meet various criteria of rationality, while other types are prerational or what I have called counterrational. Even if one were to combine the latter with the irrational type, it would seem that unanimity is not inevitably a deviation from some norm that requires majority voting (or some other decision rule) as the only legitimate form of democratic decision-making. Moreover, what was called bargained unanimity is eminently rational in the "satisficing" sense. Unanimity appears to be a legitimate form of democratic decision-making, though the kind of rationality involved always requires specification. One might well argue that it is perhaps more difficult to get men in responsible decision-making posts to disagree than to agree, just as in the world of business it seems more difficult to provide for competition which must often be "enforced" in the face of a "natural" inclination towards monopoly. But the central point to be made is that unanimity is not necessarily dysfunctional and symptomatic of a breakdown of the democratic process.

4

SOME LIMITATIONS
ON RATIONALITY

ABRAHAM KAPLAN

Few would argue that the human animal has become more rational in the twentieth century, but there can be no doubt that more than ever before we know what we're missing. Within our lifetimes the advances in the exact formulation and analysis of what constitutes rational behavior have been greater, I venture to say, than in the whole of history. The theory of games, of information, and of decision-making and associated techniques like linear programming, operations research, and data-processing all have provided us, not just with an impressive new vocabulary, but with new and profound insights into the nature of rational choice, incomparably richer and more subtle than those underlying the *mos geometricus* which defined rationality from Plato to Spinoza and beyond.[1] At the same time a new technology has sprung up, whose electronic components and magnetic tapes allow an exploitation of the theoretical possibilities incomparably beyond the capacity of a brain of flesh and blood; and if machines do not think, whatever it is they do puts our thinking to shame, given the same data and problems. More and more areas of rational decision have been brought into the domain of such theory and practice, and its frontier is expanding. A brave new world of rationality is in the making.

Now I believe that one of the functions of philosophy is this, that somebody must be willing to stand aside and say "However. . . ." The intent of such head-shaking is neither to derogate what has been done nor to discourage further endeavor, but only to restore a sense of perspective and, by heightening an awareness of limits to contribute, perhaps, to their expansion.

The irony that the new rationality owes much to problems of the design and use of engines of destruction need not detain us, though the hint may be kept in mind. The fact is that the technology of data-processing has proven itself beyond cavil, and the associated techniques of decision-making have contributed impressively to the solution of problems in business, industry, and the military. Our question is, what is its promise for enhancing the rationality of decisions in law and politics? And what are the difficulties in the way of fulfillment of that promise? We can process the information contained in the statutes and court records; how shall we use the data to increase the rationality of legislator, judge, and jury? Our computers will predict elections from early returns, and even before the balloting; how can we use them to decide how to vote?

That we cannot achieve everything does not imply, of course, that nothing can be done, nor do I in the least intend this implication. I want to direct attention to the reasons for moderating our expectations—surely itself a component of rationality. I shall consider some difficulties in three areas: with respect to the theory of rational decisions, in the application of the theory, and in behavior itself.

Whatever theories are formulated to schematize rational choice, some set of values must play a part in the analysis. The preferred

---

[1] D. Blackwell and M. A. Girshick, *Theory of Games and Statistical Decisions* (1954); H. Chernoff and L. E. Moses, *Elementary Decision Theory* (1959); R. D. Luce and H. Raiffa, *Games and Decisions* (1957); John von Neumann and O. Morgenstern, *Theory of Games and Economic Behavior* (1944).

terms are "utilities" and "social welfare functions," but the labels themselves solve no problems. There is first the task of determining what values are in fact being pursued, to be entered in the payoff matrix. Economists have become increasingly sensitive to the fact that the ends of economic action are not all commensurable in a single index, that even if there were one it cannot be identified with money prices, and that other utilities must also be taken into account, of the kind which social philosophers have discussed as alternatives or supplements to those reflected in the pricing system. How to measure or even unequivocally identify the utilities of political action I do not know. I believe, for example, that there is a species of political hypochondria for which anxiety provides a masochistic gratification, and which aims, therefore, at a condition of permanent crisis. Does this define a utility? Decisions of judges and juries are motivated by a complex of utilities, in which moral, social, and even religious values play a part, and many of them—perhaps the most decisive—are at work below the level of awareness. It is not clear to me what values rational decisions in law and politics are presumed to aim at.

Rationality, I should suppose, is more than a matter of acting so as to secure the values pursued. Would we not also want to say that reason judges them to be worth pursuing? I need not rehearse here the decades of discussion of the mutuality of ends and means.[2] What seems to me unexceptionable is that rationality is not limited to a choice among means. The paranoid who waits till dark before turning on his persecutors may be a master strategist; he is surely not a paragon of rationality. A theory which demands only consistency of preference scales (a stable transitivity of utilities) is grossly inadequate to the political process. Political theorists have recognized at least since Burke that the decision-maker has a responsibility beyond giving the people what they want; he owes them also his own best judgment of what they *should* want. It could be said, to be sure, that rationality is not the only desideratum for political decisions, and that what I see as a problem for rationality lies, in fact, beyond its limits. But that Satan has a fine mind and is lacking only in heart is more than I am willing to admit; I believe he is a fool from beginning to end.

In politics, above all, decision-making cannot escape the respon-

[2] John Dewey, *Theory of Valuation* (1944); C. I. Lewis, *An Analysis of Knowledge and Valuation* (1946).

sibility of judging the relative worth of disparate and perhaps conflicting values. Even decisions affecting only ourselves may involve this problem, for we are individuals only by courtesy; in truth the individual is a congress of selves, each pursuing values to which the other selves may be indifferent or hostile—if, indeed, they are even aware of the pursuit. In politics, there is no lack of such awareness, nor of such conflicts either. For theory, the difficulty is known as the "aggregation problem": how to combine a set of individual preference scales into a single group preference. Majority rule is not necessarily the rational procedure for such aggregation; it is easily shown that consistent individual scales do not necessarily yield a consistent scale for the majority.[3] There is a related problem of dividing the loot among the members of a winning coalition. To my knowledge, this problem has not been solved in game theory in any generally acceptable way; it is *the* problem of politics.

Values enter into our calculations only as expectations; they are associated with probabilities. This of itself does not impose limits on rationality; rationality does not require that we know everything, but only that we make the best use of what knowledge we have or can get. It has been well said that though the race is not to the swift nor the battle to the strong, that's the way to bet. The problem is how to fix the odds. A priori probabilities require the assumption of equiprobable alternatives, and though Carnap has developed a powerful theory of this type, it is restricted to languages of the very simplest formal structure, most unlike legal and political discourse.[4] Theories of "personal" probability, such as Savage's, allow, I think, a denial of rationality to all but me and thee, and *thy* probability estimates do not comfort me.[5] As for frequency theories, though they are intersubjective and empirically based, they need long-run sequences as subject matter.[6] Keynes must be quoted again—"In the long run we are all dead"—so that we can add, "If not sooner!" In fact, some decisions, just those we call "crucial," concern a run so short that it consists of but a single case. In sum, a theory of rational decision requires a more generally acceptable treatment of probability than I believe is now available.

Given determinate values as well as the probabilities of their

[3] Kenneth Arrow, *Social Choice and Individual Values* (1951).
[4] Rudolf Carnap, *Logical Foundations of Probability* (1950).
[5] L. J. Savage, *The Foundations of Statistics* (1954).
[6] Hans Reichenbach, *Theory of Probability* (1949).

attainment by alternative courses of action, there is still the question of the criterion by which a rational choice is to be made. Risks can vary though expectations remain constant; what is a rational valuation of the element of risk itself? Gambling has a positive utility for players of Russian roulette, a negative utility for the young man in De Maupassant's story who is so afraid he might die in a scheduled duel that he kills himself the night before. The political game of "Chicken!" is grossly irrational, Bertrand Russell has tirelessly argued; under the designation of "brinkmanship" it has been defended by others as rational indeed. Agreement on expected outcomes might still lead to different decisions. The mathematical expectation is the same whether we match pennies or hundred-dollar bills, it being zero in both cases; for my part, the smaller stake is the more rational. This example is complicated by uncertainties as to the utility of money, but the excitement of the gamble itself also plays a part.

A criterion must also make some assessment of the value of the future, that is, of how utilities are affected by the mere fact that they lie in the future. A miser saves all he can, spends only what he must; a child does just the reverse. We might all agree with Aristotle that the rational course lies somewhere between these extremes; but where? I am not raising the problem of hedging against inflation, for example; expected changes of this kind can be discounted. The question is how to allocate resources between consumption and capital goods—as it were, how to choose between consuming something now or more later, how to decide how much the generation of the revolution should sacrifice to ensure the great leap forward. For a democracy the formulation is that the welfare of the unborn must be taken into account even though they cast no vote. What is the basis of a rational assignment of such utilities or, for that matter, a rational assignment of the utilities for our own future selves? Is it rational to decide now in terms of what I may want then? Love's way never changes of promising never to change, but those unblinded by love know better.

There is a more general problem of the criterion, most easily put in terms of our optimism or pessimism. Game theory usually applies the criterion of minimizing maximum losses, apparently in the spirit of Damon Runyon's counsel that in human affairs the odds are always 6 to 5 against. But what of maximizing maximum gains? Shall we pursue the general welfare by improving the lot of those worst off or by making possible even greater achievements by those at the top? I imagine we would be inclined to use different criteria in different circumstances, according to whether it is a question of taxation, for instance, or of educational policy, making more shoes, or bigger Sputniks. Many criteria have been discussed in the literature; choice among them is one of the most vexing problems in the theory of rational decision-making.

I believe that the application to law and politics of such theories suffers from a certain formalism which so often characterizes them. There is a profound difference between the logic-in-use in rational decisions and the reconstructed logic which purports to give an account of the process insofar as it is rational. Even if the account is a good one, it must not be confused with its referent; in John Locke's memorable words, "God has not been so sparing to men as to make them barely two-legged creatures and left it to Aristotle to make them rational." In fact, most of the reconstructions are at best crude approximations. They are determined as much by the techniques which the theorist has at his disposal as by the demands of his subject matter, in accord with what I have called "the law of the instrument": Give a small boy a hammer, and he will find that everything he encounters needs pounding. Also at work is the principle of the drunkard's search: He looks for his house key, not where he dropped it, but under the street lamp, because "it's lighter there." There are fashions in styles of thought as in everything else; I have nothing against the modern mode, but I am still interested in what lies beneath it.

Theories of rationality inevitably introduce gross simplifications. Human values, in the concrete, are indefinitely extensible, both as to their causes and their effects. In political decisions, nothing is so common or so pernicious as the utilitarian fallacy, assessing effects in terms of ends that have been isolated in our thinking for the sake of the calculation, but which in fact are attended by side effects of quite comparable significance. A public-housing project which does not restrict rentals may strengthen the ghetto walls it was designed to destroy, for it will quickly be filled by the minorities for whom housing is hardest to find. The unanticipated consequences of decisions may in retrospect be seen as decisive. Matters are not improved when abstracted values are reassigned to an artificial context conforming to assumptions also made for the sake of the calculation: that functions are linear and continuous, distributions normal, operations additive, relations binary, forces independent in their action, and so on.

Of course, every theory simplifies. The condition that must be met, however, is that we have some notion of at least the direction, if not the amount, by which our conclusion must be corrected to take account of the errors introduced by the simplifying assumptions. How shall we correct for the distortions in the simple assumptions that lawyers are concerned only with truth, judges only with justice, legislators only with the general welfare, and the citizenry only with their own best interests? The most common procedure, I am afraid, is to select those factors in a decision problem which are most amenable to exact treatment, make them the substance of the theory, and leave the rest to the "psychology" rather than the "logic" of the situation. The dangers were clearly foreseen by John Stuart Mill:[7]

> It is unphilosophical [he writes] to construct a science out of a few of the agencies by which the phenomena are determined, and leave the rest to the routine of practice or the sagacity of conjecture. We either ought not to pretend to scientific forms, or we ought to study all the determining agencies equally, and endeavour, so far as it can be done, to include all of them within the pale of the science; else we shall infallibly bestow a disproportionate attention upon those which our theory takes into account, while we misestimate the rest, and probably underrate their importance.

Of particular relevance here, I think, is the effect of the quantitative idiom. Current theories of rational decision-making are from the outset quantitative in form, and while I have no use for the mystique which insists that some things are inherently qualitative, I do not see that much is gained by pretending to measures that in fact we do not have. Kenneth Arrow, who has himself made notable contributions in the application of mathematics to these problems, warns that the question is not whether there exists an appropriate mathematical expression in some Platonic realm, but whether we actually have the mathematics and measures called for.[8] The range of possibilities is greater here, however, than many people seem to appreciate; exact analyses can be made even though available scales do not permit all the arithmetical operations, or even any of them. Money and votes can both be counted, but even a campaign manager has other things to think about. What I have been getting at is

---

[7] John Stuart Mill, *A System of Logic* (1936 edition), p. 583.

[8] In *The Policy Sciences,* ed. Daniel Lerner and H. D. Lasswell (1951), p. 130.

something beyond Aristotle's caution that it is the mark of an edu-cated man not to demand more exactness in the treatment of a sub-ject than the subject allows. It is that a preoccupation with even the exactness that is possible does an injustice to less glamorous but none-theless important components of the problem of rational decision-making.

For one thing, decisions are often not even identified as such, and so tend to elude conscious aspirations to rationality. Administration, for instance, is not an inert form encasing a fixed content of policy; the executive and judicial functions are inescapably also legislative. I believe that a better fix on the locus of political decisions may contribute to making them more rational. In particular, the expand-ing role in our society of consultative bodies and expert advisers, from cyberneticists to psychoanalysts, gives the problem of locus increasing urgency. What should be the role of the physicist in de-termining rational policy on arms control or the role of the psychia-trist in the legal defense of insanity? We must appreciate, moreover, that decisions are by no means always reached in circumstances as formally defined as for "decisions" in the juridical sense. A man's character is formed and displayed more in the succession of his little, nameless, unremembered acts than in the rare dramatic moments of an agonizing choice. The rationality of a person or an institution lies in the whole way of its working, in the style of its performance; it is this that must find a place in our reconstruction.

Our usual reconstructions, I am afraid, beg the question of the range of their applicability by tacitly identifying rationality with what is self-conscious, deliberate, calculated, and controlled. But it is perfectly rational not to be *perfectly* rational. Reason itself sets limits on itself, not to make room for a Kantian faith, but, less metaphysically, simply to allow for the values in other modalities of experience. The computers may yet make Spinozists of us all, iden-tifying freedom with the determination of action by the recognition of deductive necessities. But spontaneity is also a value, and un-planned pleasures may be more gratifying even than unearned increments. The florist who ensures us against forgetting thereby destroys the meaning of remembering. Overarching plans, whether for scientific advance or for economic development, are in their very nature insensitive to what can be achieved by *un*organized effort; the anxious hostess trying to decide how to make the party go would be more rational if she left her guests alone—with the food and drink, I must add. More generally, the calculation of an optimal strategy has its own costs not represented in the payoff matrix on which the calculation is based. It may be more rational to take political and judicial errors as they come than to adopt procedures recommending themselves as more "efficient." There is much wisdom in the characterization of democracy—was it by Mark Twain?—as sailing on a raft: Your feet are always wet, but the thing doesn't sink.

I believe that, just as the bottleneck in the use of computers is the human programmer, so the key to enhancing the rationality of decisions in law and politics lies as much in the human psyche as in the mathematics of choice or in the technology of data-processing. What makes a brave new world, after all, is that it has such *people* in it. By and large, our irrationalities do not stem from inadequacies or errors in our theories of decision-making, but from the fact that these theories have no purchase in personality. We are all in a condition, more or less, of human bondage, and subject what reason we are endowed with to the shackles of anxiety and guilt. In politics, as Harold Lasswell pointed out long ago, private motives are projected onto public policy, and no doubt this is quite as true of the legal process as well.[9] The irrationality of the performance of courts and legislatures on matters involving the relations between the races or the sexes is only more conspicuous, but I venture to say no less pervasive, than when they involve the relations between labor and management, or between the United States and the Soviet Union. If only we could nullify the belief in the magic of symbols—to mention but one infantilism—we would do more for rationality in law and politics than by adding game theory to every legal curriculum and installing computers in every judge's chambers.

Though the focus must be on the individual, plainly the rationality of decisions is also very much a matter of social patterns. The division of labor in a complex society imposes on all of us real dependencies, but these easily regress to a pathological state as we abdicate our individual responsibilities. Decisions reflect only conformity, according to what Carl J. Friedrich has called "the rule of anticipated reaction," while personal preferences are expressed in a feat of ventriloquism which attributes them to the common will.[10] Autonomy both before and after the decision, awareness, and acceptance both of the self which makes the decision and of the con-

---

[9] H. D. Lasswell, *The Analysis of Political Behavior* (1947).
[10] C. J. Friedrich, *Constitutional Government and Politics* (1937).

sequences which follow from it are necessary conditions of its rationality. A society in which information must be transmitted through increasingly noisy channels, both interpersonally and within the personality, does not nurture awareness either of the world within or of the world without. Such rationality as our decisions do manifest is, I think, remarkable for a culture which spends three times as much on advertising as on all its colleges and universities, public and private, put together.

None of these strictures is intended as a counsel of despair. I hope I have given no comfort at all to the obscurantists who resist every idea beyond their limited understanding, or to the reactionaries who resist every social reform which transcends their limited interests. My intent has been rather to indicate the need for reinterpreting "rationality" as we move from the sort of problems with which current theory is largely occupied to those arising in the contexts of legal and political behavior. The Zen master who was asked whether he believed in God replied, "If you do, I don't; and if you don't, I do." My present disbelief is not a lack of faith, but my way of saying "However . . ." to the faithful.

The application of mathematics and machines to human decisions is already a triumph of the human mind and may ultimately release our energies for greater triumphs of the human spirit. But I believe that the greater the promise, the greater the humility with which we must set about securing its fulfillment. "Be not overly wise," saith the preacher; "why should you destroy yourself?" I have no quarrel with the great rallying cry of rationality, Freud's watchword, "Where id was, there shall ego be!" I ask only that first we be sure that we have cut our egos down to size.

LAW AS DECISION-MAKING

5

THE LIMITED RATIONALITY OF LAW

GOTTFRIED DIETZE

I

Law is a limitation upon rationality.

At first, this statement puzzles. It contradicts prevalent beliefs that law is a rational means for the elimination of irrationality and is the very offspring of rationality. How can, it will be asked, something rational be a limitation upon rationality? Law, it is generally believed, transforms disorder (said to be irrational by definition) into order (said to be rational by definition). Diderot's statement in the *Encyclopédie,* "Je ne veux ni donner, ni recevoir des lois,"[1] became a slogan for anarchists, people who, because of their rejection of law and order, are believed to be irrational. If anarchists reject law, we may argue, because they consider it a limitation upon their

[1] Quoted by Oscar Jászi, "Anarchism," *Encyclopaedia of the Social Sciences* (1930), II, 47.

rationality—a rationality which by nonanarchical standards equals irrationality—then law cannot very well be a limitation upon rationality.

The thesis that law constitutes a limitation upon rationality is contested on still other grounds. Concrete orders are considered rational because they are ruled by law. The cosmic order is conceived to be rational because it is believed to function by virtue of natural laws. The earthly order appears rational because it is under law, be it that of God, or nature, or man. Men are said to have left the irrational state of nature, characterized by anarchy, in order to live in a rational society, characterized by legal order. Societies appear rational to the degree to which they are ordered and organized by law. Carl Schmitt pointed out that the modern state is more rational than its medieval predecessor because there exists no doubt as to the law.[2] For Max Weber, the modern state is the "rational state," a state based upon "rational law."[3]

The rational quality of the law has always been recognized. Anarchies, irrespective of how much they may have been praised at times, usually were considered utopian—irrational. Plato, whose ideal state is one without law, came to realize that such a state hardly could exist. He finally admitted that a state under law was more feasible.[4] Though less ideal, such a state was more rational. In our time, the utopian character of Marx's ideal of a society without law has been generally acknowledged.

The preceding discussion indicates that a thesis, "law is a limitation upon rationality," is not undisputable. It is the purpose of this paper to marshal support for that thesis. The arguments advanced will basically turn around the proposition that men, while they are rational, are not just that and that human rationality finds its limits in more or less irrational forces. Law, being recognized and made by men, must reflect these forces and must, therefore, be a limitation upon rationality.

The not quite rational quality of the law is evident in all laws recognized and made by men.

Law has been called "reason unaffected by desire."[5] Thus ideal-

---

[2] Compare Carl Schmitt, *Legalität und Legitimität* (1932), p. 15.

[3] Max Weber, *Wirtschaftsgeschichte* (1923), pp. 289–290.

[4] These views were taken, respectively, in the *Republic* and the *Laws*.

[5] Coke's *Institutes of the Laws of England*, I, §138, refer to the law as "perfection of reason."

ized, law appears as the *ultima ratio*. However, this high evaluation is rather dubious. For neither is law as men know it usually unaffected by desire, nor can it be an unadulterated reflection of the *ultima ratio* even if it were unaffected by desire. To turn to the latter proposition first, it cannot be seen why absence of desire alone should make law an embodiment of the *ultima ratio*. In our human existence, there exist many factors which determine human action, factors that are often irrational. Taken into consideration by more or less irrational men, these factors contribute to errors in the discovery as well as the creation of the law, and prevent law from being something merely rational. A fortiori, law affected by desire can hardly be something merely rational. For it is improbable that desire equals rationality.

Law as men recognize or make it, be it unaffected or affected by desire, is thus not something merely rational. The saying, *error multiplex, veritas una*, could be complemented by the dictum, *lex multiplex, ratio una*. We know the law, but we are unable to discern the *ultima ratio*. This applies to all types of law, divine or natural, common or customary, written or codified.

Natural law as seen by men is a limitation upon rationality.

Irrespective of how much man will strive to discover natural law —and the "eternal recurrence of natural law"[6] shows that his striving has been perpetual—man's limited rationality will only find part of that law's truth and perceive a more or less subjectivized natural law. In search for natural law, man, hoping that such law is omnipresent in the sky,[7] "confidently reaches for heaven."[8] However, if

[6] Compare Charles Grove Haines, *The Revival of Natural Law Concepts* (1930); Heinrich Rommen, *Die ewige Wiederkehr des Naturrechts* (2nd ed.; 1947).

[7] Compare Oliver W. Holmes's statement in *Southern Pacific Co.* v. *Jensen*, 244 U.S. 205, 222 (1917).

[8] Compare Stauffacher's words in Friedrich Schiller's *Wilhelm Tell*, Act 2, Scene 2:

> Nein, eine Grenze hat Tyrannenmacht:
> Wenn der Gedrückte nirgends Recht kann finden,
> Wenn unerträglich wird die Last—greift er
> Hinauf getrosten Mutes in den Himmel
> Und holt herunter seine ew'gen Rechte,
> Die droben hangen unveräusserlich
> Und unzerbrechlich, wie die Sterne selbst—
> Der alte Urstand der Natur kehrt wieder
> Wo Mensch dem Menschen gegenüber steht—
> Zum letzten Mittel, wenn kein andres mehr

the reader will permit a continuation of Holmes's and Schiller's language, the sky will not always be clear. If it is overcast, man cannot be sure whether, when reaching into the clouds, he reaches in the right direction. For even above the clouds, light may be in some places, and not in others. Chances are that he will not grasp the absolute truth. He will hardly be in a better position with a clear sky. The sun might blind him. Great as his hopes of finding the *ultima ratio* may be, he will probably not succeed in seeing it, even if his search is not affected by desire.

However, since in most instances man's search for law is motivated by desire, the probability of finding the right natural law is further diminished. Natural law largely becomes what we want it to be. Our search for it is often motivated by our more or less egoistic version of the *Zweck im Recht.*[9] Since the purpose of the law will be conceived of differently by different people at different times, there is bound to be, as such relativizers of natural law as Stammler, Saleilles, and Holmes maintained, a natural law with a changing content.[10]

This relativized concept of natural law is not as revolutionary as it may have appeared some generations ago. For it only recognized the truism that not quite rational man is unable to find what is absolutely rational. This recognition came at a time when many people had become aware of the fallacy of the belief in the infallibility of human reason, a belief that had gained ascendancy during the Enlightenment and found expression in Rousseau's idea of the infallibility of the *législateur* of the *volonté générale.* By the end of the nineteenth century, one knew that the legislator often had failed in his attempts to transmute natural law into positive norms simply because he had been unable to discover the *ultima ratio* of natural law to begin with.[11]

Verfangen will, ist ihm das Schwert gegeben—
Der Güter höchsten dürfen wir verteid'gen
Gegen Gewalt.

[9] When Rudolf von Jhering spoke of "the purpose of the law," he had in mind the whole legal order. *Der Zweck im Recht* (3rd ed.; 1893), II, viii. As to his admission that the purpose of the law also applies to natural law, see *ibid.,* pp. xiiff.

[10] See Rudolf Stammler, *Die Lehre von dem richtigen Rechte* (1902); Raymond Saleilles, "Ecole historique et droit naturel," *Revue trimestrale* (1912), p. 80; Oliver W. Holmes, "Natural Law," *Collected Legal Papers* (1920), p. 310.

[11] On the decline of natural law since the nineteenth century, see the author's *In Defense of Property* (1963), pp. 149–152.

Customary or common law is a limitation upon rationality.

Common law is often considered to be a transmutation of reason into custom. Due to this transmutation, it is more specified and more tangible than natural law. And yet, common law is not clarified beyond doubt. Its backbone, the rule of precedent, includes the right of overruling precedent. Common law cannot be completely clear because it is made by not quite rational man. And age by itself cannot transform the partly irrational into the absolutely rational. Even the so-called "artificial reason" of the common law, that is, the most rational common law, cannot be absolutely rational. For it came into being through constant growth and thus was constantly modified by man's "natural reason," that is, by more or less subjective views, views held by not quite rational, and often interested, men. Sir Edward Coke, though he was convinced of the great rationality of the artificial reason of the common law, agreed with this proposition. For him, neither the common law as temporarily conceived by man's natural reason, nor the accumulation of such natural reasons, the "artificial" reason of the law, could be perfectly rational. This was evident in his stand against James I. When the jurisdiction of the ecclesiastical Court of High Commission was at issue, James I took exception to Coke's view that the clergy's Roman interpretation was not acceptable under common law. But Coke reminded the King that "the common law protecteth the King." Thereupon the King shouted back at Coke that "the King protecteth the law, not the law the King."[12] Later, a controversy arose over the question whether the King had the right to stay a court proceeding, a right which, according to the judges of King's Bench, he was denied under common law. Coke, speaking for the judges, rejected James's idea that "natural reason," unrelated to a knowledge of the law of the land, could be lawfully employed in the interpretation of the common law: "The common law itself is nothing else but reason; which is to be understood as an artificial perfection of reason, gotten by long study, observation and experience, and not as every man's natural reason; for, *Nemo nascitur artifex . . . neminem oportet esse sapientiorem legibus:* 'no man out of his private reason ought to be wiser than the law, which is the perfection of reason.' "[13]

[12] See Carl J. Friedrich, *Constitutional Government and Democracy* (rev. ed.; 1950), p. 105.

[13] Coke, *loc. cit.*

Given in reply to James's admission that he had "never studied the common law of England,"[14] Coke's dictum denied that the natural reason of those untrained in common law could discover that law. However, it did more than that. When Coke says that *no man*, and not, *no man untrained in law*, ought to be wiser than the law (which, since man is either superior or inferior to the law, means that no man can be as wise as the law), then he states that nobody, including those trained in law, can be as wise as the law: According to Coke, common law is wiser—more rational—than the natural reason of all men, including jurists.

As to the question whether the artifical reason of the common law, which "by many successions of ages . . . has been fined and refined by an infinite number of grave and learned men, and by long experience grown to . . . perfection," can be absolutely rational, Coke, much as he is convinced of that reason's relative perfection, implies that it cannot. This follows from his admission that the "artificial" reason of the common law is common law refined by "grave and learned men," that is, by their natural reason. When he says that, "if all the reason that is dispersed into so many several heads, were united into one, yet could he not make such a law as the law of England is," he denies human beings, irrespective of how well they might be trained in the law, the ability of making a perfectly rational common law. When he considers the artificial reason of the law as *summa ratio*, he has in mind only a *summa ratio* that can be perceived by fallible man—by the natural reason of man. This *summa ratio*, being nothing but a perfection of *natural* reason, cannot be absolutely rational. Nothing else could Coke have had in mind when he called law "the perfection of reason."[15] Otherwise, he would not have stated that the common law had throughout the ages grown to *an* artificial perfection of reason; he would have said that it had grown to *the* perfection of reason,—to an absolute perfection.

The improbability of discovering the absolutely rational in the common law is also demonstrated by the judicial process, a process that is basic to the common law. For that process is too tenuous to guarantee a revelation of the absolute. Like other human beings, judges have their limitations and thus cannot produce what is abso-

---

[14] *The Works of Francis Bacon*, ed. Basil Montagu (1842), II, 493.
[15] Coke, *loc. cit.*

lutely rational. Justice Cardozo describes their dilemma in his book on *The Nature of the Judicial Process:*

> I was much troubled in spirit, in my first years upon the bench, to find how trackless was the ocean on which I had embarked. I sought for certainty. I was oppressed and disheartened when I found that the quest for it was futile. I was trying to reach land, the solid land of fixed and settled rules, the paradise of a justice that would declare itself by tokens plainer and more commanding than its pale and glimmering reflections in my own vacillating mind and conscience. I found "with the voyagers in Browning's 'Paracelsus' that the real heaven was always beyond." As the years have gone by, and as I have reflected more and more upon the nature of the judicial process, I have become reconciled to the uncertainty, because I have grown to see it as inevitable.[16]

Cardozo does not only discuss "the forces of which judges avowedly avail to shape the form and content of their judgments." While he feels that "even these forces are seldom fully in consciousness," he unequivocally admits that "deep below consciousness are other forces, the likes and dislikes, the predilections and the prejudices, the complex of instincts and emotions and habits and convictions, which make the man, whether he be litigant or judge."[17]

Deriving from human action, common law cannot be absolutely rational. It thus shares with natural law the quality of being a limitation upon rationality.

Codified law is a limitation upon rationality.

Bentham denounced unwritten law as a "law which is uncertain in its essence—law without beginning and without end—law by which animals are governed, and which is disgraceful to men." In his opinion, "written law is alone deserving of the name of law," because it alone possesses "a certain manifest foundation" and "certainty."[18] But is codified law free of the irrationalities we found in natural and common law? Is it absolutely rational and thus no limitation upon rationality? We do not think so.

A passage in Goethe's *Faust* suggests that written law is as much

[16] Benjamin N. Cardozo, *The Nature of the Judicial Process* (1921), p. 166.

[17] *Ibid.,* p. 167.

[18] Jeremy Bentham, "A General View of a Complete Code of Laws," in *The Works of Jeremy Bentham,* ed. John Bowring (1843), III, 206.

a limitation upon rationality as unwritten law.[19] One may perhaps venture to claim that written law proves better than natural and common law that law is a limitation upon rationality.

Just as the adherents of customary law claimed the greater rationality of that law vis-à-vis natural law (a claim that was matched by the claim of the *Naturrechtler* that natural law was more rational than customary law), in a like manner the friends of codified law have claimed that theirs is the most rational law of all. The history of law is characterized by continuous conflicts between, or superiority claims of, natural, customary, and codified law. In his constant desire to improve things, man has wavered between the acceptance of various types of law and attempted to outrationalize one type through another.

Natural law became, as Radbruch puts it, "a magnificent historical fact owing to an absolute necessity of reason."[20] This was due to attacks upon natural law by the historical school as well as by codifiers. Customary law did not fare much better. In spite of the boom of the historical school in the first half of the nineteenth century, it was unable to halt the march of legislation. Hegel expressed thoughts similar to those of Bentham when he maintained that customary law was barbarian and that justice could only be achieved through codification.[21] The remarks of these two men reflect the general feeling of those favoring codification over customary and natural law.

The attacks against natural law and customary law often went parallel. In some cases, they first concentrated upon natural law,

[19] Faust, Part I, Studierzimmer scene:
    Es erben sich Gesetz' und Rechte
    Wie eine ew'ge Krankheit fort
    Sie schleppen von Geschlecht sich zum Geschlechte
    Und rücken sacht von Ort zu Ort.
    Vernunft wird Unsinn, Wohltat Plage;
    Weh dir, dass du ein Enkel bist!
    Vom Rechte, das mit uns geboren ist
    Von dem ist, leider! nie die Frage.
[20] Gustav Radbruch, *Rechtsphilosophie* (4th ed.; 1950), p. 305.
[21] Hegel wrote:
Barbaren werden durch Triebe, Sitten, Gefühle regiert, aber sie haben kein Bewusstsein davon. Dadurch, dass das Recht gesetzt und gewusst ist, fällt alles Zufällige der Empfindung, des Meinens, die Form der Rache, des Mitleids, der Eigensucht fort, und so erlangt das Recht erst seine wahrhafte Bestimmtheit und kommt zu seiner Ehre. Erst durch die Zucht des Auffassens wird es der Allgemeinheit fähig.
Grundlinien der Philosophie des Rechts (Lasson ed.), p. 340.

and later, upon customary law. In others, the process was reversed. However, the codifiers' arguments were always about the same: Rational man could transmute what is rational into written norms. Rationality was better reflected and more safely secured in definite norms than in unwritten law. Written law had a clarity which could be understood by everybody. Statements that the legislator purged the law of confusing elements, that he purified and demystified it, that he made it less obscure and more comprehensible, that he *rationalized* the law, abounded. Some people even went so far as to follow the most ancient of the modern codes, that of Denmark of 1683, in asserting that codification was complete and without gaps. The legislator appeared to be infallible. But was he? Had he succeeded in rationalizing the law to perfection? We do not think so.

A first indication that legislation is a limitation upon rationality, it could be argued, lies in the fact that different people at various times have had different codes, all of which cannot possibly have been absolutely rational. We need not press this point. If law, as is usually believed, is a mirror of society, then different mores, circumstances, and times may rationally require different codifications.[22]

And yet it is doubtful whether some of the differences in legal codes can be rationally defended on the grounds of mores, traditions, and times. There is, for instance, no apparent reason why certain principles should not exist in all codes, irrespective of circumstances. For example, it cannot be seen why such principles as *pacta sunt servanda, rebus sic stantibus,* or *nullum crimen nulla poena sine lege* should be recognized in some codes and not in others. To turn to more particular provisions of substantive law, it can, from a rational point of view, not be seen why under the Roman law of sales the rule prevailed that upon conclusion of the contract the goods were at the risk of the purchaser, and, if they perished accidentally, the seller was absolutely free. The buyer was bound to pay the price, although the goods had not been delivered and the property in them had not been transferred, whereas the German Civil Code (BGB) provides that the risk is transferred to the buyer only when he takes possession of the bought article. To give a few examples of criminal law, it cannot be seen why some codes provide that the instigator to a crime shall be punished as severely as the person who commits the crime, and why other codes provide for a more lenient punish-

---

[22] Characteristically, old Germanic codes were called "mirrors" (*Spiegel*), the most famous of them being the *Sachsenspiegel.*

ment. Preventive versus punitive justice; criminal law as deterrent versus that of reformation; the strict-law principle versus that of the individualization of punishment; the problem of capital punishment —all these features are represented in modern criminal codes, and it is hard to tell which codes are the most rational.

The situation is similar in the case of procedural law. Anglo-Saxon nations provide for trial by jury; most of the continental nations do not. In both instances, it is claimed that justice is served best. Actually, justice is probably served equally well under both systems. This was admitted by Anglo-Saxons when they granted the right to waive trial by jury, and by continentals when they occasionally adopted some form of jury trial. Also, in Anglo-Saxon nations, the judge plays a rather passive part in court proceedings, whereas under continental codes he is assigned a more active role. Again, it is hard to tell which method is more rational. A diversity that can hardly be explained on rational grounds also exists *within* the various systems of law. To mention just one example, it cannot be seen why the German *Zivilprozessordnung* of 1877 pushes the French device of oral allegation and debate to an undue extreme and why it should be more rational than French civil procedure. It can also not be seen why the Germans would retain their practice until 1924, whereas the Austrians recognized the shortcomings of the German method as early as 1895, when they adopted their own code of civil procedure.

Seen merely from the point of view of rationality, different statutory provisions must appear even less justified in the member states of a federal union, especially if these states have a common heritage, language, and ethnic composition. In the United States, for instance, the various states do not only have their own kind of common law[23] (which is another proof of the irrationality of that law!), but also, their own statutes. There is, for instance, no apparent reason why states should fix the minimum age for marriage differently and have different laws on divorce; why criminals should get different penalties for the same crimes; why they should be executed in some states by hanging, in other states by gas poisoning, and in still others by electrocution. The various states can defend the diversity of their laws on grounds of freedom and states' rights, but hardly merely on grounds of rationality.[24] On these grounds there is no apparent rea-

[23] *Erie Railroad Co.* v. *Tompkins,* 304 U. S. 64 (1937).
[24] See George C. S. Benson, *The New Centralization* (1941). My own

son why the ethnic melting pot should not be complemented by a legal one. Some federal states, such as Germany and Switzerland, adopted uniform codes in order to "rationalize" their law. Whether or not they succeeded in this undertaking is open to doubt. Certainly, their national codes, adopted within a short span of time, cannot be considered absolutely rational. Otherwise, they would hardly differ as much from one another as they do.[25]

In his well-known study, *On the Vocation of Our Time for Legislation and Juridical Science,* Savigny shows how defective "enlightened" and "rational" legislation can be by examining the outstanding codes of his time, the Prussian General Land Law (ALR), the Napoleonic Code, and the Austrian Civil Law Code (ABGB). We are inclined to agree with his assertion that only times that abound in great jurists can afford making codifications, although even then the results will hardly be perfect. We also share his opinion that in normal times the chances of creating good statutes are slight indeed, irrespecuive of how prevalent the belief in the rationality and perfectibility of man may be.

Legislative shortcomings are proven by the existence of so-called gaps. The lawmakers, being unable to perceive all possible legal problems, cannot totally cover exigencies that might exist in the future. Often devices such as the rule of analogy, the *argumentum e contrario*, and the *argumentum a maiori ad minus* will help. Often, they will not. The judge will then wonder what rule he should apply to the case before him. The inevitability of gaps was sometimes admitted by the legislator himself. Provision was made on how gaps should be filled. In most cases, this function was left to the judge.[26]

---

disposition in favor of federalism as a means for the achievement of freedom can be seen in *The Federalist* (1960).

[25] Thus the two major codifications, the German *Bürgerliches Gesetzbuch* (BGB.) and the Swiss *Zivilgesetzbuch* (ZGB) became effective in 1900 and 1912, respectively. The German code is more individualistic than its Swiss counterpart, although one can entertain doubts about the rationality of that important difference in view of the fact that the Swiss could hardly be called more social-minded in 1912 than the Germans in 1900. The Swiss codifier left considerably more gaps in the ZGB than did the German lawmaker in the BGB. It is hard, again, to explain this difference on grounds of rationality.

[26] Classic examples: *Code Civil*, Art. 4: "Le juge, qui réfusera de juger, sous prétexte du silence, de l'obscurité ou de l'insuffisance de la loi, pourra être poursuivi comme coupable de déni de justice;" ZGB, Art. 1: "Das Gesetz findet auf alle Rechtsfragen Anwendung, für die es nach Wortlaut oder Auslegung eine Bestimmung enthält. Kann dem Gesetz keine Vorschrift

Thus, a paradoxical situation existed: The statute, supposedly an incarnation of rationality, had defects that were to be healed by what, from the codifiers' point of view, is supposedly less rational than the statute—judicial precedent! And all this was prescribed by the "rational" statute!

Friends of legislation, recognizing the shortcomings of the legislator, have attempted to exonerate legislative fiat by the fiction that the law is wiser than those who make it. Radbruch, for instance, assumes that with its passage, a bill becomes independent of and wiser than the lawmaker. Consequently, the interpreter of the law can recognize something "as the will of the legislator which never conscientiously occurred to the legislators." Such interpretation is not merely "rethinking what has been thought before, but completing a line of thought." It is as if "a ship, when leaving port, is guided by the pilot on a prescribed course through harbor waters, until, in the open sea, it pursues its own course under the captain." Such interpretation, Radbruch continues, "imperceptibly proceeds from interpretations in the spirit of the legislator to rules which the interpreter would make as a legislator."[27] But does this conception of the written law guarantee rational justice? We do not think so. For who guarantees that the ship of which Radbruch speaks will not find itself without a rudder and that the captain will steer his boat on the right course? To use Cardozo's language again, isn't it probable that the captain will find out how trackless the ocean is on which he has embarked?

Clearly, interpretation does not necessarily make statutes more rational than they were conceived by legislators. For like lawmaking, interpretation is still in the hands of human beings. Thus the problems inherent in the judicial process which Cardozo described with a view mainly toward the application of common law also exist when statutes are applied. Interpretation of written law is "an insoluble mixture of theoretical and practical, finding and creating, reproductive and productive, scientific and meta-scientific, objective and subjective elements."[28] The idea that court opinions and *herrschende Lehre* are the only rational interpretations of law is a fiction,

entnommen werden, so soll der Richter nach Gewohnheitsrecht und, wo auch ein solches fehlt, nach der Regel entscheiden, die er als Gesetzgeber aufstellen würde. Er folgt dabei bewährter Lehre und Überlieferung."

[27] Radbruch, *op. cit.*, p. 211.
[28] *Ibid.*

as is proved by the existence of concurring and dissenting opinions, as well as by the fact that court decisions are constantly overruled and *herrschende Lehren* are always replaced.

To conclude, it can be said that no type of man-conceived law so far mentioned is absolutely rational. All types are limitations upon rationality. This applies also to combinations of these types. For there is hardly a civil-law country in which statutes are not to some degree complemented by customary and natural law, and, to go a step further, in which statutes themselves are not influenced by custom and natural law. Likewise, there is hardly a common-law country in which custom would not to some degree be complemented by statutes and natural law, and in which common law would not in some way reflect natural law and statutory law. Considering the relationship of these three types of law, it is as if natural law were constantly haunting common as well as statute law, and as if common law were always casting its spell over statute law, with neither one of these kinds of law being absolutely rational. Our belief in the rule of law is thus a groping for a rationality that is shrouded in mystery. We are captivated by something that does not quite reveal itself. Due to human shortcomings in the discovery and making of the law, Justitia can indeed only appear as she usually is depicted—blindfolded. In that condition, she cannot determine what the scales she holds contain. We, in turn, are unable to look into her eyes to find the *ultima ratio*.

II
Constitutions are limitations upon rationality.

In the foregoing, we were mainly concerned with law as it is commonly classified according to its sources. We shall now deal with a more specific type of law. We shall examine why constitutional law is a limitation upon rationality, and, furthermore, whether constitutions are perhaps greater limitations upon rationality than other law. The first question will be answered by the argument that the diversity of constitutional law proves the absence of absolute rationality in it. The answer to the second question will follow from the character of constitutional law as public, as distinguished from private, law.

The irrationality of constitutions is reflected in their forms.

A convenient way of proving that constitutions are limitations upon rationality is the formalistic one of simply showing that they consist of written, customary, or natural law, or of combinations thereof. For if all these types of law are limitations upon rationality, then constitutions, based upon them, must also be such limitations.

It is not difficult to prove that constitutions are written, or based upon custom or natural law. The American constitution is generally considered a written constitution, and that of England a customary one. Both constitutions are credited with containing natural law. But such classification is actually an oversimplification. The American constitution is not merely "written," just as the English constitution is not merely "common." Like other constitutions, both contain a bit of every type of law.

Thus the English constitution is considered to be sanctioned by natural law, a feature that was emphasized throughout the constitutional struggle between king and Parliament. Blackstone's *Commentaries* state that the common law embodied in the English constitution is in conformity with natural law and the law of God.[29] At the same time, the English constitution is, in a sense, also a statutory constitution. Documents such as Magna Carta, the Bill of Rights, the Act of Settlement are part and parcel of it. We may even say that every act of Parliament is an ingredient of the English constitution. In turn, such acts are supposed to be in conformity with common and natural law.[30]

The American constitution is generally believed to be a transmutation of the English constitution into written norms. In the debates between the colonists and Parliament, one party accused the other of not honoring the English constitution.[31] The Philadelphia Convention was to a large extent called because state legislatures interfered with the individual's rights under common law. Its delegates pinned down these rights in specific clauses of the Constitution. As a matter of fact, the whole document can be considered a guaranty of the rights of Englishmen. Also, the Constitution has a higher law back-

[29] Blackstone's *Commentaries* (12th ed.; 1793–1795), I, 41.

[30] Blackstone, the advocate of the supremacy of Parliament, wrote, concerning rights "which God and nature have established and are therefore called natural rights," that "no human legislature has power to abridge or destroy them, unless the owner shall himself commit some act that amounts to a forfeiture." *Ibid.* I, 54.

[31] Compare R. G. Adams, *Political Ideas of the American Revolution* (1922); Charles H. McIlwain, *The American Revolution, A Constitutional Interpretation* (1923); Alpheus T. Mason, *Free Government in the Making* (1949), pp. 81–141.

ground.[32] Just as the Declaration of Independence shows that the historically grown rights of Englishmen were natural rights of man, the Constitution protects the natural rights of life, liberty, and property.

The situation is similar in the case of continental constitutions. Although written, they are usually tuned to local customs and institutions. Even the French constituent assembly during the Revolution, probably the most revolutionary of all constituent assemblies, was unable to completely extricate itself from tradition. The situation is not much different in respect to other European constitutions. Continental constitutions also contain natural law. Most bills of rights, like the French Declaration of the Rights of Man and Citizen, reflect the natural law of the age of reason. Some of them also show an influence of theistic natural law.[33]

In tune with the mixed character of constitutions, constitutional interpretation in common- as well as civil-law countries has admitted the importance of natural, common, and codified law. In spite of the idea that Parliament under the British constitution is omnipotent, English jurists have not lost sight of the common-law heritage and of natural law, just as in the United States the "rights of Englishmen" and the "rights of man" were taken into consideration. In spite of the ascendancy of legal positivism on the continent, the awareness of the values of customary and natural law remained alive. It reached a climax after World War II when German jurists admitted the possibility of unconstitutional constitutional norms.[34] Under that doctrine, even acts of the constituent power can be checked for their compatibility with higher law.

It could be argued that constitutions, containing natural and common as well as codified law, could perhaps be a mere accumulation of the rationality of these types of law, and contain none of their irrationality. But this argument is weak. For who could have purged these types of law of their irrational elements? Only not quite rational man. And it is beyond his ability to absolutely purify law from irrational elements. We may conclude that if the parts of a constitution—natural law, common law, and codified law—are not abso-

[32] See Edward S. Corwin, "The 'Higher Law' Background of American Constitutional Law," *Harvard Law Review*, XLII (1928–1929), 149, 365.

[33] Compare the author's "Natural Law in the Modern European Constitutions," *Natural Law Forum*, I (1956), 73.

[34] See the author's "Unconstitutional Constitutional Norms? Constitutional Development in Postwar Germany," *Virginia Law Review*, XLII (1956), 1.

lutely rational, then the whole constitution can hardly be so.

The fact that constitutions are limitations upon rationality also follows from the discussions revolving around the merits of unwritten and written constitutions. In these discussions, the adherents of each kind of constitution advanced rational arguments in favor of their respective stands, accusing the other party of irrationality.

Paine, who admired the American state constitutions because they were written, denounced the British constitution because it was un-written.[35] In the American and French revolutions the belief pre-vailed that written constitutions are more rational than unwritten ones.

On the other hand, Edmund Burke, favoring unwritten consti-tutions, denounced the written French constitution as evil and politi-cally false.[36] De Maistre scolded those who pretended that they could "make a constitution the way a watchmaker makes a watch."[37] It was felt that unwritten constitutions are created by history, tradition, and Providence.[38] Man is nothing but an instrument of these forces. "Far from being able to constitute society, man's intervention can only prevent that society constitutes itself," for there exists only one constitution of political society, which results from human nature "just as gravity results from the nature of matter."[39] "One cannot write the constitution, for the constitution is existence and nature. And one can write neither existence nor nature: writing the consti-

[35] See Thomas Paine, *Rights of Man* (1791). In that work, Paine also credits the written French constitution with being rational:

> In contemplating the French Constitution, we see in it a rational order of things. The principles harmonize with the forms, and both with their origin. It may perhaps be said as an excuse for bad forms, that they are nothing more than forms; but this is a mistake. Forms grow out of principles, and operate to continue the principles they grow from. It is impossible to practise a bad form on any thing but a bad principle. It cannot be ingrafted on a good one; and wherever the forms in any government are bad, it is a certain indication that the principles are bad also.

The Works of Thomas Paine (1925), pp. 849–850.

[36] Edmund Burke, *Reflections on the Revolution in France* (1790). Paine's *Rights of Man* was a rejoinder to that work.

[37] J. de Maistre, "Etudes sur la souveraineté," *Oeuvres* (1884), I, 344. See also his "Essai sur le principe générateur des sociétés politiques," *ibid.*, I, 243.

[38] Compare Georges Burdeau, *Traité de science politique,* III (1950), 15–16.

[39] De Bonald, "Théorie du pouvoir politique et réligieux," *Oeuvres* (1854), I, 99.

tution means to turn it upside down."[40] No severer doubts about the rationality of written constitutions could be voiced.

Thus, at the height of the Enlightenment, rationalist philosophers were at odds as to the rationality of written and unwritten constitutions. The dilemma these rationalists found themselves in is reflected in an exchange of words that occurred in the constituent assembly. When Volney, addressing the friends of the *ancien régime*, asked, "I ask, where is our Constitution? Who made it? When was it made? Where is the code that contains it?"[41] he received the answer that it was absurd to maintain that a state which had flourished for thirteen hundred years should never have been constituted.[42]

In view of these remarks made by rational men it appears to be futile to discuss whether a written or an unwritten constitution is more rational. By the same token, it seems to be indisputable that neither written nor unwritten constitutions, both being the work of man, can be absolutely rational. Therefore, they must constitute a limitation upon rationality.

The irrationality of constitutions is reflected in their substance.

The fact that constitutions are not absolutely rational cannot just be gathered from their forms. It can also be seen in their substance. Again, we can draw this conclusion by simply referring to the diversity of the substance of constitutions. The history of constitutions is largely a history of rationality claims, of claims that one type of constitutional order is more rational than another type. Democratic constitutions adopted in the democratic revolutions were mainly defended because they were considered more rational than the *ancien régime*. In turn, advocates of absolutism claimed that the *ancien régime* was more rational than popular government. In the twentieth century, democracy was attacked on the same grounds by modern totalitarians. Since, from the seventeenth century on, authoritarian governments have existed next to democratic ones, and since in the twentieth century totalitarian governments have existed next to nontotalitarian ones, the claim of all these systems to rationality must be disputable.

But this is not yet the whole story. Within each one of these sys-

[40] *Ibid.*, I, 210.

[41] Volney, *Des conditions nécessaires à la légalité des Etats-généraux* (1798), p. 5.

[42] "Cahiers de la noblesse du Bugey," quoted by A. Lemaire, *Les lois fondamentales de la monarchie francaise* (Diss. Paris, 1907), p. 2.

tems, different constitutional orders can be found, each claiming superior rationality. Thus the French democratic constitution-maker was asserted to be more rational than his American counterpart. The democratic rationality of the Weimar constitution was said to be superior to that of other constitutions. These examples indicate how questionable democratic claims of rationality are, a fact that is borne out by an observation of the making and interpretation of democratic constitutions. For reasons of space, the discussion shall be confined to the situation in the United States.

The student of that situation cannot be but surprised at the great diversity that exists within the scope of democratic rationality. The Philadelphia Convention, it is generally agreed, was determined to secure free government. Although the remark of one of its members that it was "the wisest council in the world"[43] might be exaggerated, the convention was on the whole composed of first-rate, highly rational minds. The delegates wanted rational deliberations and excluded the public for fear that its irrationality and passions might prevent rational discussion. And yet—how different were the supposedly rational arguments advanced by the delegates! This can be seen in the discussion of broader principles as well as in that of specific provisions of the new Constitution. Randolph, advancing the Virginia Plan as a rational solution for a more perfect Union, was as much of an adherent of free government as was Patterson, who, again on rational grounds, proposed a plan diametrically opposed. The rational compromise suggested by William Samuel Johnson, known as the Connecticut Compromise, was as much motivated by the desire to create a more perfect Union for the sake of free government as were the Virginia and New Jersey plans. To turn to more specific provisions of the constitution, it cannot be seen why adherents of free government, favoring the omission of a bill of rights, should be more rational than those favoring the inclusion of such a bill; why those in favor of an indirect election of senators and the president should be more rational than those favoring direct election. Certainly, events have proved that those who had their way in the Convention because their arguments were considered more rational by the majority of delegates, later were refuted, on supposedly rational grounds. A bill of rights was soon added to the Constitution, the Sixteenth Amendment provided for direct election of senators,

---

[43] The statement was made by William Pierce of Georgia, one of the delegates. Quoted in Mason, *op. cit.,* p. 190.

and the election of the president by an electoral college has become a mere formality. The Constitution is a "bundle of compromises"[44] of various democratic rationales. The Philadelphia Convention did not assert that their work was, from a rational point of view, perfect. They readily provided for the possibility of amendment.

The diversity of democratic rationalization is also evident in the outstanding commentary on the Constitution, *The Federalist*. While its authors agree upon the need for, and essential features of, free government, as well as upon the fact that the Constitution is conducive to that form of government, they differ in their rational evaluation of general as well as specific constitutional devices such as federalism, the separation of powers, the necessary and proper, and supremacy clauses.[45] It would be unfair to deny the individual author's claim to rational, "scientific" arguments.[46] And it is hard to tell which of these arguments are the most rational.

The conflict of democratic rationales that is evident in the Philadelphia Convention and *The Federalist* became reflected in later constitutional interpretations. Again, these interpretations were claimed to have been made on rational grounds. But it is hard to tell to what degree they really were rational, when, for instance, the pendulum was permitted to swing back and forth between the doctrines of nationalism and dual federalism, or between the protection of property rights and civil rights, or between narrow and wide interpretations of the general welfare and commerce clauses. When Chief Justice Marshall stated, "It is a constitution we are expounding, . . . intended to endure for ages to come, and, consequently, to be adopted to the various crises of human affairs,"[47] he referred to the need for a constitutional flexibility beyond that provided by the amendment process, a flexibility that made possible *Verfassungswandlung* as distinguished from *Verfassungsänderung*.[48] Did Marshall's dictum propose a safety valve for rationality or irrationality? Probably for both. A constitution, not being something absolutely rational, hardly can become so through interpretation, even if such

[44] Alpheus T. Mason, "The Nature of Our Federal Union Reconsidered," *Political Science Quarterly*, LXV (1950), 503.

[45] See the author's *The Federalist*, pp. 260–275.

[46] Hamilton's and Madison's trust in political science can be seen in essays 9 and 37. *The Federalist* (Modern Library ed.; 1937), pp. 48, 229.

[47] *McCulloch* v. *Maryland*, 17 U.S. (4 Wheat.), 316, 407, 415 (1819).

[48] See Georg Jellinek, *Verfassungsänderung und Verfassungswandlung* (1906).

interpretation would be absolutely rational. But the chances are that constitutional interpretation will be as devoid of rationality as that of statutory, common, or natural law.

Constitutional law being a limitation upon rationality, the question arises as to whether it is not a greater limitation than other kinds of law. Marshall's dictum, quoted above, draws the distinction between public and private law, suggesting a greater flexibility of the former. Having seen in the American and French revolutions how public law vanishes and private law lasts,[49] the great Chief Justice recognized the disadvantages for legal security of the transitoriness of public law. This situation, he felt, could be meliorated by permitting public law to vanish by adjustment rather than abolition. But such adjustment is likely to be less rational than the interpretation of private law, just as the creation of public law is generally less rational than that of private law.

Public law, laying down the law of the superior public power to the inferior private individual, usually is more affected by desire and interest than private law, a law which merely establishes rules for the fair play among equal individuals. Reflecting power rather than freedom, public law, we may conclude from Lord Acton's statement that power corrupts, is, to a large extent, corrupt law. As such it is less rational than private law. Made by an interested legislator, public law is oriented toward subjective rationality. Its rationality is not on a par with that of private law. For that law, made by less interested men, is more oriented toward objective rationality.

Constitutional law, being public law, is afflicted with all the shortcomings of that law. The student of constitutional law is constantly aware that its making and interpretation are motivated by political rather than legal considerations, by an interested, subjective, rather than a disinterested, objective, rationality. Consequently, constitutional interpretation has been delegated on the Continent to special constitutional courts.[50] The United States Supreme Court, which is not a special constitutional court, often has been tainted with politics.[51] But subjective rationality hardly is rationality in the sense in

[49] "Öffentlich Recht vergeht, Privatrecht besteht," is a German saying.

[50] Compare the author's "Constitutional Courts in Europe," *Dickinson Law Review,* LX (1956), 313.

[51] See Charles G. Haines, *The American Doctrine of Judicial Supremacy* (2nd ed.; 1932) and *A Government of Laws or a Government of Men* (1929); Edouard Lambert, *Le gouvernement des juges et la lutte contre la législation sociale aux Etats-Unis* (1921) and *La lutte judiciaire du capital*

which that word has been used in this essay. And if private law constitutes a restriction upon rationality because, as law, it cannot be absolutely rational, then constitutional law, being less rational than private law, must constitute such a limitation a fortiori.

III

In the preceding pages, an attempt was made to show that law is a limitation upon rationality. It is hoped that the author's arguments did not convey the impression that he is a relativist. He is opposed to relativizations of the law. He believes that there is such a thing as a perfect law, a law that is no limitation upon rationality. As a matter of fact, his attempt to show that law is a limitation upon rationality was designed to prove that such a perfect law exists. The very fact that law as recognized or made by men is, due to human shortcomings, irrational, unjust, wrong, and, thus, a limitation upon rationality proves that there must be a rational, just, right law which does not constitute such a limitation. For the existence of anything imperfect presupposes the existence of something perfect. On rare occasions, perhaps the perfect law may be revealed to men. In that case men would possess more than *"jurisperitia"* and even more than *jurisprudentia,* for even human wisdom is not necessarily identical with rationality. They would possess a law that is identical with rationality. However, it is so improbable that this will happen that the Romans did not even coin a word for it.

It appears doubtful whether a law that constitutes no limitation upon rationality can be recognized or made by man. The science of the law will remain a mysterious science,[52] not only because irrational people will continue to irrationalize and mystify the law, but also because they will remain unable to penetrate the mystery of the law and see the law's pure rationality. The belief that man could perceive and make perfect law ran high in the Age of Reason. Today, we no longer are so confident. It appears as if with the advance of science law has become more and more a limitation upon rationality. It has been remarked that at about the middle of the last century, law entered a crisis because it was split up into nonproblematic and

---

et du travail organisés aux Etats-Unis (1923). These works accuse the Supreme Court of being opposed to social legislation. For a criticism of the Court for being in favor of social legislation, see the author's "America and Europe—Decline and Emergence of Judicial Review," *Virginia Law Review,* XLIV (1958), 1233.

[52] See Daniel J. Boorstin, *The Mysterious Science of the Law* (1941).

problematic law.[53] That crisis cannot be seen merely in the fact that *Gesetz* remained no longer identified with *Recht* and that the latter became increasingly relativized.[54] It can also be seen in the fact that law became less and less rational, that is, more and more a limitation upon rationality. This decline of the law[55] was due mainly to a lowering of the caliber of the lawmakers and to an undue increase of the number of laws. Whereas formerly lawmaking, largely consisting in the discovery of natural and common law, was mainly in the hands of the learned and select, nowadays lawmaking, largely consisting of legislation, is mainly in the hands of the not-so-learned and not-so-select, some of whom even have criminal records. As a result, the quality of laws has deteriorated. Laws that were rational to a high degree have become replaced by laws that are irrational to a high degree, laws motivated by human passion rather than reason. This qualitative deterioration was aided by a quantitative acceleration of lawmaking which, in turn, was not conducive to the quality of laws. For whereas learned and select lawmakers were, on the whole, conservative and thought twice before making a new law, their less learned and less select successors were, on the whole, more radical and had no inhibitions to pass as many laws as possible. The situation became such that the legislature, in spite of its obvious lust for lawmaking, soon found out that it could not completely satisfy increasing desires for new laws and delegated part of its authority to various agencies. These bodies, usually composed of men who are as little learned and select as the members of the legislature, tried to outdo the latter in quantitative lawmaking, often subdelegating their legislative power. As a result, a veritable deluge of norms which, by standards of rationality, left much to be desired, was showered upon the public. It became harder and harder for those applying and interpreting the law to disentangle themselves from the labyrinth of a rather irrational mass of irrational norms and to see the light in this veritable legal mess. In our time, the dictum *summum ius, summa iniuria*[56] shows its validity largely because law has become a greater limitation upon rationality than ever before. *Homo homini homo?*

[53] Carl Schmitt, *Die Lage der europäischen Rechtswissenschaft* (1949), p. 25.

[54] For the change in the meaning of *Rechtsstaat,* compare the author's *In Defense of Property* (1963), pp. 150–151.

[55] Compare F. A. Hayek, *The Constitution of Liberty* (1960), pp. 234–249; Georges Ripert, *Le déclin du droit* (1949).

[56] Cicero *De officiis,* i.10.33.

6

THE SEPARATION OF LEGAL
AND MORAL DECISIONS

MURRAY L. SCHWARTZ

My comments are intended to examine the problem: What is a legal decision? Although this exposition may seem to complicate what might for some purposes be treated as a relatively simple definitional problem, it is important to make clear that, for the purposes at hand, the concept of a legal decision—one of the essential elements of the inquiry—is indeed a complicated one.

Consideration of the theme of the separation of moral and legal decisions would seem to require the identification of both moral and legal decisions. What this paper attempts is to identify certain features of a legal decision, thereby making the task of separating legal from moral—and perhaps other—decisions a more manageable one.[1]

---

[1] Many of the ideas in this paper have been expressed more fully and elaborately elsewhere. See, for example, the introductory comments in the

Quite apparently, with a concept as complex as a human decision, whether it be legal, moral, or political, it is not very likely that a neat set of characteristics will be found which is applicable to one particular type of decision, such as a legal one, and not to any other. One may also predict that each characteristic or feature will generate doubtful areas. But, despite the absence of simplicity or certainty of any conclusions which may be reached, the effort may produce clarification which, in turn, may prove helpful in considering other aspects of the relationships between law and morality.

Perhaps the issues can be best introduced by an illustration: the execution of John Smith for the murder of his wife. What decisions preceded this event? Consider the following:

The delegates to a state constitutional convention draw up and approve a constitution to be submitted to the voters for ratification. This constitution expressly empowers the legislature to adopt a penal code. The constitution may also contain limitations on this legislative body—prohibitions against ex post facto laws, a due process clause, or the like.

After the constitution has been ratified by the people of the state, the legislature meets and duly enacts a penal code. That code provides that the punishment for the crime of first degree murder shall be the electric chair or life imprisonment, as the jury shall decide. It further provides that "insanity" at the time of the commission of the offense shall be a complete defense.

John Smith is accused by neighbors of killing his wife. The conflicting reports suggest that John may have been "insane" at the time, with the consequences that he is to be acquitted of the criminal charge, but possibly to be committed to a mental institution. He may have been "legally provoked," with the consequence that the crime may be mitigated from first degree murder to voluntary manslaughter. He may have premeditated and deliberated, a classic instance of first degree murder. There is even some evidence that John did not kill his wife.

After reviewing the reports and interviewing the various witnesses, the prosecuting attorney decides to submit the case to the

---

unpublished, mimeographed materials of Professors Hart and Sacks of the Harvard Law School, "The Legal Process" (1958). The concept in the text illustration of the criminal process as a series of decisions is developed in Donnelly, Goldstein, and Schwartz, *Criminal Law* (1962); see also my own *Professional Responsibility and the Administration of Criminal Justice* (1962).

grand jury, which, after hearing the evidence presented to it by that official, decides to indict John Smith for first degree murder. He, through his attorney, pleads not guilty and also not guilty by reason of insanity.

At the trial the judge makes a number of rulings on matters of procedure and evidence. After all the evidence is in and the concluding arguments of counsel have been heard, he submits the case to the jury with appropriate instructions. The jury finds the defendant guilty and imposes the death sentence.

John's attorney appeals to the appellate court, challenging the existing legal standard for insanity on the basis of which the jury was instructed. The conviction is affirmed by the appellate court. In its decision it states that the present insanity standard is appropriate and that it is in no way convinced, despite the moral, psychiatric, and legal arguments presented to it by John's attorney, that the standard should be altered.

John's attorney files a petition for a writ of certiorari in the Supreme Court of the United States, requesting that Court to exercise its discretion and review John's case. The Supreme Court, whose criterion for exercising its discretion is the "importance" of the question, denies the review requested.

John's attorney petitions the governor of the state for a pardon or for mitigation of the sentence, which the governor is legally authorized to grant. The governor rejects the plea and John is executed by the state penal authorities pursuant to the trial judge's warrant.

The above illustration is a routine description of a criminal case. It could be embellished with other parties and decisions; examples are the police decision to arrest and the Parole Board's possible role in the sentencing process. Moreover, confining the illustration to criminal proceedings eliminates a wide variety of other types of decisions such as administrative agency rule-making or adjudication and arbitrators' decisions. But the illustration should provide a suitable vehicle for the discussion of the main question: Is it possible to extract from the many decisions described the features of a "legal decision" so as to assist in the differentiation of other types of decisions such as moral ones?

Four such features are proposed for discussion:

 (1) Who makes the decision;
 (2) What procedures, if any, are or must be followed in coming to the decision;

(3) What guides are provided for the decision-maker;

(4) What types of consequences follow from the decision.

THE CHARACTER OF THE DECISION-MAKER

The decisions presented in the illustration demonstrate that legal consequences may follow from decisions made by private persons as well as by public or official institutions. Yet it is doubtful whether decisions by individuals are generally thought of as legal decisions. For such individual decisions could encompass the entire range of human conduct, such as a decision to pass through a stop sign, an offer to sell a car, or inattention (negligence) resulting in injury. Consequently, it would seem, both as a matter of popular understanding and as a matter of appropriate description, that one feature of a legal decision is that it is made by an "official" or "public" institution or agency, that is, by an institution or agency created for the purpose, perhaps among others, of making decisions which affect the legal status of others.

Two possible consequences follow from describing one feature of a legal decision in this way. First, it of course excludes the host of decisions made by individuals in their private or nonofficial capacities—decisions which may ultimately have legal consequences.

The second consequence is the differentiation of a legal decision from other types. For example, it is not generally considered that a moral decision (however that may be defined) must be made by a rule-defined office or position. Indeed, it is fair to say that anyone may make moral decisions. Can this feature be used to differentiate among different kinds of decisions made by the "public" agency: the one created to make decisions which affect the legal status of others? This question has two aspects. The first is whether such an agency can make moral, as opposed to legal, decisions; the second is whether a particular decision by the agency may be both moral and legal.

With regard to the first aspect, it would seem to follow from the assertion, that anyone may make moral decisions, that the official agency also may make them. Thus, whereas this feature may assist in excluding the decisions of nonpublic institutions from the category of legal decisions, it does not, of itself, help to distinguish among the various decisions which might be made by the public institution itself.

The second aspect, whether legal decisions may also be moral ones, depends upon how one defines the phrase "moral decisions." Certainly, a legal decision may be influenced by moral considerations or moral principles; it may affect moral ideas in its practical impact. A few examples of the intimate involvement of moral principles in what appear to be legal decisions are the choice of the standard of insanity and decisions to prosecute, to impose capital punishment, and to refuse a pardon.

In sum, this feature of the official character of the decision-maker is helpful in excluding a wide body of decisions (by "private" persons), but it does not serve as a distinguishing feature among decisions made by an official agency itself.

DECISION-MAKING PROCEDURES

One particular emphasis which lawyers tend to place upon decisions is upon the process itself, that is, upon the procedures by which decisions are reached. The law's concern with procedures is perhaps unique among the possible kinds of decisions. The question which this emphasis presents is, to what extent is procedure, or a particular procedure, a feature of a legal decision?

The illustration presents a great diversity of procedures, including the carefully prescribed adversary judicial procedure and the parliamentary procedure of a legislative body. It is therefore difficult to propose that a feature of a legal decision is its conformity to any particular type of decision-making process. At the same time, it does seem appropriate to suggest that one expects of a legal decision that it be arrived at after *some* procedure has been followed. One way to express this thought is: A legal decision must adhere to whatever procedure has been legally prescribed for the decision.

As Procrustean, if not tautological, as this may seem, it does call attention to two important points. The first is that it is to be expected of a legal decision that some procedure has been prescribed; and second, that for a decision to be recognized as a valid one, the decision-maker must have followed a prescribed procedure.

These points can serve to distinguish legal decisions from other kinds. Although moral decisions, for example, may in fact be reached after some procedure has been followed, one does not usually consider that procedure either particularly significant or required in the moral decision process. Of course, it could be argued that before a moral decision is reached, the decider should take into consideration all relevant arguments, in a sense internalizing the adversary process. Yet, again, this does not seem to be essential for a moral decision.

GUIDES FOR DECISION

The possibility of identifying particular kinds of guides (standards, principles, or rules) for legal decisions is frequently the issue which is discussed when the question of separation of legal from other kinds of decision is presented. To a large extent, this is the topic to which other contributors to this volume are addressing themselves. At the risk of encroaching upon their territory, a few comments seem in order.

The specific question is whether a feature of a legal decision is that it is made by reference to purely legal guides, as distinguished from political, moral, economic, or other kinds. In the illustration, it is apparent that a wide variety of guides could have been used by the decision-makers. Is it possible to identify purely legal guides by which the decisions were or should have been made? If we consider the substantive content of the guides, it seems clear that it is not possible. What would be the legal guides which would determine what provisions should be included in a constitution or a statute, a grand jury's decision to indict, a trial judge's decision that certain evidence is relevant, or an appellate court's determination that the existing standard for criminal responsibility should be retained? True, when these decisions are articulated, they may be couched in legal phraseology. But surely it would be incorrect to suggest that the legally phrased conclusions are what determined the result.

Much of the emphasis on the legal nature of the guides for a legal decision seems to derive from the existence of decisions for which there seems to be only one applicable guide—one principle or standard or rule. In the typical judicial expression: The application of the law to the facts is clear. Such situations seem to engender the notion that the only appropriate guides for decision are pre-existing legal rules.

But there are serious objections to establishing this notion as a feature of legal decisions, even if limited to the context of judicial decisions. It does not advance the analysis very far to refer to decisions about which there can be no reasonable dispute, the uncontroverted case. The problem becomes real only when there is something to decide. There are at least the situations where the existing legal principles conflict in the context of the case or issue; where the existing legal principle does not seem to go far enough to cover the situation; where the argument is made that the existing principles should be changed. In each of these cases, the selection of the guide or principle on which to base the decision cannot be made by reference to purely legal criteria.

It is possible to express this thought in a slightly different way, by the assertion that the guides for a legal decision must be relevant to the issues presented. Such a formulation quite obviously presents some major difficulties. What would be meant by the assertion that a legal decision has been made by reference to irrelevant guides? Simply that in the speaker's judgment the guides which were employed were not sufficiently related to the issues. But the criteria for making this judgment cannot be purely legal ones. How does one decide that one principle or guide or another is relevant to a legal decision? There would not seem to be peculiar formulas for legal relevance. Relevance would therefore seem to be a concept which merely serves to raise the question, once again, of what guides are appropriate.

CONSEQUENCES OF THE DECISION

The existence of the foregoing features would not seem to suffice for the description of a legal decision. One additional feature involves the consequences of the decision. Can this feature be defined so as to make the task of identifying legal decisions an easier one? One possible definition would take the following form: To constitute a legal decision, the decision must affect a legal status or a legal relationship as a proximate consequence of the decision. This definition presents a number of problems including at least: Is it tautological? Does "affects" include decisions which leave the legal relationships as they were before the decision? Is the term "proximate" helpful?

To say that a legal decision must affect legal relationships does appear tautological; nevertheless the word "legal" in the phrase "legal status" or "legal relationship" does connote considerations which are different from those which are suggested by terms such as moral or political status or relationship. Again, relationships may be both moral or political and legal. At the same time, it would seem possible to ascertain whether a particular relationship is a "legal" one or not, regardless of its coincidence with other types of relationships.

The second problem is simpler. To "affect" a legal status or relationship can be defined to include decisions which appear to make no change—so long as they are rendered by authorized bodies pursuant to prescribed procedures. For example, the dismissal of a complaint filed by a plaintiff on the ground that it fails to state a cause of action is a legal decision even though the parties seem to remain as they are. There has been a legal change: The decision itself has determined that the prior relationship is the correct legal one.

The third problem, the significance of the word "proximate," raises the question whether decisions such as legislative acts are to be included in the phrase "legal decision," that is, whether the concept of legal decision is to be limited to such decisions as judicial or administrative ones where the decision is intended to affect particular parties directly. The word "directly" has been used here to point out that, although this is a matter of definitional stipulation, it does afford an opportunity to exclude nonadjudicatory decisions from its ambit. It may be, with regard to this feature, that a habit of mind or general understanding is determinative. For what seems to be the implication of the more limited interpretation is the exclusion of all types of decisions except those which are adjudicatory or, perhaps, those which the Constitution of the United States terms "cases or controversies."

Be that as it may, and despite the difficulties and possible ambiguities raised above, the inclusion of legal consequences as a feature of a legal decision may be helpful in the more general inquiry of separating legal from other types of decisions, for, to repeat, no matter how other types of decisions may be defined, clearly there is no requirement that they have legal consequences.

In sum, the foregoing discussion of a legal decision has emphasized three features: the official or public or rule-defined nature of the decision-maker; the procedural requirements for decision-making; and the legal consequences of the decision. What follows from this is, at least, that when these features are present, a paradigm of legal decision exists. It bears repeating, however, that there will be cases where not all these features appear and doubt will arise whether a legal decision has been made. However, these features would seem to be helpful in separating legal from moral decisions—the original purpose of the inquiry.

This attempt to identify the features of a legal decision has, at several different points, referred to the unavailability of purely or solely legal guides for decision and to the probable relevance of other types of considerations for legal decisions. This discussion suggests a different question: Are the existing legal decision-making institutions appropriate for their functions? More specifically, to what extent are the various decision-makers presented by the illustration and the procedures which they follow adapted to arriving at the "best" decisions? This, of course, is a question of what is desirable.

The fact is that a legal decision-maker in a controverted-case context simply cannot rely upon "legal" ideas alone. He must consider a wide range of ideas. Whether he is the best qualified to do so and whether he is operating under the procedures best calculated to arrive at the appropriate results is the significant question of the discussion over the difference between legal decisions and moral decisions.

7

REASON IN LEGISLATIVE DECISIONS

J. ROLAND PENNOCK

Men used to argue about whether man is rational and, if so, to what extent. Today they are more likely to assume that he is, in some sense, rational, but contend about the meaning of reason or of rationality. Probably few of us would agree with Hobbes that reason is naught but calculation. We would not confine it to the selection of the most efficient means for the attainment of predetermined ends, although probably not many would go all the way with Michael Oakeshott and deny the possibility of this kind of calculation (or at least of activity growing out of such calculation).[1] I shall essay no careful definition of "reason" or "rationality." I believe my understanding of the terms is in accord with Professor Freund's remarks (Ch. 8), which prompt my own. It is practical reason of which we speak here, and I agree further with Paul Diesing's formulation of

[1] See Michael Oakeshott, *Rationalism in Politics* (1962), p. 100.

that concept as involving three aspects, related and each ultimately including the others: reason as creativity; reason as adherence to the principles of generality, regularity, and consistency (he speaks of the discovery and application of rules to cases); and reason as calculation.[2] I consider the first of these, which Diesing defines as "the making of order," as including the weighing and ordering of values. One thing that distinguishes a "rational" being from other beings is the capacity to reflect, to weigh the relative values of, say, writing an article or playing tennis, and then to make a judgment and act accordingly.

Let us begin with the generality-regularity-consistency aspect of rationality. Legislatures, like courts, are enjoined to treat like cases alike. Courts are finding this standard increasingly difficult to apply. As society grows more complex and as tests of relevant differences are expanded progressively beyond the formal (*vide* the demise of "separate but equal"), general rules for the application of general principles become increasingly difficult to articulate. For the legislature, too, this problem nags. Rousseau's declaration that the General Will could speak only in terms of general rules was always (without further elucidation) vacuous, but in two centuries the problem of giving it content has grown at an exponential rate. It is not solely because of the resistance of vested interests that the task of revising our national tax structure has proved to be so baffling. We may say that classifications should be relevant to some socially approved purpose, that, when legislators vote price supports for agricultural products and not for manufactured goods, they must justify their discriminatory treatment; but these statements only frame the problem. It is worth incidental notice that the example illustrates how the three aspects of rationality are related. If the justification of price supports for certain commodities and not for others is necessary to establish whether the principle of generality, or equal treatment, is being observed, it cannot be accomplished without both calculation of consequences and weighing values (e.g., the efficient allocation of resources versus the virtues of communities of family farmers).

How can the modern legislature cope with the problem of developing general rules for an increasingly complicated world? One way is to divide itself into specialized committees and subcommittees, to equip these committees with staff experts, and then to enact legislation the complexity of which matches that of the situations to which

[2] Paul Diesing, *Reason in Society* (1962), pp. 244–247.

it applies. To an important degree we in the United States have followed this pattern. The other alternative, principally relied upon in Great Britain and also extensively used in the United States, is to delegate discretionary authority to administrators. The former runs the risk of irrationally treating unlike cases alike. Each new particularization in a statute or appropriation act is likely to create as many problems as it solves. On the other hand, delegation that amounts to buck-passing, to evasion of responsibility for resolving policy issues, is both an invitation to administrative arbitrariness and a weak link in the chain of accountability. But delegation may, of course, be accompanied by adequate policy directives, and, in any case, the delegated power may be exercised with substantial rationality even though rules, the hallmark of formal rationality, are lacking.

The test of generality, or consistency, may be applied vertically (over time) as well as horizontally. It is as irrational, other things being equal, to treat two successive cases differently as it is to discriminate contemporaneously. This consideration is what gives the doctrine of *stare decisis* such force as it has in the United States. A legislature is less bound by this aspect of rationality than are the courts. First, it is not applying rules, but creating them. More fundamentally, its action is prospective, whereas that of courts is, to an important degree, retrospective. When the courts interpret the law in a way contrary to what prior decisions have led people to expect, the rationality of the system has broken down, and injustice may be done to those who have invested funds or made other commitments on the assumption that the law was other than what it has turned out to be. Legislative decisions are normally taken within a wider context of fixed anticipation. Legislative "precedents" are properly less binding than judicial precedents, if only because they are *understood* to be less binding. Moreover, the legislature is freer than is the judiciary to distinguish between its prospective and its retrospective effects. It can grant exemptions for actions taken or enterprises embarked on under the pre-existing state of the law. Yet we must be on our guard against making too much of an obvious difference. Legislatures as well as courts are, in important measure, captives of their own history. It is not always feasible to limit retrospective effect, if only because it is often impossible to determine what actions were taken on the assumption that existing law would prevail. If Congress wished today to repeal outright all agricultural price support legislation but felt that to do so would be unjust to those who have invested money on the assumption that present policies would not be suddenly jettisoned, it would hardly be feasible to draft legislation that would distinguish those cases from others. Moreover, the element of utility as well as justice may make a rational legislature seek to maintain continuity of policy. Tax legislation designed to encourage industrial development, for example, would lose its efficacy if legislative policy in such matters notoriously vacillated.

Calculation is perhaps the least interesting aspect of rationality. Clearly it is important for both court and legislature. It probably plays a larger role in the work of the legislature just because the legislature's work is completely prospective and because it has a greater range of discretion, being less hedged about by precedent. For these reasons it is especially important that it be guided by a calculation of the probable consequences of its action. It should be noted, however, that in this respect the legislature enjoys an advantage over the courts; if its calculation proves to have been incorrect, it can more freely amend or reverse its action in the light of experience.[3]

If calculation is the simplest aspect of rationality, certainly that group of functions combined under the heading of creativity is by all odds the most complex. Here the decision-maker must weigh and order values. Of course, in the process of seeking to maximize social utility, calculation and the deliberate commensuration of values are inextricably intertwined. A decision as to whether to decrease the present oil depletion allowances involves calculations as to what the effect of a given decrease would be on the development of new oil resources and on public revenues and at the same time entails judgments as to the relative importance (value) of the production of oil today and its production at some future date, perhaps for our children. (Many other calculations and evaluations are also involved in this decision.)

For all the room that the modern American appellate judge has

---

[3] It appears to follow that courts should be more careful in calculating the consequences of their action insofar as a calculation of consequences is relevant to their decision. This conclusion prompts the further thought that courts are less well equipped for this task than are legislatures. Perhaps we have here a justification of the common-law doctrine that courts should strive to avoid passing on the interpretation or validity of legislation until it is actually in operation, so that its effects may be as accurately as possible appraised or forecast.

for creativity, he is confined within a relatively restricted sphere as compared to the range open to his legislative counterpart. But the legislator's freedom of choice is constricted by factors we have not yet considered (and which do not apply to the judge). His role calls for him to be responsive to public opinion, particularly to the opinions of his own constituents. He also owes some deference to the views of his party leaders, locally and nationally, and to those of the chief executive if he is of the same political party. For present purposes, we shall lump these factors together as all constituting links between the legislator and the public he is supposed to represent. It is certainly rational for the legislator to take them into account, whether in terms of his self-interest or in terms of his duty as a legislator. But in many, probably most, cases, the legislator does not know what a majority of his constituents would wish him to do. Probably they do not know themselves. Party leaders, seeking the guidance of "electoral considerations," are faced with the same difficulty. But, neither the rational leader nor the rational legislator is completely thwarted in his search for electoral considerations by the absence of a known public will. He may and should still make an estimate of how the probable consequences of a particular policy choice will be received by the electorate. This factor does complicate the task and restrict the options of the rational legislator. Yet an estimate of the probable reaction to a given policy choice is different from a response to a known attitude toward it in advance. It differs by the measure of the potential difference between an abstract public opinion and one that is confronted with a *fait accompli* and is informed by some experience with the results of the policy in question.

It will be noted that the last two paragraphs have slipped from discussion of the legisla*ture* to talking about legisla*tors*. We here must deal with an important distinction that has been thus far avoided. It points to a difference not so much between legislative and judicial rationality as in the means by which the two are to be attained. Where a court consists of more than one judge, presumably each of the judges, if acting with complete rationality, would arrive at the same decision in a given case. The same rule does not hold for a legislature. The fact of distinct constituencies makes the difference.

Initially, this difference between court and legislature appears to inject an unavoidable element of irrationality into the legislative output—constituents may be wrong and yet their representatives may feel compelled to bow to their will. Yet, even granted this factual situation, the net result need not necessarily be irrational. First, suppose the simple, if rather artificial, case in which only two alternatives are open to the legislature. Alternative A is more favorable than Alternative B to the interests of six of the ten constituencies, while the contrary is true of the other four. We may further assume that the size of the constituencies is the same and that the interests in question are of equal intensity. Finally, we must make the important assumption that no values are involved for the entirety other than the summation of the values and disvalues for the constituent parts. In the situation described, the interest of the majority of the constituencies would be the general interest, and the varied behavior of the individual legislators would produce the rational result.

Take another situation. The majority of the voters in four constituencies have an irrational prejudice against Alternative A, while the opposite situation prevails in another four constituencies. In the other two constituencies, however, sweet reason, in all possible senses, prevails. All representatives vote accordingly. The ultimate decision is rational because of a fortuitous mutual canceling out of irrational elements. A process of this kind is one of those upon which Rousseau relied for his argument that the Will of All would *tend* to give expression to the General Will. In any given case, the perfect cancellation hypothesized above would have to be described as "fortuitous," but, where large numbers are involved, the laws of chance favor random distribution of irrational factors.

Now consider a slightly more complicated situation. The question at issue itself, we assume, is complex. A rational solution involves bringing to bear on the decision process a vast array of facts, a number of complicated lines of reasoning about probable consequences of the alternative solutions, and a weighing of values that involves a subtle appreciation of the impact of a particular state of affairs on each of a number of variously conditioned groups of people. Which is more likely to arrive at a rational conclusion, an individual or small group of individuals, similarly circumstanced and all trying to see the whole picture and arrive at an over-all judgment? Or might it rather be a larger group, with each member arriving at his judgment at least partly on the basis of his special knowledge of the needs and wishes of his constituents and then reaching a collective decision by counting heads? The sum or resultant of these partial views might well contain more of the elements of rational decision, properly

weighted, than could conceivably have been obtained or comprehended by a single mind.[4]

In the various ways suggested above, a collective body made up
of individual members who arrive at widely differing conclusions as
to the right policy may tend to make more rational decisions than
could otherwise be obtained. One may even venture the statement
that the best route to rational decision-making may be by way of
assembled and integrated partialities. How they are organized, how
they are informed, what procedures they follow, and how they deliberate will have much to do with how effectively this process works.

Still another aspect of the legislative process both serves to distinguish it from the judicial process and to account the type of
creativity that is especially characteristic of reasoning as it operates
in a legislature. A court, as we artificially assumed for the legislature
in the discussion above, is typically confronted with only two possible decisions; it must decide for the plaintiff or for the defendant.
In determining what rule should govern or in fashioning a new rule,
it has room for creativity, as Professor Freund has shown, but its
scope is still restricted as compared with the legislature. The latter
is confronted not with a contest to be decided but with a problem
to be solved. A Congressional committee may have before it a dozen
different proposals all directed at the same situation. Or, beginning
with a single bill, it may consider, perhaps even adopt, scores of
amendments, while a similar process may be repeated on the floor
of the House. Clearly the net result of this process may be good or
bad, rational or filled with inconsistencies and biased evaluations.
The point is simply that the opportunity for problem-solving exists.
The judge seeks the right result for the instant case and for the
future, within flexible limits set by the values of certainty and continuity of legal development. Moreover, he can deal only with the
case before him, not with the one he would like to have. In these
respects the legislature has far greater scope—for reason as well as
for unreason. By the same token it has a greater responsibility, and
one that takes it beyond consistency, beyond calculation, and even
beyond evaluation—and yet still within the broad ambit of "creativity." It is not enough to imagine a great number and wide variety
of solutions in hopes that it will prove to be right. It must also
find a solution that is acceptable to a majority. In other words, it is

---

[4] Or by a small group of similarly circumstanced individuals, all seeking
to accomplish the same result in the same way.

part of the task of the legislature, in particular of legislative leaders, to build consensus. This task may be partly accomplished by reason in the most common sense of the word: by invention of means that will satisfy the ends of groups hitherto opposed to one another because the only means that anyone had proposed for satisfying their various ends had been mutually conflicting. In default of such a happy, integrative solution, however, resort must be had to persuasion, to bargaining, and to "politicking." These devices properly come under the heading of rationality, not simply because reason is required for their successful employment, but more fundamentally because they are part of the process of bringing about an effective integration or "rationalization" of a society.

The last note is perhaps the key to the distinctive role of reason in the legislative process. Here, in the formulation and authentication of fundamental policies for the state, reasoning is likely to be diffuse, partial, and incomplete in its ultimate result. At the same time it is here that rationality, in the polity, meets its greatest challenge and enjoys its greatest achievements. If those achievements often appear to be filled with flaws and incompletenesses, the charitable critic must remember the enormity of the task.

When one reviews the task of the legislature and of legislators from the point of view of the role of rationality, what special problems call for discussion? Two may be singled out for brief mention: (1) the problem of the tension between responsiveness and responsibility and (2) the search for the right locus for authority. To a certain extent all forms of government confront both of these problems, but the first is especially characteristic of democracy. It is a matter of finding the means for making the processes described above operate most fully—in Rousseau's terms, of making the Will of All accord with the General Will, that is, with the objectively rational. About this problem—almost coterminous with the problem of democracy!—we shall here remark only that its extent in any particular case is a measure of the need for leadership in that situation. It is for leaders, official and unofficial, at all levels from nationwide to the most parochial, to help bridge the gap. They can do so in many ways. It is partly a matter of identifying problems, analyzing them, calculating, and proposing solutions. It partly involves calling attention to the problems and the proposed solutions in a dramatic fashion, in ways that enlist support by aiding weak imaginations, by showing ties of interest hitherto unrealized, or by enlisting concerns for wider spheres of welfare. By such means as these the building blocks of rational public policy are fashioned. The better this job is done, the less is the tension between responsiveness and responsibility, between what is demanded and what is right, between desire and reason.

Another aspect of rational decision-making at the political level has to do not with particular decisions about substantive policy but rather with decisions as to where and how decisions are to be made. What decisions should be made by the legislature itself? When should authority be delegated to the chief executive or to administrators? In the latter case, should it be delegated to administrators who are direcly accountable to the executive or to semiautonomous agencies? Or should general rules be left to the courts for interpretation and application? To say that decisions of this kind call for a high level of the statesman's art is not to deny that they must be guided by reason. It is partly a matter of the appropriate degree of remoteness from the instruments of popular control. What kinds of information and expertise are required? How effective are the standards of professionalism, judicial or administrative, for the subject matter in question? Discretion unbounded by either legislative or professional standards imposes too great a strain on integrity. But discretion too restricted by either general rule or legislative specificity produces instruments too blunt for rational discrimination in the handling of complex factual situations. The facts of a given type of problem, whether it be the regulation of the securities industry, the application of antitrust legislations to the banking industry, or interpretation of income tax legislation, tend to produce and encourage their own peculiar discipline. This need for decisions by specialists in a given area does not necessarily mean that courts must give way to administrative boards and commissions. It may be that specialized courts in many areas—sometimes as reviewing agencies and sometimes as agencies of original jurisdiction—provide the answer. Those in search of a rational allocation of authority should not allow themselves to be governed by old dogmas about the role of courts, dogmas that may no longer be sound guides for decision. Within reasonable limits specialization in the judicial system may be as valuable, as rational, as is administrative specialization.

JUDICIAL DECISIONS
AND THEIR RATIONALITY

8

RATIONALITY IN JUDICIAL DECISIONS

PAUL A. FREUND

I

When James I royally maintained that he was perfectly competent to decide questions of law by the exercise of reason, Sir Edward Coke respectfully protested, if we can accept his account, that such decisions must be reached by the "artificial reason" of the law, which the King was scarcely qualified to pursue. There have been some who doubted the force of Coke's rejoinder in the context of the common law. Max Weber, for example, regarded Anglo-American law as distinctly inferior in rationality to the systems derived from the Roman law.[1] The common law, he argued, is too akin to the layman's ideal of the practical, the expedient, the expectable, and rests too heavily on the charisma of the judges, while the continental systems are more truly rational in their relentless application of for-

[1] *Max Weber on Law in Economy and Society,* ed. Max Rheinstein (1954), pp. 307–308, 316–318.

mulated rules to the facts of particular controversies. This is not the place to consider the verisimilitude of Weber's picture of the two legal worlds, but one or two points can be made that will perhaps illuminate in a preliminary way the dimensions of the problem of rationality in judicial decisions.

Weber, as might be expected, denigrated the jury as an irrational intrusion. But it may well be that the rationality of a system as a whole is maintained by the deliberate employment of a less rigorous element at a chosen stage: for example, the assignment by lot of a particular judge to hear a case, the intervention of an executive pardon, or the informed hunch of a probation board. Weber, too, selected for illustrative praise the decision of a German court that, under a code provision punishing the larceny of a chattel, the stealing of electric power is not an offense; it was a case of an omitted class of acts that must be rectified by new legislation. One might agree with the conclusion, but for more expedient reasons: though the term "chattel" could be applied sensibly to electric power in some contexts (e.g., in a comprehensive constitutional grant of authority to the government to sell publicly owned chattels or real property), in the context of a criminal law a more restrictive meaning may be called for in the interest of a general policy that crimes shall be strictly defined.

What I have tried to suggest in this preliminary way is that rationality has some important relation to the context of a system and of a particular class of problems. I find it less helpful to essay a definition than to examine a process in operation. Nevertheless one should, I suppose, indicate broadly the nature of the concept under examination. Rationality, I take it, is a term of commendation, though not of ultimate praise; a decision may be rational and yet not command approval as a necessary truth or even as right. It is set off against nonrational modes like will, power, caprice, or emotion, against irrational modes, like recklessness of means or ends or their relation, against rapacity or opacity. It is a warrant not so much of the soundness of a decision as of the course pursued—that the course of inquiry has been kept open and operating in appropriate ways and within appropriate termini. A principal aim of this paper on judicial decisions is to stimulate comparisons with the ways and the termini of the rational process in political and scientific thinking.

II

A convenient framework is at hand in Cardozo's analysis of the judicial process.[2] There are, he suggested, four elements in judicial reasoning: logic, precedent, history, and social utility. It may be useful to consider these (taking the first two together) from the standpoint of rationality and the limitations on it.

First, then, is logic, which embraces the notions of generality, consistency, deduction, and induction.

Generality. In ethical reasoning (of which legal reasoning is essentially an instance, for judicial decisions are aimed at the norm of justice), it is often said that propositions should be general, should not contain proper names, or should be capable of universalization. In the law, at least, a maxim of this sort is little more than a restatement of problems. Consider the following series of statements beginning with the words "A judge always ought to":

(1) decide by whim

(2) decide for the plaintiff in a negligence case

(3) stretch a statute (Maitland's self-professed rule as a member of the Senate of Cambridge University)

(4) give preference to an injured child in a negligence case

(5) give predominant weight to the welfare of a child in a custody case

(6) uphold an agreement as a valid contract

(7) uphold an agreement as a valid contract if it would be such by the law of any state having relation to the transaction

(8) impose stricter procedural safeguards in capital than in noncapital cases.

The form of these statements is general throughout. Does not their rationality depend on the relevance of the proclaimed standards to the classes described? And does not this first depend on an understanding of the sectors of the law with which the statements are concerned? And does not an understanding involve a good deal

[2] Benjamin N. Cardozo, *The Nature of the Judicial Process* (1921).

of feel for the traditions, assumptions, and practices of the discipline?

Consistency or Transitivity. A rational decision, it may be suggested, will respect the principle that, if A is preferred to B and B to C, then A must be preferred to C. But this also tends to obscure the real problem, which is whether to view the choices as part of a single field or in pairs which may alter the relevant fields. Anatol Rapoport has put the case of a man faced with the choice of living with one of three women. He prefers A to B and B to C. Is it, then, irrational to prefer C to A? Not if C is insanely jealous of A, so that to live with A rather than C would provoke an overhanging threat of murder. The law can furnish less fanciful illustrations. A federal statute provides that a lien for federal taxes shall be subordinate only to a pre-existing lien of a mortgage. Thus if there are three claims, that of a prior mortgagee (M), of a tax due to the United States (U), and of a tax lien of a state (S), the priorities would seem to be M, U, S. But suppose the state has a statute, enacted within its acknowledged powers, giving priority to state tax claims over the claims of a mortgagee. To follow the state rule would produce the series S, M, U. There is circuity here which somehow has to be resolved. One way of doing so might be to interpret the federal rule as not applying where the claim of a mortgagee and of the state coexist. Another solution might be to preserve the place of the federal claim by giving first priority to the amount and only the amount of the mortgage, but subjecting that amount to the tax lien of the state.[3] In any event, the analysis must go deeper than a principle of transitivity and must take account of policies made acutely relevant by what is on the surface a logical dilemma.

Deduction. One need not dwell on familiar logical troubles of deduction: what the tortoise said to Achilles in Lewis Carroll's fable or how deduction from a rule involves the problem of sameness in classifying phenomena under a major premise. In the legal process the difficulties are compounded by virtue of the fact that premises tend to be not so much rules as principles or standards and by the correlative fact that there are commonly two or more such premises available arguably as starting points for reasoning. In this respect judicial decision tends to resemble efforts at decision by maxims: when we remember that the early bird catches the worm (a rule, to begin with, for the birds), we are at once reminded of the cog-

---

[3] Cf. *U.S.* v. *City of New Britain,* 347 U.S. 81 (1954), and the discussion in *University of Pennsylvania Law Review,* XCV (1947), 739.

nate truth that haste makes waste. I hope to illustrate what it means to "apply a rule" by the analysis of a case at the end of this paper.

Induction. One need not dwell here on induction as the "scandal of philosophy" nor on the general observation that inductive reasoning is not self-starting or self-limiting—that, as Charner Perry put it some years ago, in beings who act and know there is an irreducible element of chance or will, of intellectual violence in the process of decision.[4] In the legal process induction proceeds from precedents and from facts of life. The use of precedents raises again the problem of sameness and also the problem of the range within which precedents should be re-examined. There is here a parallel with the method of science, since every experiment involves in principle a testing not only of the immediate hypothesis but also of the whole series of postulates of the system within which the experiment is performed. In the law the problem is complicated by the assignment of roles: a trial judge has much less freedom than an appellate judge to re-examine precedents, and there is a difference in role between judges and legislatures. The problem is further complicated by the relative importance of stability and justice (of which stability is, to be sure, an element) for different classes of legal transactions and events. A planned transaction, like a mortgage or a marriage, calls for more stability in the use of precedents than, say, a collision (though the making of settlements argues for some stability even here).

When one turns from precedents to facts of life as elements of induction, one must recognize that the facts are not given in a raw sense but are themselves part of a social system which makes them intelligible and which must itself be understood. Facts, to be sure, are rarely as raw as we carelessly assume. As recent studies by Jerome Bruner, George Miller, and others have shown, personal values or the norms of syntax and semantics affect the threshold of perception, and "concernedness" helps to define perception's span.[5] Social phenomena as the facts of law call for a special sensitivity and sophistication. Whether baptism and pagan initiation rites are viewed as parallel phenomena will depend on the orientation of the ob-

---

[4] "Knowledge as a Basis for Social Reform," *International Journal of Ethics* (April 1935), pp. 267, 276.

[5] Thirty years ago Alfred North Whitehead is reported as saying, " 'Concernedness' is of the essence of perception." *Journal of Philosophy,* **XXIX** (1932), 97.

server.[6] Judicial review of state taxation in Australia and the United States will be best understood in the context of the whole federal system of each country. On a more elemental level, the claims with which the law deals are not raw demands, but demands that have been shaped by a legal system itself, not the raw appetites for goods or association, but the claims of legal personalities, of debtors and creditors, buyers and sellers, husbands and wives. In this respect the legal process resembles the social sciences and is marked with similar entanglements in building on empiric evidence.

Of history it may be said briefly that its usefulness varies inversely with the weight of the demands made on it. The judge can learn relevant things from a narrative (how habeas corpus began and the functions it served) and, with luck and discretion in interpreting social facts, some things from the history of institutions about the strengths and weaknesses of certain forms of order (arbitration, judicial review of legislation). When he looks to history for a scaling of values, he is confronted, besides all this, with the problem of differentiating history from the historians: in Yeats's phrase, how to know the dancers from the dance; in Santayana's, looking over a crowd to find one's friends. Judges, said Holmes, are apt to be naïve, simpleminded men; they need a touch of Mephistopheles. In any search for objectivity through history, they need a touch—perhaps it is the same thing—of philosophy.

Social utility, the fourth of Cardozo's elements, is in a broad sense, as he acknowledged, an inclusive criterion, and it is of this that I want to speak more at length. In the law its limitations are near the surface. Law is a system for imposing a modicum of order on the disorder of human experience without disrespecting or suppressing a measure of spontaneity, diversity, and disarray. How and how much order to impose are questions that cannot always be answered by a utilitarian calculus. Order and freedom are mutually reinforcing to a degree, but at some point become incommensurables. Apparent allegiance to a common ideal of freedom may conceal deep divisions in the valuing of order and disorder: when Benjamin Franklin declared, "Where freedom is, there is my home," Tom Paine answered, "Where freedom is not, there is mine." Similarly with the sanctity of life and the preservation of lives. Is a man justified on utilitarian principles in killing an innocent person in order to save the lives of

---

[6] See Peter Winch, *Idea of a Social Science and Its Relation to Philosophy* (1958), p. 108.

two others? Of course, utilitarian considerations of a long-run kind may enter into a rule; a legal justification in so plainly stated a case might encourage homicides in situations whose exigency is less clear, where a deterrent is wanted. But these long-run considerations can be tenuous at best, and a more intuitive basis for a rule in this case is probably more realistic.

We are concerned, however, with the judicial process rather than with law as a whole, and here the practices of the discipline afford some escape for the judge from the problems of valuation.

First, the judge may take refuge in a rule of more-or-less generality already formulated, either by his predecessors or by the legislature. The starting point or points, in other words, are not at large but are within limits determined. Some rules embody a resolution of values, as in the homicide case. Others are prophylactic in the sense of forestalling the resolution of wasteful and difficult controversies of fact. The inquiry whether an alleged oral agreement was in fact made or is actually a trumped-up claim may be bypassed by a general provision of the Statute of Frauds requiring a writing for certain kinds of promises. Thus, problems of cogency in the establishment of truth are replaced by those of consistency in the application of rules. Such statutes, more often than is generally supposed, leave much to interpretation and thus a fathoming of purposes, but at least they circumscribe the scope of inquiry at the outset. In the formulation of such general rules by legislatures or courts, a good deal of nonrigorous empirical assessment of need and of consequences is indulged in. Social scientists, by and large, have concerned themselves very little with the formation and functioning of rules of substantive law. The reasons for this inattention to a rich quarry of experience are probably various. The problems do not readily lend themselves to experimental study save on a relatively trivial level from which it would be risky to extrapolate. Systematic observation would be costly and often inconclusive because of the number of variables. And, not least, opportunities seem too rare for results that carry a promise of being counterintuitive.

A second delimiting factor for the judge is the scope of the hearing or trial, as shaped by rules of evidence and procedure. The issues are defined in legal terms, with all that this implies for the exclusion of "remote, collateral, and prejudicial" evidence that might be of interest to an ethicist bent on fixing moral responsibility. As a judge, Holmes tried to remember, he said, that he was not God. However unsatisfying judicial judgments may be under the aspect of eternity, if they purported to assess responsibility in a more supernal way, they would become intolerable in a community where society and the state are not identical and where first or final causes are not a subject of easy consensus. This may take some of the edge off T. R. Powell's barb: "If you can think of a thing, inextricably attached to something else, without thinking about the thing it is attached to, then you have a legal mind."

The subject of the trial or hearing opens up the familiar issues of the expert witness, cognate to the issue of the social scientist at the rule-making stage. This is surely one of the least satisfactory phases of the judicial process. If the establishment of official, nonpartisan experts as an adjunct of the court seems an obvious remedy, it must be remembered that the authority of such officials might in practice be excessive and that differences among experts on ostensibly technical issues may subtly reflect honest divergencies within their profession on more nearly ultimate judgments, whether of the role of punishment, the desirability of patent privileges, or the virtues of economic competition.

A third delimiting factor for the judge—in addition to the reception of rules and the contours of a trial—is the form of his judgment or decree. For reasons which may be bound up with historic procedures, a judge at common law is limited, in general, to categorical sanctions; the defendant is liable to pay the plaintiff's damages, or he is not. In admiralty more flexibility is recognized, as in the assessment of damages on the basis of comparative fault. In equity, too, there is more flexibility, notably in the conditional decree.

Flexibility is a desideratum in the arsenal of sanctions, but a judge does well to respect the limitation of the role of his office, of the record on which he acts, and of his capacity for supervision of a decree. The attractions and the cautions surrounding a flexible decree are put in a strong light in the Associated Press case.[7] The AP sued to restrain members of the INS from copying news from AP bulletin boards and from early editions of AP member papers. A majority of the Court granted the relief. In a dissenting opinion Justice Brandeis, while recognizing the wrongfulness of the defendants' conduct narrowly viewed, raised the question of the public interest in the dissemination of news, the restrictive membership provisions of the AP's bylaws, and the dominant position of the AP as

[7] *International News Service* v. *Associated Press,* 248 U.S. 215 (1918).

a newsgathering medium. He argued that more comprehensive justice would require that relief be conditioned on AP's opening up its
membership on reasonable terms, but he acknowledged that this
restraint-of-trade aspect of the case had not been developed in the
pleadings or the record and that such a decree would entail supervision of services and dues that the Court was not prepared to
administer. His final conclusion was that the Court should abstain altogether, lest by doing partial justice, it reinforce other injustices that
it could not then eliminate. This seems an appropriate last word on
the judicial pursuit of social justice: a reminder that the judge is,
for good and ill, circumscribed by his station and its duties—that he
is not God or even the legislature.

III

Two special problems deserve attention in a study of rationality: creativity and bias.

To be creative in a discipline is in some sense to remain within it.
Creativity involves a tension between vitality and technique, as Jerome Bruner puts it, between passion and decorum, between the
frenzy of a mathematical insight and the decorum of an equation.[8]
The legal order, particularly the judicial process, puts a premium on
continuity in the midst of change; no Nobel prize is awarded to a
judge for the most revolutionary decision of the year. And yet, in a
deeper sense, creativity in judicial thinking may not be radically
different from that in science; both depend on seeing new connections, on re-examining postulates, on formulating new statements
that promise to be more satisfying (because more inclusive or eco-
nomical or fruitful) than the old. The amount of innovation in a
discipline may be obscured, magnified, or minimized by forms and
manners. (A Latin American visitor once remarked, "In my country
we boast of being socialist, but we are not; in your country, you
boast that you are not, but you are.") Ancestral voices and communal ghosts may be more powerful in science and in the arts than
a new generation may understand or care to acknowledge. "Coper-
nicus and Kepler," as Michael Polanyi has written, "told Newton
where to find discoveries unthinkable to themselves."[9] Of innovation
in literature, Harry Levin has observed:

Literary achievements are never quite so personal or original as they

---

[8] *On Knowing: Essays for the Left Hand* (1962), pp. 24–25.
[9] "The Republic of Science," *Minerva*, I (1962), 54, 69.

may seem, and generally more traditional or conventional. The most powerful writers gain much of their power by being mythmakers, gifted—although they sometimes do not know it—at catching and crystallizing popular fantasies.[10]

In law, particularly in the judicial process, the voices and the ghosts are proudly echoed and paraded, often disguising stranger accents and shapes. Creativity that is too upsetting to legitimate expectations may be left by the judges to the prospective operation of legislation. There are many factors that properly enter into this balance: how firmly grounded, how just, are the expectations; how much dislocation will result from the decision; how amenable might the subject be to the rule-making of general legislation; how feasible would it be to enter a judicial declaration applicable only to future transactions?

A vexing problem of rational creativity is the extent to which the new position should be formulated or may properly be left inchoate. In *Hamlet,* that tragic encounter of reason and passion, of intuition and rational proof and spectral evidence, the hero speaks mordantly of "a beast, that wants discourse of reason," and again,

> Sure he that made us with such large discourse,
> Looking before and after, gave us not
> That capability and god-like reason
> To fust in us unus'd.

"Discourse," articulation, the embodiment of a decision in a reasoned opinion or the amenability of a decision there and then to such an embodiment—how essential is this to rational creativity? Much current criticism of judicial decisions as unprincipled or unarticulated tends to overlook the useful part played by decisions in the past which were fraught with creative ambiguity, which moved in a certain direction but left open the turns that might be taken. One need not subscribe to all of Michael Oakeshott's critique of rational intervention and his enshrining of communal ways to appreciate the force of his observation: "Those who look with suspicion on an achievement because it was not part of the design will, in the end, find themselves having to be suspicious of all the greatest human achievements."[11] Of writing the law of torts in England at the end of the nineteenth century, when the notion of absolute liability

---

[10] "Some Meanings of Myth," in *Myth and Mythmaking,* ed. Henry A. Murray (1960), p. 112.
[11] "The Universities," *Cambridge Journal,* II (1949), 532.

was making inroads on the unifying concept of blameworthiness and when the academic jurists were disturbed at the resulting impurity and imprecision of doctrine, Professor Fifoot of Oxford has recently said:

> Faced with the fragments of life, the current law of any place and time can but approximate to a principle or indicate a tendency. Looking back upon the individual torts as they had emerged at the end of the nineteenth century, it requires an act of faith to postulate that principle or to indicate the goal to which they were tending.[12]

Professor Fifoot was referring, among other things, to the celebrated case of *Rylands* v. *Fletcher,* decided by the House of Lords in 1868, which has been the subject of an extensive literature and whose potentialities are even now far from settled. Because the case is not charged with political excitement and because it has become an influential precedent in a major area of private law, there may be value in examining it as an instance of judicial creativeness whose rationale, to say the least, was not clearly articulated.

The facts were not complicated. The defendant, a mill operator in a mining area, maintained on his land a reservoir for whose construction he had engaged an independent contractor. The contractor negligently failed to discover some abandoned mine shafts which threatened the stability of the reservoir. In time water escaped through the shafts and flooded a neighboring mine owned by the plaintiff. An action was brought against the defendant for damages. Various conventional bases of liability were argued, but none quite fit the case. Though there was culpability on the part of the contractor, the defendant himself was not negligent and was not chargeable by imputation with the fault of an independent contractor who was not strictly an employee. Vicarious liability without fault was therefore inapplicable. Other limited forms of liability without fault were likewise an awkward fit. Trespass on another's land entailed a willful entry, and here the defendant did not deliberately discharge the waters. Nuisance entailed a continuing or abiding noxious condition maintained by a defendant, and here the reservoir was not noxious in itself and the flooding was a completed event. To be sure, the escape of cattle would involve liability for their trespass, but to identify escaped water with wandering cattle would compound the animism that led to liability in the latter case. And yet there was

[12] C. H. S. Fifoot, *Judge and Jurist in the Reign of Queen Victoria* (1959), p. 56.

something about the Rylands problem that impelled the English court to transcend the limits of the precedents and impose liability. The court spoke of a "non-natural use" of the land for purposes of collecting water in a reservoir and a consequent liability for the escape of the dangerous substance so collected on the land.[13]

A host of questions perplexed the commentators who tried to fathom the principle underlying the decision. What is a "non-natural use"? Suppose the area were devoted more largely to mills than to mines? What if nothing escapes, but damage is done, say, by the vibrations of a blasting operation? What if the plaintiff, too, were engaged in an unnatural use of his land? How "absolute" is the liability? Suppose the barriers were broken by the action of a stranger or by an act of God? More broadly, could the decision in principle be confined to landowners? Did it entail, rather, a doctrine of responsibility for the consequences of highly hazardous undertakings? These questions, implicit from the beginning, have been answered over the succeeding decades, so that the "principle" of the decision is as much its eventual product as its original ground.

After the foregoing paragraphs were written, I rediscovered a passage in the early writings of Holmes which is itself an ancestral voice that will be legitimating as it may have become legitimated:

> It is the merit of the common law that it decides the case first and determines the principle afterwards. Looking at the forms of logic it might be inferred that when you have a minor premise and a conclusion, there must be a major, which you are also prepared then and there to assert. But in fact lawyers, like other men, frequently see well enough how they ought to decide on a given state of facts without being very clear as to the *ratio decidendi*. In cases of first impression Lord Mansfield's often-quoted advice to the business man who was suddenly appointed judge, that he should state his conclusions and not give his reasons, as his judgment would probably be right and the reasons certainly wrong, is not without its application to more educated courts. It is only after a series of determinations on the same subject-matter, that it becomes necessary to "reconcile the cases," as it is called, that is, by a true induction to state the principle which has until then been obscurely felt.

[13] The case is reported in (1868) Law Reps. 3 House of Lords 330. Professor Francis Bohlen sought to explain it by an economic or class-interest interpretation of the judicial process. "The Rule in Rylands v. Fletcher," *University of Pennsylvania Law Review*, LIX (1911), 298, 318–320. This view was vigorously disputed by Dean Roscoe Pound, "The Economic Interpretation and the Law of Torts," *Harvard Law Review*, LIII (1940), 365, 383–384.

cisions before the abstracted general rule takes its final shape. A well settled legal doctrine embodies the work of many minds, and has been tested in form as well as substance by trained critics whose practical interest it is to resist it at every step. These are advantages the want of which cannot be supplied by any faculty of generalization, however brilliant. . . .[14]

This is not to exalt blind groping or mystical intuition as marks of a creative judge, but to suggest that insight may outrun foresight, that there may be a time for sowing and a time for winnowing, that the advancement of doctrine need not await an exposition of its full reach, so long as judges are reasonably satisfied that it will not prove to be intractable. These are metaphors which could be annotated extensively from the law of the past.

To turn from creativity to the problem of impartiality or neutrality or bias, a judge's root beliefs or presuppositions or, in Holmes's phrase, his can't-helps: What is the role of reason in the congeries of selves, the congress (of Vienna or otherwise) that constitutes the personality of the judge? I would suggest four functions that reason might perform to cope with the problem of bias.

1. Distinctions must be drawn between legitimate and illegitimate biases, as the list of statements above was meant to indicate. It is one thing to indulge a bias in favor of injured children; it is another to be guided by the child's welfare in a custody suit. These often come down to the received traditions of the discipline, subject, to be sure, to modification like other parts of substantive law. Sometimes two legitimate biases may conflict. In a case of prosecution for bigamy following a marriage after a migratory divorce, working in favor of the validity of such a divorce is the bias against uncertainty in the criminal law and working toward its invalidity is the bias against competitive depreciation of moral standards through the avenues of a federal system. Neither bias is disreputable, each is relevant, and, if all other indicia leave the mind in equilibrium, the one more strongly held may prevail.

2. But reason should not lightly assume that one's biases deserve the strength they have or that they would not be amenable to further scrutiny. Is not this what needs to be said about the noncognitive character of values? To flaunt one's biases as can't-helps assumes

---

[14] "Codes, and the Arrangements of the Law," *American Law Review,* V (1870), 1; reprinted in *Harvard Law Review,* XLIV (1931), 725.

that they are like saying "I dislike asparagus" when they may only be of the order "I dislike Picasso."

3. Related to the previous point is the possibility of rationally finding a ground of agreement short of a collision of root beliefs. The judicial process is full of devices for this cushioning: burden of proof, presumptions, delimitation of issues, and so forth—institutional arrangements that have been referred to earlier in connection with social utility and intuition. Moreover, agreement on the facts may forestall a conflict of biases. If I am a vegetarian and you are not, we may agree that a given piece of meat is unfit for consumption without agitating our basic difference, and reason should explore such grounds of consensus to the full (though it is entirely possible that one's assessment of the facts will be somewhat affected by one's general bias).

4. The most troublesome role of reason in coping with bias is an endeavor to offset an illegitimate one by self-awareness and deliberate counterbias. How delusive or self-defeating may this be? May it produce a counterdistortion rather than neutrality? And may the self-analysis be too superficial, disguising a deeper desire to arrive at the counterbias? These psychological questions might be illuminated by that discipline in a way helpful to students and practitioners of the judicial process. The late Judge Jerome Frank suggested psychoanalysis for all judicial appointees. My present question is simply whether self-concern with bias, adding oneself to the problem, may involve a significant risk of distorting oneself, the problem, and the decision.

IV

Some general observations on rationality may tentatively emerge from a study of the judicial process. Rational thinking is to be understood in the context of an activity or set of practices; relevance and bias are meaningful in that context; and this is true also of creativity. Rational thinking involves respect for roles, not only for the place of a given discipline in society, but also for the allocation of functions within the discipline.

It has been said (in Paul Diesing's recent book, *Reason in Society*[15]) that the concept of practical reason has taken one or another of three forms among philosophers from Plato on: creativity (Plato, Hegel, Whitehead); the discovery and application of rules

[15] (1962), p. 244.

(natural-law theorists); calculation (Hobbes, the utilitarians). The judicial process, at least, suggests that these are interacting and, to a degree, interfused.

Sinclair Refining Co. v. *Atkinson,* decided by the Supreme Court of the United States on June 18, 1962, is an interesting and not atypical case presenting problems of rationality in decision-making that may illuminate the meaning and relation of creativity, the application of rules, and calculation.[16]

The facts were not in dispute for purposes of the case. The company and a union of its employees entered into a collective-bargaining agreement which provided for arbitration of grievances and renounced strikes or slowdowns over any causes that were arbitrable. In violation of the agreement the union repeatedly engaged in work stoppages on account of arbitrable grievances and did not resort to the arbitration procedure. The company brought suit in a federal court to enjoin such work stoppages. For its defense the union relied on the Norris–La Guardia Act of 1932, Section 7 of which prohibits the federal courts from issuing injunctions against a union's concerted nonviolent activity growing out of a labor dispute.

If this were all, it might appear that the course of decision is plain, that the rule of the Norris–La Guardia Act compels the Court to refuse an injunction. The "rule" is clear; it need not be extracted from decisions, it is actually codified; and it is not of convenient vagueness like standards ("due process" or "prudent investment") or principles ("no one may profit by his own wrong at the expense of another"). And yet this result might well cause disquiet. Does the act really fetter the courts in enforcing the obligations of a collective agreement? The background of the act was a history of federal courts' intervention to restrain strikes and picketing in an era before rights of union organization and bargaining were secured; injunctions served to intensify the inferior position of workers and caused widespread hostility and disrespect on the part of labor toward law and courts. So viewed, would not an application of the act in the circumstances of the present case be perverse? Already the neatness of "applying a rule" is becoming blurred. The calculation of consequences and the investigation of purposes suggest the possibility, at least, that the rule is more complex than it seems. Any reformulation must not do violence to the potentialities of the language used; but the term "labor dispute" may be sufficiently protean

[16] 370 U.S. 195.

to exclude cases where there is a breach of an arbitration agreement and of a no-strike clause. Whether this would involve too much creativity on the part of judges is the resulting question. If this were the whole case, the justices might well have concluded unanimously that on balance this degree of creativity should be left to Congress.

But that was not the whole case. Other data were at hand that bore some relevance to the process of decision. In 1934, without amending the Norris–La Guardia Act, Congress provided in the Railway Labor Act for compulsory arbitration of certain disputes, and the Supreme Court thereafter held that despite Norris–La Guardia an injunction could be issued against a strike in violation of the later statutory plan. At this point in the analysis, the present Court might rationally have (1) overruled the railway labor decision as an excess of judicial lawmaking, (2) followed it as a precedent where, as here, a plan of arbitration (though here voluntarily adopted) was in force, or (3) distinguished it as apposite only to a legislative scheme of arbitration. The "rule" of the precedent might have been either (2) or (3), depending on the emphasis placed on the factor of legislative intervention.

But there was, in fact, additional legislative intervention in the background. In 1947, the Taft-Hartley Act conferred authority on the federal courts to entertain suits for the violation of contracts between employers and employees. This provision, the Court had held, authorized mandatory orders compelling a union or an employer to submit a dispute to arbitration. But did it authorize the kind of negative injunction forbidden generally by the Norris–La Guardia Act? Now, obviously, the decision could not even in form be rested on "application of a rule." There was at least another coordinate rule to be taken into account, that of the 1947 Taft-Hartley Act.

In the actual decision, the Court divided. The majority opinion was written by Justice Black, who had been a member of the Senate in 1932. The dissent, joined in by Justice Douglas and Justice Harlan, was written by Justice Brennan, who had extensive experience in labor law before going on the bench.

The difference in approach of the two groups loses its significance if it is looked at simply as a difference in the application of a rule. Justice Black took the Norris–La Guardia Act as the primary datum; held the railway cases inapposite; and stressed what would be the legislative character of a repeal of Section 7, which Congress had declined to do. The calculation of consequences was for Congress; in any event they were not too serious, since an action for damages and a mandatory order to arbitrate were still available. Justice Brennan took as his primary datum a pattern of legislation and asked not whether the earlier provision had been repealed but whether it could be "accommodated" with the later legislation. This he did because the consequences of the Norris–La Guardia Act on the beneficent practices of arbitration agreements he regarded as deeply upsetting. And so he essayed a more creative role, seeking to find connections and reconciliation between otherwise discrete legislative provisions, converting inharmonious rules, if you will, into a more refined and comprehensive principle whose touchstone would be the promotion and safeguarding of collective bargaining. This he attempted to achieve by regarding the Norris–La Guardia Act as a nonrigid direction, to be followed generally but not in the special circumstances of a case falling within the fostering policy of the Taft-Hartley Act.

It is not important here to appraise the two opinions in their outcomes. What is of interest, I believe, is the fusion in actual practice of the types of rationality classically described as rule application, creativity, and calculation. In that fusion each element, while not losing its distinctiveness, takes on some of the qualities of the others. That this is psychologically true, it may be argued, does not establish that it is logically valid or philosophically useful; perhaps the psychological impurities ought to be burned away in the interest of clear and distinct ideas. It is really, I suggest, a matter of pragmatic emphasis: Which aspect, the distinctiveness or the interaction, is it more useful to stress? I can say only that I believe the interaction to be not merely a valid description, but a process the receptive awareness of which can enrich the resourcefulness and fruitfulness of the judicial process.

9

THE PLACE OF PRACTICAL REASON IN JUDICIAL DECISION

JOHN LADD

Nowadays, philosophers usually expect the words "rational" and "irrational" to generate more heat and noise than light—especially in mixed company, that is, when we meet our brothers in disciplines outside academic philosophy. Rationalists and irrationalists alike claim to be on the side of the angels, or, in more acceptable jargon, they both claim to be the defenders of the humanity of man. There are so many different issues clothed in these names that it is impossible to discuss "rationality" in general. What I want to do is to discuss rationality in the judicial process, which I take to be a kind of deliberative process that is similar to, if not a species of, ethical deliberation. I shall make no attempt to provide standards or criteria of rationality in judicial decision, for that, I believe, is a function of the legal specialist. My principal concern will be with the role, the function, or the place of reasons in a judicial decision. In other words, I want to ask how a judicial decision can be a rational decision.

From a philosophical point of view, we are interested in whether rationality is a logical requirement or an ethical requirement or not a requirement at all of a judicial decision. And from the jurisprudential point of view, the question leads in one form or another to the problem of the nature of logic in the law: whether judicial thinking is deductive, inductive, calculative, reasoning by analogy, or whether it has a special logic of its own or no logic whatsoever. Some jurists think that judicial thinking ought to be scientific and experimental, whereas others maintain that the scientific model does not apply to law, on the grounds that law individuates rather than generalizes, uses inexact concepts, and so on. All these issues arise, I believe, from the obsession with science and with scientific models of reasoning. I shall try to show that these difficulties can be resolved only if we free ourselves from the assumption that there is only one kind of rationality, namely, that represented by formal logic and the scientific method. Along with this assumption, we must get rid of the associated philosophical doctrine, of ancient ancestry, that rationality is a property of beliefs and not of actions or attitudes. (In ethical theory, these are the assumptions of what is often called "cognitivism.") The fundamental mistake on which these two related and mutually supporting assumptions rest is the reduction of practical thinking to some form or other of theoretical thinking.

Once we acknowledge the existence of what Aristotle called "practical reason"—that is, reasoning that issues in action rather than belief, we will, I believe, be able to understand what is involved in a "rational decision." In particular, I shall contend that we will be better able to understand the nature and logic of the judicial process if we recognize it to be a mode of practical reasoning. The model I propose to substitute for the scientific model is that of an individual engaged in explaining and justifying his actions in the past and in deliberating about what to do in the future. I propose, then, to consider a judicial decision as a kind of act proceeding from practical reason, that is, as a rational *action*.

By a "rational decision" I mean a decision for which the agent can give good reasons. A nonrational decision would be one for which the agent has no reasons, whereas an irrational decision would be one for which he has only bad reasons, that is, one which, though ostensibly rational, actually violates the norms of rationality and thus conflicts with rationality. (I shall have more to say later about these distinctions.)

It is important to distinguish between a rational decision and a correct or right decision; for a decision may be rational and yet wrong, or it may be right without being rational. In this respect, our use of the term "rational" to characterize decisions is analogous to its use in connection with beliefs: a belief may be false though rational (given the evidence available) or true though irrational or nonrational (by chance, as it were).[1] This distinction allows one to admit that a decision is rational while at the same time consistently denying its rightness, just as one can admit a belief to be rational and yet deny that it is true. Nevertheless, although one can quite consistently repudiate the decision itself in a rational decision (or rational belief), it is clear that calling the decision "rational" is a way of commending it. Just how and why it is possible at the same time both to reject and to commend a decision will be explained later.

A JUDICIAL DECISION IS AN ACTION

The best way to bring out the issues involved in explicating the nature of rational judicial decision is to consider one rather extreme theory of the judge's function. For want of a better name, I shall call it the "Platonic theory." According to this theory, the function of the judge is to determine, in the sense of *find out*, what is right or just in particular cases of conflict between two parties. Moreover, the theory maintains that his conclusion, if rational, is derived from a certain body of knowledge, including knowledge of the laws. (In order to bring the theory up to date we may admit all kinds of logical and scientific techniques, calculi, and psychological and sociological information, so that the nature of the resources on which the judge draws in order to reach his conclusion is not a point at issue.) Thus in the Platonic theory the judge's function may be compared to that of the physician, the clinician, who brings his knowledge to bear on the particular medical problem before him.[2]

---

[1] Perhaps the distinction between right and rational cannot be carried through all the way in practical discourse, and so, in the final analysis, it does differ from the distinction between true and rational.

[2] Plato himself, it will be recalled, was fond of comparing judges to doctors and even speaks of judges as doctors of the soul. See the *Republic* III.409; *Gorgias* 478a, 480b.

The judge, then, on this theory is the legal expert par excellence, and the worth of his decision, indeed, its validity, is determined by its rationality, that is, by the extent to which it is the most reasonable conclusion that can be reached from the knowledge available.

It is clear that the Platonic theory of the nature of the judicial function does not correspond at all to the judge's role in any of the legal systems we know. No one can pretend that judges have more knowledge of the law than, say, lawyers and jurists who, indeed, may even be specialists in the branch of the law that is involved in the case to be decided; nor, indeed, is it even necessary to assume that judges are wiser than other men. Nevertheless, the decisions of a judge possess a kind of validity and authority that the conclusions of the legal expert on exactly the same subject do not possess; for, albeit with certain qualifications, we have to agree that "the law of any case is what the judge decides."

The idea that the law is determined by what the judges decide is, of course, double-barreled, for through it, its advocates are both asserting a logical truth and making a plea for judicial reform. However, we are at present concerned only with its logical side, namely, the proposition that the validity of a judicial decree derives from the judge's authority, from his legal powers, rather than from the rationality of the decree itself. We must also recognize that the decree, the decision, is itself different from a simple conclusion from a body of knowledge; for it effects certain changes (or nonchanges) in the legal situation, that is, through his decision the judge changes the legal relations of the parties involved (or else he acts to sustain them as they are). For example, a decision may impose a new obligation, say, a fine, on the accused. Thus, the judicial decision differs from the conclusion of a mere legal expert in two ways: first, in the source of its validity, that is, what makes the decision binding on us, and second, in what the decision does, that is, its legal effect.

It is clear, then, that, when the judge renders his decision, he is not asserting a proposition at all. His decision is an action, not the assertion of a proposition. In this respect, what the judge, in rendering his decision, is uttering is what J. L. Austin called a "performative," that is, he is doing something, performing an action—and in contrast to what the legal expert says, what the judge says is neither true nor false.[3] The judge, in other words, is an actor who does

---

[3] J. L. Austin, *Philosophical Papers* (1961), chap. 10, and *How to Do Things with Words* (1962), *passim*. "Only the still widespread obsession

something; he creates new legal relationships, and what he does only a judge clothed with judicial authority is able to do. The legal expert may know what it would be most reasonable to do, but only the judge is able to do it. Thus, even when the judge only applies a rule in a mechanical way, the applying itself is an act, a performance, and not merely a logical operation of subsuming a particular case under the rule.

It follows therefore that there is something paradoxical about asking whether the judge's decision was the right decision—whether, for example, the Supreme Court's interpretation of the Constitution is the right interpretation—because it is, after all, the judge (or the court) that determines what is legally right and binding *by making it so*. On the other hand, when all is said and done, we still want to be able to evaluate and to criticize a judicial decision; we must do so, I submit, by using the standard of legal rationality rather than the concept of legal rightness (or validity).

Now if, as has often been maintained, the function of the judge is to make the law for particular situations, or, as I prefer to say, to perform an operation on the legal situation, then it follows that what he does is not at all like what the scientist does, nor, for example, the same thing a doctor does when he diagnoses and prescribes for a particular situation. The rightness or wrongness of the doctor's diagnosis and prescription depends solely on his knowledge and his use of it, and not at all on a commission of authority which has been given to him by someone else. Hence, we cannot accept the Platonic analysis of the nature of judicial decision.

The analytical view that the law is what the judges decide is often taken to exclude the view that the law itself is what determines the judges' decision. Thus has been generated a fallacious either-or: Either the judge determines what shall be law, or the law determines what the judge shall decide. Even if we admit with Kelsen that the law itself, that is, the basic norm (constitution), confers upon the judge his authority to make decisions and prescribes the procedures he is to follow and the limits within which he is to decide, the possibility of judicial discretion or creativity destroys the contention that

---

that the utterances of the law, and utterances used in, say, 'acts in the law,' *must* somehow be statements true or false, has prevented many lawyers from getting this whole matter much straighter than we are likely to—and I would not even claim to know whether some of them have not already done so" (*Ibid.*, p. 19).

what the judge decides (or ought to decide) is completely determined by the law; for if and when he is creative, to that extent he is doing something, performing an act, rather than reaching a conclusion.

The legal realists have concluded from the fact that the judicial decision is creative and determines the law that, therefore, it cannot be the law that acts to determine his decision, and so we can only ask for the "sources" (Gray) or the causes thereof. Since law is, as it were, the product of the judge's decision, all we can do is to ask for the causes of his decision. Hence, we have various sociological studies of judicial decisions and the plausibility of the so-called gastronomic theory: the idea that the judge's decision is determined by what he ate for breakfast. But apart from such absurdities, the realist movement (perhaps for the wrong reasons philosophically) has succeeded in opening up broader questions concerning the grounds for judicial decisions and has encouraged the judges to look beyond the strict rules, even to the facts of psychology and sociology, for a basis for their decisions. In doing so, they have not, of course, actually repudiated the rationality of the judicial process, but have only shown the inadequacy of what Pound calls "mechanical jurisprudence."

The view that judicial decisions have causes but not reasons to explain them has, of course, an analogue in philosophy, for there is an ancient prejudice that reasons can only be construed as the premises from which a conclusion is drawn by means of logical rules and that logic requires both premises and conclusion to be propositional, if not truth-functional. The argument is that, in order for anything to be a reason (or a conclusion), it must involve the principles of logic, and the principles of logic apply only to propositions or mental states with propositional content. Hence, since neither actions nor the determinants of action like wants, desires, purposes are propositional, they cannot serve as conclusions or premises, and so the concept of a reason does not apply to them. The view that all knowledge and reasoning is theoretical may be regarded as equivalent to holding that all knowledge and reasoning is propositional. It follows from this view that actions and other nonpropositional occurrences cannot have reasons; they can only have causes, although, of course, if a belief that is the conclusion of a line of reasoning is the immediate cause of an action, we might say that it is a kind of reason *sensu lato,* a reason by marriage, so to speak.

It is not evident, however, that one cannot give and demand reasons for things other than propositions and propositional attitudes. Aristotle's doctrine of the practical syllogism is an attempt to show how there can be reasons for action and that among such reasons we have to include ends, desires, and wants, as well as beliefs. Von Wright also has recently defended a brand of inference that he calls "practical inference."[4] The very fact that we can ask intelligibly for a reason for an action seems to me to be ample proof that the whole notion of there being reasons for actions is an intelligible one. It is common to ask: "Why did you do it? For what reason?" (This is true, by the way, of attitudes, as well. We ask: "Why do you feel that way about him? What are your reasons?") Furthermore, the reasons which are asked for in such questions are directly reasons for the action or attitude concerned and do not require the causal mediation of a propositional conclusion of some kind.[5]

If all this is granted, then we can consider a rational action to be an action for which the agent has good reasons, and a judicial decision, regarded as a very special sort of action, will be rational insofar as the judge has good reasons for it. I now propose to explore the consequences of assimilating judicial decisions to rational actions in general. In order to do so, I shall, first, explain more fully the logic and function of reasons for actions; second, show how the reasons given by a judge to justify his decision can be construed as similar to the justification offered by an agent of his actions; and, third, relate the justification procedure, which I regard as the essence of the judicial process, to the requirements of morality.

REASONS AND ACTION

Following Aristotle, I shall assume that the fundamental schema of practical reasoning is the means-end schema, so that, in terms of the practical syllogism, the major premise is an end (or expresses a want), the minor premise concerns the means to that end, and the conclusion is the action itself. Now, many refinements

---

[4] Aristotle's clearest exposition of the practical syllogism is to be found in *De Motu Animalium* 701ᵃ ff. It is also discussed in *Ethica Nichomachea* 1147ᵃ1–ᵇ19. G. H. von Wright, "Practical Inference," in *Philosophical Review*, LXXII, No. 2 (1963), 159–179. I have also discussed the practical syllogism in my "Reason and Practice," in *The Return to Reason*, ed. John Wild (1953).

[5] They are *rationes agendi*, and not *rationes cognoscendi*. See my *Structure of a Moral Code* (1957), pp. 163–164. I have also argued for this view in my "The Desire to Do One's Duty for Its Own Sake," in *Morality and the Language of Conduct*, ed. H.-N. Castaneda and G. Nakhnikian (1963).

and qualifications have to be made, and, indeed, some were made by Aristotle himself. I shall only point out a few ways in which this basic schema changes as it is applied differently, since my principal object here is to elucidate the role of reasoning in judicial decision. The two facets of practical reasoning to which I want to call attention concern, first, the different modes of assent (types of acceptance) and, second, some of the logical peculiarities relating to the premises (reasons) themselves.

Aristotle and von Wright both recognize that practical inference operates differently for the agent and for the onlooker, that is, the practical syllogism differs in its first-person form and its third-person form. (I shall assume that a person's attitude towards his own past actions is like that of an onlooker.) Aristotle called the excellence of the agent's reasoning that eventuates in action *phronesis*, practical wisdom, whereas he called the ability of the onlooker to grasp and follow the agent's reasoning *synesis*.[6] We may ask: If the practical syllogism eventuates in action for the agent, what does it do to the onlooker who does not act? Even though he does not perform an overt action, we want to say that he accepts the inference in some sense and that something happens to him as a result. Consider, for example, A's giving B his reasons for doing X, that is, A is attempting to justify his doing X to B. What happens to B if A succeeds? I think it will be clear that there are many different possible outcomes for someone who accepts, but is not in a position to act on, a practical syllogism: imitation, approval, acceptance, sympathetic understanding, and so on.[7] These are all what might be called practical acceptance falling short of action. We may, perhaps, stay with Aristotle's term "understanding," of which he says: "Practical wisdom is imperative, understanding only judicial. I mean that, whereas

---

[6] See Aristotle, *Ethica Nicomachea* 1143ª1–20. The exact interpretation of Aristotle's doctrine in this passage is a matter of dispute. St. Thomas Aquinas and his followers regard *synesis* as the last cognitive judgment before preception (the command to act). See Aquinas, *Summa Theologiae* I–II. Q. 57, a. 6 ad 3; II–II. Q. 51, a. 3; II–II. Q. 48, *passim*. This interpretation is too cognitivist, in my opinion. J. A. Stewart writes: "[Synesis] is the faculty of understanding and appreciating good advice laid before one by another person. The *synetos, qua synetos*, does not initiate policies, or schemes of conduct, but has the intelligence to recognize good ones when they are presented to him. . . ." *Notes on the Nicomachean Ethics* (1892), II, 84. Stewart and others seem to agree with my principal point here, namely, that *synesis* is an excellence in the onlooker.

[7] See my "The Desire to Do One's Duty for Its Own Sake," pp. 333 ff., for more detail concerning my notion of qualified acceptance.

practical wisdom gives orders, its end being a declaration of what we must or must not do, understanding is content to pass judgment."

It is important to note also that practical reasoning of the sort under consideration does not relate solely to actions yet to be undertaken. Aristotle and others have emphasized the process of deliberation in their accounts of practical reasoning, but I believe that we use this same form of reasoning when we give reasons for actions that are already completed. When we ask a person to explain why he did something, we are usually requesting him to give a reason for his action, a reason which operates, as it were, to justify the action. Thus, explanations of past actions, although they may be causal explanations, typically take the form of a justification. Such explanations may be called *justifying explanations*.[8] Accordingly, a person may use a justifying explanation to explain his past action or a contemplated action to others, or his past action to himself, or the actions of others to himself or to others. Justifying explanations, according to this analysis, use practical syllogisms of the sort under discussion.

It is clear, then, that practical reasoning has a much wider use than its use for discovering what to do. Indeed, discovery, that is, the satisfactory resolution of practical problem-situations, is probably not even the principal way in which it is used. More often it is used to defend one's acts, whether they be past or merely contemplated, in the sense that the aim of the person presenting the reasons is to procure acceptance of some sort on the part of others: this may be action, imitation, acquiescence, or perhaps just understanding. I think it is also obvious that a person is able to explain (that is, justify) a past action by using a practical syllogism, even though the premises of the syllogism were not consciously in his mind when he performed the act; for example, we have no difficulty in giving reasons for many of the things we do automatically without thinking —lighting a cigarette, putting on one's shoes, shaking hands, and so on. Reason has a use here, but its relation to action is more indirect than just being the cause of it. There is, therefore, nothing strange in acting, perhaps even deciding, and then becoming aware of the reasons for it later. In this sense, then, we could say that an action is rational even if, at the time of acting, the agent is not consciously aware of his reasons.

---

[8] *Ibid.*, p. 326, for more detail concerning justifying explanations.

All of this, of course, applies to judicial decisions and the judge's reasoning, for, I contend, in presenting his opinion, he is offering a justifying explanation of his decision, that is, he is, in a way, out to defend his decision as a rational act. Moreover, the fact that the immediate cause of the decision was a hunch or, say, an unarticulated feeling that one side was right and the other wrong does not impugn its rationality.

I now want to call attention to some of the logical peculiarities of practical reasoning and practical syllogisms, for I think they also throw some light on the nature of the judicial process. One of the most interesting and important peculiarities of practical reasoning is what might be called its "pluralism," that is, the way it admits and deals with conflicts of premises or reasons. In terms of the means-end schema of the practical syllogism, the conflict can be expressed as a conflict of ends. Suppose, for example, that A wants both X and Y, and he knows that M is a means to X and N is a means to Y and that he cannot do both M and N; so he has to choose. Perhaps his desire for X overrides his desire for Y so that he ends up by doing M. Now his desire for Y, Y considered as an end, is not eliminated nor in any way refuted or repudiated by his choice of the means to X; the premises of the practical syllogism, (1) I want Y, and (2) N is a means to Y, are still perfectly good premises, but the act that is the conclusion of that syllogism is frustrated by the fact that A chooses to do something else that is incompatible with it, namely, M. Given the choice of, say, the X-M set, then the Y-N set that is incompatible with it is rendered impossible, and the conclusion of the incompleted syllogism takes on a form resembling the form it has for the nonagent onlooker: an acceptance short of action.[9]

The interesting logical feature of this analysis is that, although an action that is based on one end X is incompatible with the pursuance of another end Y, the choice of that action does not eliminate or render unacceptable the end Y. This feature of practical inference stands out in contrast to the principle of ordinary propositional logic, which holds that, if two different premises entail contradictory

---

[9] The logical status of the Y-N set that is rendered impossible is similar to that of an "ought" statement when one is unable to fulfill the "ought." It is held in abeyance, so to speak. For more detail concerning unfulfillable "oughts," see my "Remarks on the Conflict of Obligations," *Journal of Philosophy*, Sept. 11, 1958.

conclusions, then one of them must be false, that is, is unacceptable. (If p implies q, and r implies not q, and p, then not r.)

Elsewhere I have called the reason which is thus overridden by another reason an inadequate reason and the overriding reason an adequate reason.[10] The fact that there are inadequate reasons in practical discourse explains how it is possible to accept a certain practical argument as rational and yet not act on it, and indeed, even repudiate the conclusion. This, I submit, is what happens in the judicial process: Arguments are advanced on both sides, and they are good arguments in the sense that they fit into the scheme we have been considering, and yet, of course, both sides cannot win. The deliberative process in which an agent weighs the mutually exclusive courses of action in terms of the ends to be achieved by each thus finds an analogue in the court where the decision for or against the plaintiff is weighed in terms of the different principles favoring each side. As in the deliberative process of a private person, the judicial procedure makes sense only on the presumption that a case can be made out for both sides, notwithstanding the fact that one side may be clearly superior to the other. It is easy to see why this presumption on which judicial procedures rest is justified once we look on the judicial process as a type of practical reasoning involving the weighing of conflicting ends or principles. Theoretical models of reasoning, such as the scientific model, are not, I submit, capable of explaining this significant feature of the judicial process.

Let us consider for a moment how one could overturn a practical syllogism. There are two ways of doing this: first, by producing a premise (an end) that *overrides* the premise (end) of the original syllogism. For example, A might want to buy a certain house because it is on the seashore, and against this B might point out that it costs too much, and, as a consequence, A's desire to save money might override his desire to own the house, so that, as a result of B's counterargument, the conclusion not to buy wins out over the conclusion to buy. Overturning a practical syllogism by overriding a premise in this way I call *confutation*. The second way of overturning a practical syllogism is by showing, for example, that the house A wanted to buy was not on the seashore. This mode of overturning by attacking the premises I call *refutation*.[11] Now from a rhetorical point of

[10] "The Desire to Do One's Duty for Its Own Sake," p. 329.

[11] It is obvious that this distinction between confutation and refutation has further ramifications. The whole subject of the logic of refutation in

view, that is, if one is interested in a fine knock-down argument, the method of refutation is more effective. Returning to our example, if B shows that the house A wants is not actually on the shore, that ends the discussion, whereas if he merely shows that the house is costly as well as desirable, he invites a weighing of the desirability of the house against the cost, and the final outcome of the procedure is not nearly as obvious and certain as in the case of the refutation. For this reason, in legal argumentation the method of refutation is generally preferred to the method of confutation—explicitly, at least. But although refutation is the ordinary procedure in legal debate, it takes a very peculiar form: namely, what Karl Llewellyn calls a "juggling" of concepts.

This leads us to the second peculiarity of practical syllogizing— the methods of formulating the minor premise concerning the means to the desired end. There are two entirely different kinds of means, which may be called *extrinsic* and *intrinsic* means. An extrinsic means is nothing more than an external cause of the end sought; Dewey calls it a "mere means"—an instrumentality. A means may, however, be intrinsic to the end in the sense of being part of the end. Thus, moving one's feet is an intrinsic means to dancing, and telling the truth is an intrinsic means to living a virtuous life. (This, I believe, is what Mill meant when he said that virtue was a means to happiness because it was a part of happiness.) Now, the interesting practical syllogisms are those which refer to intrinsic means: I want, say, to be an honorable man, and I regard a certain act as a means to that end because I regard it as an honorable act. Whether or not to accept the minor premise relating to the means depends on how the end itself is interpreted, since the means itself is part of the end. In other words, in practical syllogisms involving intrinsic means, the question whether or not to accept the minor premise is itself a valuational problem, for the minor premise provides content for the major premise and in a sense defines the end itself.[12]

For the same reason, judicial thinking often turns on the meaning of legal concepts, the middle terms which refer to what might be called intrinsic means. If we consider the general rules of law as the major premises, that is, as expressing ends, then it is clear that much

---

ethics and practical discourse in general is a fascinating and unexplored subject.

[12] This is explained in more detail in my "Reason and Practice," pp. 253–254, and in my *Structure of a Moral Code,* pp. 159–162.

if not most of legal thinking relates to the minor premises—for example, what is or is not to be included under, say, trespass, negligence, nuisance, freedom of contract, commerce, and so on.

In a disparaging way, it has been said that all that lawyers and judges do is manipulate concepts. The judge, says Llewellyn, is a juggler, but, he adds, he should do it like Our Lady's Tumbler in the medieval tale: "Let him tumble and juggle reverently; let him turn upon his juggling all that is best in him and all his skill. . . . The quarrel which one has with the judges is . . . [that] the sleight of hand is not always lit by passionate, conscious battle with the problem of ends and purposes which presents itself before honest juggling can begin."[13] But the need to juggle, as it were, with basic concepts is as important in morals as it is in law; surely Christ was doing a good bit of juggling with the concept of neighbor in the parable of the good Samaritan. There is, of course, bad juggling as well as good juggling, foolish juggling as well as wise juggling, irrational juggling as well as rational juggling. But creativity in morals, as in law, is certainly closely related to the juggling of concepts, which, of course, can be described more pretentiously as using persuasive definitions.

Once again, it is clear that the way in which judicial thinking makes its reasoning depend upon the meaning of legal concepts brings it closer to moral and practical thinking in general than to science, where disputes over words are easily settled—or comparatively easily.

It can now be seen how and why legal thinking uses the method of refutation rather than the method of confutation in its argumentation. By making the point at issue a question of the meaning of a legal term, the jurist is able to avoid the lesser certainties involved in the comparative evaluation of the rules themselves, or, in our language, of the ends of practical syllogisms. The question that naturally arises is whether, in the end, the subterfuge of manipulating concepts has any different outcome from the explicit recognition that, in certain contexts, one principle (end) overrides another. The preference of the method of refutation, one suspects, is based on the desire, in Llewellyn's words, to stay "within the bounds of legal decency."[14]

[13] Karl N. Llewellyn, *Jurisprudence* (1962), pp. 90–91.
[14] Loc. cit.

THE JUDGE AS A RATIONAL AGENT

Although there does, indeed, seem to be an analogy between the judge and the deliberating rational agent, we might still want to ask whether or not the rationalizing that the judge does is really like the rationalizing of an individual agent when he gives a justification of a planned course of action or a justifying explanation of a past action.

Let me put the question in the form of an objection: It might be argued that the procedures are not at all analogous, since the individual agent reasons from his own personal ends and the means open to him to the action to be undertaken, whereas the judge, on the other hand, does not introduce his own ends and actions into the discussion at all, but is concerned instead with the actions and interests of the parties before him. Thus, we might say that the individual is thinking *subjectively,* whereas the judge is thinking *objectively,* since the point of reference for the former is what belongs to him personally, that is, his own wants and actions, whereas the point of reference of judicial thinking is the concerns of others, their wants and actions. Furthermore, the subject matter of the judge's deliberation, his weighing of pros and cons and his evaluating, relate to other persons and not himself. His own ends are not merely irrelevant, but must be excluded.

If we examine more complex examples of deliberation by private agents, we can see that there is not, however, as great a difference as appears here. If we take simple examples like Aristotle's example of the man wanting a coat or von Wright's example of a man wanting to make a hut habitable, it surely seems that the reasoning is oriented subjectively, that is, it is related to the agent's own situation. But when we consider more complicated cases in which practical reasoning is employed, we find that they tend to become more and more oriented toward the properties of the relevant objects rather than toward the agent's ends. Take, for instance, a man deliberating about whether or not to buy a certain house: His deliberation will be oriented toward the various properties of the house—its condition, its location, its closeness to good schools, the taxes, and the cost; these are the factors on which his ultimate decision will rest, and, for the agent, they are, in their own way, just as objective as the factors that the judge must take into consideration in reaching his decision.

But, the objector might continue, what is the end that provides the ultimate major premise for the judge's practical syllogism? Here we seem to be faced with a dilemma: If the judge's end is his own end, then his decision loses its impartiality; yet, if it is not his end, then it loses its character as a practical syllogism. It would seem, then, that the judge's end cannot be his own; rather it must be, in some way or other, the ends of the respective litigants.

The answer again calls attention to the complicated character of practical reasoning. The ends of practical reasoning are multifarious; in particular, they are often defined by roles and institutions, and as such they need not be personal and private in the sense that they conflict with the ends of others or of society. Consider the end of a doctor's action, for example, which we may assume is to restore his patient to health; as Plato pointed out, he might also have a private end, say to increase his income, but qua doctor, in *that* role, his own end is one that serves the interests of others. The judge's end, which provides the major premise of his reasoning, is similarly determined by his institutional role, and it is not to be identified with any private, personal interests he may have. What, then, is the judge's end? Here we have to be vague, but we might say, perhaps, that it is the impartial administration of justice or of the law.

Furthermore, institutionally and role-defined ends like that of the judge or the doctor usually include conditions and limitations—rules, relating to the means that are to be employed in reaching these ends. Just as the football player, whose end is to win the game, is bound by the rules of the game, so also the judge, whose end is to administer justice, is bound by rules, some of which are specific and some of which are so general that they are called "principles." These rules and principles play the logical function of defining the end itself (the law), and in this respect there is an analogy between what the judge does and playing a game; for, as has been frequently pointed out, the activity, say, of playing a particular game is itself defined by the rules governing it, so that unless one plays by the rules (or a minimum set of them), e.g., of football, he cannot play the game in question; he will be playing some other game instead or no game at all. Likewise, if the judge decides a case by tossing a coin, he will be playing coin-tossing rather than acting as a judge. Thus, the judge, being bound by the rules under which he operates, has his ends and means defined in a somewhat different way from the individual moral agent, whose reasoning may involve only a private personal end.

We are now in a position to explain more fully the use of the terms "rational," "nonrational," and "irrational" as applied to actions. The terms "rational" itself is susceptible of a very broad and general use in which it is contrasted to "nonrational." "Rational" in this sense means merely having reasons, so that a "rational action" would be an action that is performed because it is believed to be a means to a predetermined end. (We might narrow down this definition by stipulating that the beliefs concerning the means to the ends themselves be rational in, perhaps, a scientific sense, which involves the use of available information, calculation of probabilities, and so on.)[15] Charles Lamb's story of the origin of roast pork illustrates this kind of rationality, since the building and burning of houses with pigs inside is a completely effective means of procuring roast pork, that is, it is rational in the broad sense.

We are, however, interested in a narrower sense of "rational," one in which it is contrasted with "irrational," since almost any action whatsoever could be construed as being "rational" in the very broad sense. I think that we usually use the word "irrational" to apply to beliefs and actions, that, although rational in the sense that they have reasons behind them, violate the canons of rationality in some way or other. As far as beliefs are concerned, we might want to say that a belief that is grounded in superstition is irrational—for example, the belief that anything with the number 13 is dangerous. I think that, when we call an action "irrational," we usually mean that, although it is an effective means to the end sought (and thus rational in the broad sense), the outrageous price that has to be paid for using that particular means is completely ignored by the agent, that is, the means are unsuitable. In this sense, a man burning down houses to procure roast pork or a man destroying a town to vent his anger against one person or a man strangling an elderly woman in order to get some money to buy a meal is irrational.[16] Irrationality, in this sense, then, involves the complete

[15] "Rationality of an action will here be understood in a strictly relative sense, as its suitability, judged in the light of the given information, for achieving the specified objective," writes C. G. Hempel, "Rational Action," in *Proceedings and Addresses of the American Philosophical Association* (1961–1962), p. 7.

[16] Thus John Dewey writes concerning the roast pork incident: "Only

disregard of the reasons against the action in the decision to perform it, a disregard that dismisses the other side from any consideration whatsoever by ignoring it or even flagrantly contemning it. If this account of irrationality is accepted, then we may consider rationality to be its opposite, so that a necessary part of rationality when applied to decisions consists in the agent's paying some heed to the claims of alternative courses of action. In particular, when we speak of a judicial decision as being rational, the least that we can mean by it is that the judge has reached it after giving due consideration to both sides of the dispute. For our purposes, then, we may regard the consideration of all the facets of a decision as a *necessary* condition of its rationality. (I might add that I do not think it worthwhile to become embroiled in a lengthy dispute concerning the correct or *real* meaning of "rational" and "irrational" as if there were such a meaning and as if it made any practical difference. My substantive contentions still hold regardless of the terminology used.)

Now it is important to realize that, many respected theories of rationality to the contrary notwithstanding, what is rational in one context, say, a game or a social gathering, will be irrational in another, say, in a court of law. Thus, as was said at the very beginning of this article, the canons of rationality and, in particular, the determination of what is to be accepted as a good reason and what is to be rejected as a bad reason are established within the discipline itself. For example, the question of whether or not an argument offered by counsel is a good or a bad argument is itself a legal question, not a logical or philosophical question. Accordingly, the demand for a set of rules or principles governing practical reasoning in general, that is, rules for the practical syllogism, is fatuous; for, as I have tried to show, the means-end schema, which I have regarded as paradigmatic of practical reasoning, takes on different forms in different contexts, so that sometimes it may call for flexibility and discretion on the part of the agent, whereas at other times all he needs to do is, say, perform a calculation. This aspect of practical reasoning, I submit, accounts for the fact that so many different methods can be used in juristic thinking and explains why in some

---

when the end attained is estimated in terms of the means employed—the building and burning-down of houses in comparison with other available means by which the desired result in view might be attained—is there anything absurd or unreasonable about the method employed." *Theory of Valuation* (1939), p. 41. In this, and in much else, I owe a great debt to Dewey for the insights that he has provided.

situations the judge may or even has to be "creative" whereas in others he merely applies the rule mechanically.[17]

MORALITY AND RATIONAL DECISION

In the account that I have offered, I have tried to show how judicial decisions can be construed as a species of rational action and how the judicial opinions supporting such decisions can be regarded as rational justifications presented by the judge to explain his decision. If my contentions are correct and judicial reasoning is a kind of practical reasoning employing practical syllogisms and the means-end schema, then we have an explanation for a very peculiar facet of the judicial process that otherwise remains unintelligible, namely, how the judicial process can be both rational and intersocial and how, as such, it can be participated in by different parties with different points of view even though it has to end in a decision favoring one party against the other. The aim of the process is to have its rationality accepted by all parties, despite the fact that the decision is regarded by one or more of the parties as wrong. In other words, we must be able to say that, although we think a decision is wrong, we accept it as reasonable, and this acceptance must be a kind of practical acceptance that amounts to much more than a purely intellectual acknowledgment of its validity. Although the usual theoretical models of rationality are unable to explain this paradoxical character of the judicial process, I hope that I have shown how the concept of practical reasoning and in particular the notion of an agent's justifying explanation for his action are able to do so.

The same considerations relate to the familiar proposition that everyone has a right to a fair hearing before the judge. This proposition, of course, rests on the presupposition that a case can be made out for both sides; for, even though in an actual situation there may not be much of a case for one of the sides, we have to assume the possibility, at least, that there are two sides. This assumption, however, is intelligible only if we accept an analysis of the judicial process as a mode of practical thinking in which there *can* be

---

[17] According to my view, then, the kinds of issues raised by Herbert Wechsler and his notion of neutrality, as well as the kind of issue raised by Charles Black and his notion of activism, are not answered by the analysis I have provided. Although philosophy may help to clarify some of the logical aspects of such issues, the issues themselves are not, in my opinion, logical, but, rather, legal in the broad sense.

reasons on both sides. Theoretical thinking, as I have pointed out, is not able to accommodate this assumption in the form that is required here. On our analysis, then, it is possible to explain why the judge can decide for one side without having to deny the merits of the reasoning of the losing side, and the losing party can similarly repudiate the judge's decision while, in a sense, accepting the reasoning he gives to support it.

It is hardly necessary to point out the importance of these interesting aspects of the judicial process for the relation of law and morals. The dignity of the individual and his right to a fair trial require that legal decisions affecting his basic interests be explained and justified in the way that I have indicated. Although it might be thought that the purpose of this rationalizing procedure is merely to persuade the loser to accept the decision or to convince others of its rightness, this is not the chief purpose at all. It is, rather, to treat a rational being rationally, that is, as a rational being, by *explaining* to him through reasons why a decision that adversely affects his interest has been reached. Of course, the persons to whom the judge is addressing his reasoning may not, as a matter of fact, actually have enough intellectual equipment (rationality) to be able to understand and appreciate the reasons he gives, but here, as elsewhere in morality and in the law, we are required to act on an *as if*, namely, on the injunction: Treat other human beings as if they were rational and could understand.

10

POLITICAL PRIVACY, THE COURTS, AND THE WORLDS OF REASON AND OF LIFE

A. A. MAVRINAC

Since the last years of the 1940's, the United States Supreme Court has played its role in the American version of the contemporary revolt against nineteenth-century structures, first, by the support it eventually gave to the New Deal's efforts to supplant personal government of economic units with more rational self-justifying government; second, through bringing under the protection of the United States Constitution certain aspects of individual activity and certain facets of the personality previously thought the proper concern of local government. In this rebellion of life and of reason against the restricting force of nineteenth-century mediocrity and arbitrary will, the Court has used a whole set of instruments, extending from freedom of religion to the right to anonymity and embracing freedom from arbitrary search and seizure, freedom from self-incrimination, freedom of associational privacy, and the secrecy of the ballot.

Underlying these conceptual instruments and, indeed, giving life to much of the development of contemporary constitutional jurisprudence has been the concept of the right of privacy. Some commentators, like Dean Griswold, speaking of it as "the right to be let alone," have called it "the underlying theme of the Bill of Rights"[1] and have adopted Justice Brandeis's characterization of it as the right "most valued by civilized men."[2] By 1959 a note in a leading law review was able to say that "any doubts that may have remained as to the status of the right to privacy" had been resolved.[3]

But a significant feature of the development of a right of privacy in the constitutional area seems to me to be that the concept has not been used as a focus for the disposition of parties in litigation or as a core about which conflicting parties group themselves and are assigned positions in terms of the forces of rights and duties flowing from that core. Rather, the concept has been used to bring out new riches of power residing in such classical governing principles as the right of assembly or the right to enter into contractual relations, as well as to suggest new ways of looking at the source of Congress's power over interstate and foreign commerce or at the very nature of the legislative process. Also, perhaps because it has not seemed to play the immediate role in the assignment of duties and rights, the concept of political privacy has not received a very extended explicit treatment in legal commentaries. Its qualities have been left to be developed by implication from decisions pivoted on grounds more familiar to the legal practitioner.

If we consider the concept of political privacy closely, the exclusion of it from among the pivots of judicial controversy may not be surprising. First the concept grows out of the recognition that ultimately all the different worlds of value that have been involved in constitutional litigation where right of privacy has been evoked derive their life from the individual as a whole. Each of these worlds of the political, the social, the familial, the individual, or the judicial

---

[1] Erwin Griswold, "The Right to Anonymity," *Northwestern University Law Review,* LV (1960), 217.

[2] *Olmstead* v. *United States,* 227 U.S. 438, 478 (1928).

[3] Note, "Group Action: Civil Rights and Freedom of Association," *Northwestern University Law Review,* LIV (1959), 392, referring to the Supreme Court's decision in *NAACP* v. *Alabama,* 356 U.S. 449 (1958).

provides a means by which the individual human being orients himself to other men and, in sum, finds meaning for his existence. Each of these worlds is composed of structured elements and of nonstructured, and each world attempts to provide means for effectively integrating the structured and the nonstructured.

This attempt to provide for the control of change through the harmonization of new vital forces with old arrangements of values is one dictated to us by the language of thought that is our classical heritage. For Plato the creative is the product of love, but the operative quality of the creative is its rationality.[4] That is, the creative moves an already existent artistic structure by inserting itself into that structure, by understanding itself.[5] In somewhat the same way Hobbes suggests the necessity of structure, procedure, regularity, and certainty to the effectiveness of the forces of life that operate at the "state of nature" level ever present beneath society, just as that structure cannot exist without the renewing thrust of the vital. For both, life requires channels for its action to be effective, and the channels are meaningless unless they express the demands of life. Creativity is the expression of the unique and personal, but order is the prerequisite of freedom or the condition of opportunity for creativity.

As the constitutional system develops, there appears more and more clearly as a central principle the proposition that political institutions within this system—institutions all deriving their quality from this never-ending interaction between the ordered routine and the ordered creative—should be grounded firmly, explicitly, and overtly in the individual human being as the direct and continuing source of the creative element in society, even while these institutions serve in themselves as instruments for the control of vital forces and for ensuring that these become translated into forms easily integrated into the prevailing pattern. The emergence of the concept of privacy as an ever more effective catalytic agent is a

---

[4] See here Socrates' analysis in the *Symposium,* especially *circa* 209, and the Platonic description of the relationship of reason and necessity in the *Timeaus* 48[a].

[5] In the Christian conception of the Trinity, the creative that is the Father seems to be understood as by His very nature impelled to come to an understanding of Himself, an understanding that is the second person, with the Holy Spirit the unity of love that binds the two. Ordered creativity allowing the spirit of charity to move all seems in this tradition a meaningful, analogous way in which to look at the Trinity.

result of this constitutional impulse to have all institutional life flow directly from the individual human being.

Within the legal institution itself, the jury serves the function of helping the system accommodate the forces of renewal within society to the control patterns which the law has undertaken to protect. The jury represents the felt limits of the law's effectiveness in dealing with the emerging patterns of values which new generations constantly elaborate as expressions of their meaning of selves and the world and as the instruments to that meaning. And the jury remains a good example even though at times it may seem to serve more as an instrument of defense of outmoded structure while highly trained judges serve as the sensitive agents of new social value systems.

Within the political, the universal order, free and equal participation in the voting process by each adult becomes the principal source of new structural and process orientations; in turn this force of new crystallizations of social understandings is channeled into prevailing patterns by the strength of these patterns themselves, specific institutions therein endowed with high degrees of coercive potential over one another and over individual members of the society.

Because they are all based on the individual (even while transporting values that are the refinements of the value patterns esteemed by a succession of generations of individuals), all these structural worlds—political, social, legal, familial, individual—are related to one another. They all represent, according to the specialized quality of each, the interactions of individuals attempting to impart meaning to their lives, trying, that is, to come to an understanding of the self, however impossible this might be in a time-space context that allows us to see ourselves only as through a glass, darkly.

Each system seeks internal coherence, logic, and stability. Such coherence, logic, and stability when attained mark the successful balancing by the system of the forces of an older value pattern superficially representing the forces of stability on the one hand, and of the forces of a newer value pattern superficially representing the forces of change and of the present on the other hand. That each system seeks such coherence is the observation of practically every political thinker, whether it is Aristotle remarking on the causes of revolution, Machiavelli noting the sources of discontent, or Marx expounding the weaknesses of a thought system now become ideology that serves only a long-since-surpassed system of production relationships. When a structure no longer serves as an opening to meaning for men, it is ignored, or, if it will not be ignored, it is at length jettisoned. The system which fails to make itself understandable to itself is a system that has closed off the forces of creativity. And the inability to make itself comprehended by itself is, because of the system's source in fact in the lives of living men, simply another way of representing the system's inability to serve as a means of men's orientation.

Each of these systems, from the system of the man himself to that of the family and on to that of the political order, uses a technical language appropriate to itself. It seeks to justify itself to itself through the use of this language. Beyond this, however, each system has the problem of communicating to the others, of justifying itself when it is called upon by another to do so within the framework of a coordinating order to which each system adheres.

Whatever the technical differences among the languages of the systems, because the systems in the end proceed from the same unity-seeking individual, the systems cannot retreat behind a wall that they pretend to be essential. However the general social system may assign primary responsibility to a particular system for managing certain value functions, these responsibilities are at some point bound to be open to other systems. The autonomy of systems must be respected as a necessary part of the use of structure to ensure ordered movement of the creative to the point of utility. But there is no such phenomenon as complete independence. It is only in this sense that I can find meaning, for example, in Justice Frankfurter's remarks in *American Federation of Labor* v. *American Sash and Door Co.:*

> Courts can fulfill their responsibility in a democratic society only to the extent that they succeed in shaping their judgments by rational standards, and rational standards are both impersonal and communicable. Matters of policy, however, are by definition matters which demand the resolution of conflicts of value, and the elements of value are largely imponderable. Assessment of their competing worth involves differences of feeling; it is also an exercise in prophecy. Obviously the proper forum for mediating a clash of feelings and rendering a prophetic judgment is the body chosen for these purposes by the people. Its function can be assumed by this Court only in disregard of the historic limits of the Constitution.[6]

[6] 335 U.S. 538, 557 (1949).

Justice Frankfurter's argument here in the American Sash case is not an argument in abdication, no more than the considerations advanced in *Baker* v. *Carr,* in which he urged the Court to refrain from entering the thicket of reapportionment, represented a turning away from responsibility. In *Baker* v. *Carr* he argues that "the crux of the matter is that courts are not fit instruments of decision where what is essentially at stake is the composition of those large contests of policy traditionally fought out in non-judicial forums, by which governments and the actions of government are made and unmade."[7] Courts are not fit in a case like this because "standards meet for judicial judgment are lacking."[8] That is, the judicial system does not have appropriate to it tools for properly analyzing the life of the legislative branch as manifested and impinging upon men in the districting of a state. The larger framework of the political order within which both the Court and the legislature work recognized certain categories of analysis as inappropriate to the legislature's organizing and expressing its view of the world. To look at the world in terms of individual men in their individual systems in terms of "Negroes or Jews or redheaded persons"[9] is another matter. Here is a scheme of communication among men in society forbidden to the legislature by the political order of which it is voluntarily and expressly a part.

I

The sensitive search of Court and Congress for ways in which to articulate meaningfully the relationship between the system that is the individual citizen, the system that is the Congress, and the control system that is the Supreme Court is strikingly evident in the relationship of those three systems at the point of Congressional investigations. The search here has been precisely for a way by which to protect each system in its own efforts to integrate the forces of creativity within its structure and, while sheltering this privacy, to protect the political order's own analogous effort to control the integration of social creativity and social structure.

In the area of these investigations the invoking by a person of

[7] 369 U.S. 186, 287 (1962).
[8] *Ibid.,* 289.
[9] *Ibid.,* 300. As Justice Frankfurter says, such a way of conceiving and organizing the world is what the Court struck down in *Gomillion* v. *Lightfoot,* 364 U.S. 339 (1960).

the rights of his privacy under the rubrics of freedom of speech or assembly or of freedom from illegal search and seizure means both that the committee can be called upon by the Court to verbalize its authority and sustain the coherence of its action and that the citizen must be prepared to demonstrate the quality of his participation in the political process beyond the intimate, private, and completely sheltered exercise of the suffrage. Burden of proof may lie in the first instance with the committee, but in the second with the citizen.

Although the autonomy of the legislative structure cannot permit a court to prescribe affirmatively a set of choices from which the legislature is to draw or otherwise pretend to substitute its own creative powers for those of the legislature, the court can still scrutinize the choice made in order to determine its consistency with the norms general to all structures—in this case the constitutional norms and, following on this, its consistency with the internal legislative structure. This is to say that the court can determine whether the demands of substantive and procedural due process have been met. The court can insist that the purposes of the inquiry have relevance to a purpose consistent with the political structure and consistent with the general distinction between the political and the personal area. It can further insist that the legislature give evidence regarding the situation that was structuring itself under the pressure of the legislative moving as one of the channels through which the unformed forces of change respond to shaping questions put to them. The legislature can be called on in this unified world of autonomous value structures to satisfy the court that its movement toward the articulation of a set of new norms was proceeding in a professional fashion, new elements being sought in the building of the structure by a reasoned movement forward from a sturdy elaboration already existing and not taking place fitfully, blindly, in passion.[10] Then the legislature must give some evidence that its professional judgment could reasonably justify the conclusion that the individual compelled to appear before it for testimony had himself penetrated the political area from his private world. Here the court necessarily respects the creative forces that operate within

---

[10] One of the best recent common-law examples of the analysis of a situation in this way is to be found, I think, in Judge Irving Kaufman's analysis of the Appalachin Case, *U.S.* v. *Bonnano,* 180 F. Supp. 71 (D.C.S.D.N.Y. 1960).

the legislative structure and allows them to bring to life the questions by which phenomena are ordered and values are brought to life. But as the protector of the autonomy of all structures, it insists that, where they impinge on one another, they justify themselves to one another by a rational discourse the mark of which is a general language full of bi- or multilateral terms allowing all relevant value systems to latch onto a peg joined to another peg that is the tool of another system. The language of the law in dealing with privacy problems is not the language of privacy itself, but is rather the language that binds the private and the political areas. Freedom of assembly, freedom from unreasonable search and seizure, freedom to enter into contractual relationships, all such language conveys the bipolar concerns involved. It represents, that is, in one unified expression the logic of each system involved and represents at the same time a permanent reference point in the refinement of the nature of each such value system.

In dealing with the Congressional action, the task of the United States Supreme Court is to serve as the sensitive interpreter of social norms evaluating momentary acts not only in terms of what Justice Frankfurter has referred to as their complex "associations, overtones, and echoes," but also in terms of the complex values of society, represented themselves in a myriad of such echoes and overtones. In "Some Reflections on the Reading of Statutes," Justice Frankfurter observed that the area of free judicial movement in dealing with Congressional action was considerable. Laws, he said, are not propositions. "They are expressions of policy arising out of specific situations and addressed to the attainment of particular ends." However, the central difficulty is, as he sees it, that "the legislative ideas which laws embody are both explicit and imminent."[11] He sees legislative enactments as "organisms which exist in the environment," and he reminds us that Justice Holmes said that "the meaning of a sentence is rather to be felt than to be proved."[12] As Justice Frankfurter says, "Legislation and adjudication have different lines of growth, serve vitally different purposes, function under different conditions, and have different responsibilities." Again quoting Justice Holmes, he has emphasized that "statutes are the outcome of a thousand years of history. . . . They

[11] *Columbia Law Review*, XLVII (1947), 533.
[12] *Ibid.* Quoted from *United States* v. *Johnson,* 221 U.S. 481, 496 (1911).

form a system with echoes of different moments, none of which is entitled to prevail over the other."[13]

What is it, then, that the Constitution demands of the legislature? To what has the legislature committed itself? As I have suggested, the Supreme Court cannot demand of the Congress that it allow itself to be judged by the same standards of the rational that courts use to judge their own work or the roles of personal social actors. But the Court can still insist that the action of the Congress be able to be analyzed in terms of some rational standard and that all legislative action leading to the ultimate movement of enacting the law be logically relatable to that ultimate rational structure. This I take to be the thrust of the Supreme Court's decisions in *Watkins* v. *United States*[14] and *Barenblatt* v. *United States*[15] and of the decisions on legislative inquiries since those cases. The nonlegal and creative, which in the first instance the legislative act is, must in its first impulse be assimilable to a pre-existing structure. Legislative activity cannot be like personal activity at the state-of-nature level, breaking out of old forms and spontaneously moving to set up a new hierarchy of values. New programs must be born in a more ordered way, out of the womb of the old, and every new legislative action must be based on a prior action. It must fit into a coherent structure of rights, duties, and remedies. This framework of action that is rational, that is, in Lasswell's definition, action that is consistent within the frame of an actor's reference made "while passing through a long sequence of decision"[16] still can enclose the process by which choices are shaped by the action of professional tools of the legislator, themselves given form in over a thousand years of experience in the art of creative brokerage, on the rough new models coming up out of the depths of social action.

The Court therefore cannot quarrel with the legislature's last choice, provided that it is a choice that can be shown by the legislature to be related to a structure of decision-making elaborated over time. The question is not whether the choice is a rational one, but whether there is a rational relationship to the structure built up by the Congress by itself and in terms of its own judgment.

[13] *Ibid.*, at p. 533; quoted from *Hoeper* v. *Tax Commission*, 248 U.S. 206, 219 (1931).

[14] 354 U.S. 178 (1957).

[15] 360 U.S. 109 (1959).

[16] Harold Lasswell, "Current Studies of the Decision Process: Automation versus Creativity," *Western Political Quarterly*, VIII (1958), 381–399.

II

The discretion permitted the president in certain areas, especially foreign affairs and military affairs, offers another illustration of the nature of the freedom from the requirement of self-justification permitted to a value structure. The United States Supreme Court's handling of the Japanese expulsion cases during World War II[17] shows the high degree of protection which the Court felt it must provide the president in his privacy from the need to explain his actions as a value-incarnator to any other constellation of values. Here the impact on and expressed hurt of a particular individual are analyzed in terms of the limitations which Court intervention would impose on the spontaneity of presidential expression and on the privacy of the private citizen. The impairment of the individual's ability to contribute to the political order, weighed against the extent of impairment of the ability of the presidential office to respond flexibly to threats to national order, becomes the guide to the determination of the extent to which the institution, the value world, must justify itself, express itself, and defend itself in language that is common to a number of value systems. The concept of a president always able to retreat behind the wall of prerogative and into a closed world of his own, a world where choice and decision are not rational, but arbitrary, and not related to other structures or to the general structure of society and the general interaction of structure and the creative area, is an untenable concept. It is impossible because of the relationship of the president as an amalgam of values to the individual, and it is also impossible because no action of the president is creative unless it is ordered, unless, that is to say, it is rational. Whether it is for the Court in a given instance to inquire into the rationality of a presidential act depends on the balancing qualities of the system as a whole. Other sysems will have their chance in a constitutional system to measure the rationality—the self-coherence and coherence in the estimation of other systems—of a particular presidential act or, better, of the presidential orientation. It is for the Court to use those categories developed by it for facilitating communication and control across systems and apply these general terms, which allow for incorporating the vital demands of each system, as a way of evaluating a

[17] *Hirabayashi* v. *United States,* 320 U.S. 81 (1943); *Korematsu* v. *United States,* 323 U.S. 214 (1944); *Ex Parte Endo,* 323 U.S. 283 (1944).

specific situation. *Ex Parte Endo* represents more than a shift dictated by prudence. It is the result of a sound estimation of the impact of such a decision on the strength of the presidential value structure. That any other course than the one taken by the Court in the Hirabayashi case would have extended it beyond the power of the Court to enforce its decrees is in itself no more severe a criticism than the suggestion that a court is limited in its framing of a decree in equity by its awareness of the limits to control imposed on it by the complexity of the case, the difficulty of determining the existence and extent of damage, and the impossibility of fully defining the rules of conduct to be observed by the parties.

Recent decisions of the United States Supreme Court provide a particularly rich example of the way in which situational principles of analysis and the use of the privacy concept in the way I have been outlining it can be used to determine rights and duties. In the Negro sit-in cases decided late in the 1962 term, the Court disposed of five cases in which criminal trespass actions had been brought by the state against Negroes, or whites with them, trying to obtain service at segregated lunch counters in stores in Southern cities. Such state action in other circumstances, of course, can represent an effort to protect the storekeeper's area of privacy vis-à-vis his customers. The offer on the part of a storekeeper to sell is not in itself a commitment to sell to whomever appears and indicates intent to purchase and proffers consideration. The common law and legislative action have built up over the years a structure of rights and duties that shelter the entrepreneur from contacts he might deem a threat to his self-image, while specifying the points at which his very decision to engage in a particular enterprise has committed him to communication with other men. In his brief as *amicus curiae* in these cases the solicitor-general of the United States denied that the position he was asserting "would require holding the proprietor to a duty to serve Negroes and denying their private rights to exclude them for whatever reasons they chose," a result which he said would be "inconsistent with the preservation of the private freedom of choice, sustained in the Civil Rights cases and our ensuing constitutional history."[18] In some of these cases the trespass arrest took place in a situation elaborated by local law specifically prohibiting the service of Negroes and whites at eating facilities

[18] *Peterson* v. *Greenville*, 373 U.S. 244 (1963), brief for the United States as *amicus curiae*, p. 79.

with the same utensils or in close proximity to each other.[19] In other cases the involvement of the state was less formal, though significant enough to warrant the Court's assimilating it to the involvement manifested in other cases by legislation. In *Lombard* v. *Louisiana*, for instance, Chief Justice Warren referred to the announcements, a week before the sit-in incidents in question, by the mayor and police chief of New Orleans, decrying sit-ins and referring to "the normal, good race-relations that have traditionally existed in New Orleans"[20] and announcing that no more sit-ins would be tolerated as they would be considered breaches of the peace.[21] The chief justice went on to say, "As we interpret the New Orleans city officials' statements they have determined that the city would not permit Negroes to seek integrated services in restaurants. Consequently, the city must be treated exactly as if it had an ordinance prohibiting such conduct."[22]

In these cases the equal-protection clause of the Fourteenth Amendment is therefore used to prevent the state's authority from interfering with the freedom of the proprietor to communicate with the customer should he desire to do so. Impediments to a free decision of the manner in which the proprietor will choose to express himself toward other men, the places in his own personality structure at which he will build communications bridges to other men, are voided where these impediments express a social value inimical to the fullest expression of the uniqueness that is each man. Were this attempt to build barriers to the creation of bonds of personality not present, the proprietor's right to choose the human beings with whom he would share his privacy would be unquestioned; he would not need to justify his decision to anyone.

It is this right of privacy, then, that the Court is protecting when it tears down the barriers to communication. But in attacking this barrier, the Court is pointing to the personal basis on which the equal-protection clause rests. That basis is the uniqueness of each human being and the ultimate problem each man has of giving life to that uniqueness, a problem complicated by the fact that, as the constitutional assumption has it, this uniqueness cannot grow except

[19] The terms of the Greenville, South Carolina, ordinance are fully set out in the chief justice's opinion in *Peterson* v. *Greenville* at 246–247.

[20] *Lombard* v. *Louisiana,* 373 U.S. 267, 270 n.2 (1963).

[21] *Ibid.*

[22] *Ibid.,* 273.

in its exposure to the warmth of the love of other persons, men, and God, molding it and nourishing it.

Similarly, while the proprietor as person is in this way protected in his privacy by the destruction of false obstacles to his communication with other men, he, too, as proprietor, can be called upon to exercise his individuality in accord with the logic of the structure by which, in establishing himself as entrepreneur, he has chosen to communicate qua entrepreneur with other men. As no human action is comprehensible outside a structure, indeed, is unimaginable without such a structure by which strivings are channeled and impulses are controlled, so every human action is judged as to relevance by the structure into which it seems to fit.

Now, the features of such a structure as that of interstate commerce are, of course, always in the process of refinement, their general nature defined in differing senses from generation to generation in rough accord with the logic first given extensive coherent expression by Chief Justice Marshall in cases like *Gibbons* v. *Ogden*. But a rough consensus is still possible which will accept as a logical development the assumption, by many of those who frame their lives in the commercial structure, of an obligation to turn outward and free themselves of even the self-imposed barrier of racial prejudice and so come into communion with dark-skinned men. However else they may choose their clients, by wealth or station, they can no longer ask the question of race. The groping of the system toward coherence and clarification now seems to require categorization on lines other than race, lest the system be no longer the logic by which men express themselves, but a relic, like long-displaced crank telephones hooked up to a dead switchboard. In the process of definition we exclude Mrs. Murphy and recognize that she lives by a structure other than that of interstate commerce or, indeed, by a structure hardly commercial. The demands of either system make trivial the activities of Mrs. Murphy and her family boardinghouse.

The equal-protection cases protect the very nature of a man, his privacy, by refusing to allow the community to force that man to look at other men and ask himself the question of color. Man, not God, has invented color, like everything else except the intangible human soul, and the society in consensus now creates a value in which the color of a man's skin is defined out of existence as a socially relevant phenomenon. This means, however, that

many men who have found it easy and natural to express themselves in this way will be forbidden to use the question of color by
which to orient themselves in the commercial world. No doubt
many of these will feel that some powerful force has moved to
penetrate their very own private depths and force them out of their
privacy. The thrust of the application of the "right to be let alone"
in the area of constitutional law is that one, indeed, does have a
right to be alone. But the thrust is also that this is a right that each
one of us exercises in the company of other men who are our com-
panions and in cooperation with whom we build the world of
external values in which we act out our destinies. The inarticulate
premise is that the whole structure of communications by which we
bring each other to grow is infused by the charity that is life, a
charity that moves us into a bond of love with one another. This
bond also has its logic, its movement toward coherence, its limits,
and its strivings. Though much of that logic is beyond the power of
the law to enforce or work on directly, there are analogous appearances of it, and it is through action on these appearances in the
public area that courts, like all the coercive instruments of society,
can influence the real secret life of men that is the life of love.

The area of privacy is the area of decision—of choice, judgment,
or act—that need not be justified to any other than the immediate
system by which and in which the decision is taken. Thus, privacy
is a quality of every decision-making system from the individual
through the social and to the political. But as every system derives
the energies ultimately from the individual and as every individual
is also inescapably a member of a number of systems, the area of
privacy in each system is not necessarily coextensive with the system.
The limitations of the privacy of the system are thus imposed by the
situation formed from the interaction of that system with another or
others. For example, in the familiar situation, personal privacy is
comparatively limited, though even in these limits the creative that
is protected by privacy can be, and, in the healthy situation, is,
easily accessible for orderly translation into coherent structural
patterns. In the political situation the constitutional principle insists
on the most limited impact on the privacy of the individual, indeed,
allowing none in the crucial election situation. Within the political
situation per se, specific institutions are assigned strong privacy protection by the constitutional theory in order to provide for restraints
on the relationship between the political and the personal areas.

These restraints are reinforced by an impact on the privacy of the political process permitted to such institutions as the legal.

Where two systems impinge on each other, the autonomy protecting the mover from the need to justify its decisions no longer exists. The warrant for proposing to cross the threshold of privacy must be so expressed as to be intelligible to the other system and to any mediating control systems. The peculiar and individual language of discourse by which a system reaches decision when it is operating in its privacy and which need be intelligible only to that system is no longer sufficient. The rationale of actions must now be expressed in terms comprehensible outside the system. That is, there must be a rationale, a structuring of the decision, that is comprehensible to the other systems concerned, and a language to convey this structuring and to express a sense of its proper relationship to the structuring of other value systems. We assume that no creative act even within the privacy area of a system is such without creative forces' being integrated into an orderly, coherent, and internally consistent pattern proper to the system (though this tells us nothing necessarily about the nature of the ultimate sources of creative choice). However this may be, the relations among the value systems demand that, where there is impinging of one system on another, there be a coherent, understandable justification of the choice made by the system in its decision-making process. The language among the systems is, therefore, a language which ideally seems to carry at once the sense of each system. It harmonizes in an abstract way the essentials of the decision-making process of each.

The concept of privacy is, therefore, of limited value to a mediating control system, such as the legal system, if one restricts use of the concept to the human personality. If, however, one sees the concept of privacy as applicable to every system of decision-making, then it can serve as a means for illuminating the richness of older terms mediating between decision-making systems and as a way of bringing into existence newer terms which will aid each system in presenting its decision in rational, that is, self-comprehensible and extracomprehensible, terms.

WHEN THE SUPREME COURT
SUBORDINATES JUDICIAL REASON
TO LEGISLATION

MARGARET SPAHR

That the judiciary is reason incarnate is an outgrown myth of an earlier age. No present-day legal or political theorist would evaluate the judicial branch of government in terms such as those employed by Alexander Hamilton in *The Federalist:* "The judiciary . . . has no influence over either the sword or the purse; no direction either of the strength or of the wealth of the society; and can take no active resolution whatever. It may truly be said to have neither *force* nor *will,* but merely judgment."[1] We know better but are in danger of serious error in the opposite direction. In our sophisticated certainty that courts necessarily create new law, we sometimes tend to mistake judicial legislation and legislative enactment for identical twins.

[1] *The Federalist,* No. 78, pp. 395–396 (Everyman edition).

160

Both legislative and judiciary advance the cause of justice, but by different means. It is the legislature's function to remove inequities from existing law and hence openly to introduce innovations. Reason is employed in an auxiliary capacity, as in devising the most effective means for securing desired ends. Law courts, on the other hand, best serve justice by using established procedure to assign to each that which is his due under existing law. To a court, reason is primarily analysis, analogy, and deduction, not the implementation of volition. Justice Benjamin Cardozo, in the midst of an eloquent discussion of the creativity inherent in judicial decision, uttered a wholesome caution:

> I do not mean, of course, that judges are commissioned to set aside existing rules at pleasure in favor of any other set of rules which they may hold to be expedient or wise. . . . [T]here may be a paramount public policy, one that will prevail over temporary inconvenience or occasional hardship, not lightly to sacrifice certainty and uniformity and order and coherence.[2]

Judicial legislation is characteristically retroactive, whereas legislative enactments are almost invariably prospective. The framers of the United States Constitution took great pains to avert the evils of retroactive legislation. Both Congress and the state legislatures were forbidden to pass ex post facto laws and bills of attainder. No state might pass a law impairing the obligation of contact. By the adoption of the Fifth Amendment, Congress was denied the power to deprive any person of life, liberty, or property without due process of law, and the Fourteenth Amendment eventually imposed the same restriction on the legislatures of the states. But a judicial decision, no matter how contrary to precedent, cannot be regarded as ex post facto law or impairment of contract or deprivation of property rights; the most recent decision of a court of last resort is viewed as a determination that the law has always borne the meaning that is now at last attributed to it. The disappointed party who has relied on precedent has no relief for his sense of outrage.[3]

---

[2] Benjamin N. Cardozo, *The Nature of the Judicial Process* (1921), Lect. II, p. 67.

[3] For example, plaintiffs seeking damages for the death of their children through an "attractive nuisance" lost their case when the attractive-nuisance doctrine, long followed in the federal courts, was repudiated by the Supreme Court. *United Zinc and Chemical Co.* v. *Britt,* 258 U.S. 268 (1922). Again, a conviction for perjury under a federal statute that limited the crime to willfully and falsely swearing to *"any material matter"* was affirmed

The courts of our own day, as a rule, leave it to legislatures to amend statutes and to modify common-law rules. The intricacies of the common law were created in centuries in which Parliament gave little or no attention to questions of private law. Today, in the words of Cardozo:

> There is a growing tendency in the law to leave development to legislation. Judges do not feel the same need of putting the *imprimatur* of law upon customs of recent growth . . . as they would if legislatures were not in frequent session, capable of establishing a title that will be unimpeached and unimpeachable.[4]

In this country, however, legislatures cannot modify Constitutional provisions, and formal amendment of the United States Constitution is difficult and infrequent. As a consequence, the Supreme Court is repeatedly under pressure to interpret the Constitution in accordance with policy rather than in strict conformity with the standards of judicial reason. On occasion it has yielded to the temptation to express its own views on policy, as in a number of leading cases concerning the status of the Negro under the Constitution. Let us examine a few of the decisions in which judicial reason seems to have been subordinated to other considerations.

The first case to be reviewed is the historic *Dred Scott* v. *Sanford*,[5] decided in 1857, when five of the nine justices of the Supreme Court were slave-state men. Declaring that Congress could not, by proclaiming any territory "free," exclude from its borders slave owners and their slaves, the Court held the Missouri Compromise Act of 1820 to be null and void. Further, it declared that a descendant of Negro slaves could under no circumstances become a United States citizen entitled to sue in a federal court. Yet Scott could have been remanded to slavery without reference to any Constitutional issue. He had admittedly once been the slave in Missouri of a certain Dr. Emerson, who had taken him into a free state and into territory free under the terms of the Missouri Compromise; later, Scott had accompanied Emerson back to Missouri, whose courts had subsequently held that under such circumstances there was a reversion to slavery. The Supreme Court could easily have held that the legal consequence of a voluntary return to a

---

by the Court of Appeals for the Second Circuit on the novel theory that materiality of a question established the materiality of the answer. *U.S.* v. *Siegel*, 263 F. 2d, 530, 533 (1959). [Certiorari denied, 359 U.S. 1012.]

[4] Cardozo, *op. cit.*, Lect. II, p. 60.

[5] 19 How. 393 (15 L. Ed. 691).

slave state was a question of state law. In fact, that was exactly the line of reasoning followed in the concurring opinion of Justice Nelson, a Democrat from the free state of New York.[6] The prevailing majority opinion of the Court went out of its way to determine questions of policy.

The invalidation of the Missouri Compromise stirred up a storm of outraged protest that contributed to the coming of the Civil War. Its shock to Northern opinion was the greater in that the Supreme Court had only once before declared any act of Congress unconstitutional, and that more than fifty years previously.[7] Less attention was paid to the holding that no act of any state could render a Negro capable of United States citizenship, but this was revolutionary. As noted in the dissenting opinion of Justice Curtis, free native-born Negroes had been citizens in five of the thirteen original states before the adoption of the Articles of Confederation,[8] and it had been accepted doctrine that all citizens of the several states became citizens of the United States under the Articles and later under the Constitution. If this principle must be abandoned, could anyone—except as the result of naturalization—be certain that he possessed American citizenship? In its endeavor to settle controversial issues by judicial legislation, the Supreme Court had plunged citizenship—the foundation of any republic—into a bog of uncertainty.

Because of the Civil War and its aftermath, the judicial innovations of the Dred Scott case majority had no opportunity to set the pattern for the future. On the contrary, the three postwar Constitutional amendments went far beyond restoring the balance upset by that prewar decision. The institution of slavery was completely abolished by the Thirteenth Amendment.[9] The Fourteenth, by

[6] The other free-state Democrat on the Court, Justice Grier of Pennsylvania, accepted the reasoning of the Court. The five slave-state Democrats were Chief Justice Taney (of Maryland) and Justices Wayne (of Georgia), Catron (of Tennessee), Daniel (of Virginia), and Campbell (of Alabama). Justices McLean (R., Ohio) and Curtis (Whig, Mass.) dissented.

[7] *Marbury* v. *Madison* 1 Cranch 137 (1803).

[8] "At the time of the ratification of the Articles of Confederation, all free native-born inhabitants of the states of New Hampshire, Massachusetts, New York, New Jersey and North Carolina, though descended from African slaves, were not only citizens of those states, but such of them as had the other necessary qualifications possessed the franchise of electors, on equal terms with other citizens." 19 How. 393, 572–573 (15 L. Ed. 691, 770).

[9] The Thirteenth Amendment, effective in 1865, reads:

Section 1. Neither slavery nor involuntary servitude, except as a

authoritatively defining United States citizenship and reducing state citizenship to a subordinate and derivative status, made the Negro a citizen of both nation and state; further, it prohibited state discrimination against the new Negro citizen.[10] By the Fifteenth Amendment, no citizen might be barred from the franchise on account of race, color, or previous condition of servitude.[11] In the first decision reached under the new amendments—the Slaughterhouse cases[12] of 1873—the Supreme Court called attention to the pervading purpose underlying all three newly added articles. This was "the freedom of the slave race, the security and firm establishment of that freedom, and the protection of the newly made freeman and citizen from the oppressions of those who had formerly exercised unlimited dominion over him"; the Court added that "in any fair and just construction of any section or phrase of these amendments it is necessary to look to the purpose which we have said was the pervading spirit of them all."[13]

As no Negro was in any way involved in the Slaughterhouse cases, these observations on the purpose and spirit of the postwar amendments were mere dicta unnecessary to the decision; but in

---

punishment for crime whereof the party shall have been duly convicted, shall exist within the United States, or any place subject to their jurisdiction.

Section 2. Congress shall have power to enforce this article by appropriate legislation.

[10] The significant sections of the Fourteenth Amendment, effective in 1868, are:

Section 1. All persons born or naturalized in the United States, and subject to the jurisdiction thereof, are citizens of the United States and of the State wherein they reside. No State shall make or enforce any law which shall abridge the privileges or immunities of citizens of the United States; nor shall any State deprive any person of life, liberty, or property, without due process of law; nor deny to any person within its jurisdiction the equal protection of the laws.

Section 5. The Congress shall have power to enforce, by appropriate legislation, the provisions of this article.

[11] The Fifteenth Amendment, effective in 1870, reads:

Section 1. The right of citizens of the United States to vote shall not be denied or abridged by the United States or by any State on account of race, color, or previous condition of servitude.

Section 2. The Congress shall have power to enforce this article by appropriate legislation.

[12] 16 Wall. 36 (21 L. Ed. 394).

[13] 16 Wall. 36, 71–72 (L. Ed. at 407). Nevertheless, "We do not say that no one else but the Negro can share in this protection. Both the language and spirit of these articles are to have their fair and just weight in any question of construction."

two cases decided in 1880, *Strauder* v. *West Virginia*[14] and *Ex parte Virginia*,[15] both directly concerned with Negro rights under the Fourteenth Amendment, the dicta were paraphrased or quoted with evident approval.[16] Moreover, the Court declared that the amendment must be construed liberally to carry out the purpose of its framers[17] and proceeded to apply the principle of liberal construction both to the prohibitions of the first section and to the enforcing power conferred on Congress by the final section.[18] On Congressional power under the Fourteenth Amendment, the Court emphasized:

> It is not said the *judicial power* of the general government shall extend to enforcing the prohibitions and to protecting the rights and immunities guaranteed. . . . It is the power of Congress which has been enlarged. Congress is authorized to *enforce* the prohibitions by appropriate legislation [emphasis in the original].[19]

Both 1880 cases originated in the exclusion of Negroes from jury service. In *Strauder* v. *West Virginia,* a Negro indicted for murder in West Virginia, whose statute admitted only white male citizens to jury service, sought to remove his trial to a federal court under a Congressional act permitting such removal by a defendant denied equal civil rights in a state court; the Supreme Court found the jury qualification act void and the removal act valid. *Ex parte Virginia* concerned the habeas corpus petition of a state judge who had been indicted by a federal grand jury for excluding Negroes from jury service contrary to an act of Congress that prohibited such exclusion by any officer charged with the selection of jurors; the Court decided that denial of Negro rights by the judge constituted denial by the state of Virginia and sustained the punitive enforcement act. In the words of Justice Strong:

> Whatever legislation is appropriate, that is, adapted to carry out the objects the amendments have in view, whatever tends to enforce submission to the prohibitions they contain and to secure to all per-

---

[14] 100 U.S. 303, 25 (L. Ed. 664).

[15] 100 U.S. 339, 25 (L. Ed. 676).

[16] 100 U.S. 303, 307 (L. Ed. at 665); 100 U.S. 339, 344–345 (L. Ed. at 679)

[17] "If this [the prevention of state discrimination against Negroes as a class] is the spirit and meaning of the amendment, whether it means more or not, it is to be construed liberally to carry out the purposes of its framers." 100 U.S. 303, 307 (L. Ed. at 665).

[18] *Supra,* note 10.

[19] 100 U.S. 339, 345 (L. Ed. at 679).

sons the enjoyment of perfect equality of civil rights and the equal protection of the laws against state denial or invasion, if not prohibited, is brought within the domain of congressional power.[20]

To all appearances, the Supreme Court was determined to sustain Congress in its choice of means for ensuring the Negro equal citizenship status in the United States.

Appearances proved misleading. In deciding the Civil Rights cases[21] in 1883, the Court cut itself loose from its former endorsement of the principles of liberal construction and Congressional power. The range of discrimination prohibited by the first section of the Fourteenth Amendment was restrictively narrowed, and the section authorizing Congressional enforcement was substantially obliterated from the article. The Negro was left exposed to reduction to second-class citizenship.

The legislation involved in the Civil Rights cases was the section of the Civil Rights Act of 1875 that mandated for all persons in the United States, regardless of race, color, or previous condition of servitude, the full and equal enjoyment of inns, public conveyances, theaters, and other places of public amusement. Eight of the nine members of the Supreme Court agreed that such primary direct legislation fell entirely outside the enforcement power of Congress. The Court reasoned:

> To enforce what? To enforce the prohibition. To adopt appropriate legislation for correcting the effects of such prohibited state laws and state acts, and thus to render them effectually null, void and innocuous. This is the legislative power conferred upon Congress, and this is the whole of it.[22]

Justice Strong, the advocate of broad Congressional power in the 1880 jury-service cases, had left the bench, but the majority included Justice Miller, who had spoken for the Court in the Slaughterhouse cases. A single dissenter, Justice Harlan, protested against the distinction between primary and corrective legislation:

> Under given circumstances, that which the Court characterizes as corrective legislation might be deemed by Congress appropriate and entirely sufficient. Under other circumstances primary direct legislation may be required. But it is for Congress, not the judiciary, to say

---

[20] 100 U.S. 339, 345–6 (L. Ed. at 679). The language clearly echoes that of Chief Justice Marshall in his famous construction of the necessary and proper clause in *McCulloch* v. *Maryland*, 4 Wheat on 316, 421 (1819).

[21] 109 U.S. 3 (27 L. Ed. 835).

[22] *Ibid.*, 11 (L. Ed. at 839).

what legislation is appropriate; that is, best adapted to the end to be attained.[23]

The Civil Rights cases, restriction of Congress to corrective legislation did not overrule *Strauder* v. *West Virginia* or *Ex parte Virginia*. On the contrary, both decisions were expressly reaffirmed.[24] The first had involved an act of Congress correcting discrimination by a state legislature, and the second a Congressional act punishing discrimination by a state through an official. But the Court reasoned that no *state* action was involved in the denial by an *individual* of access to a railroad, an inn, or a theater. It was unequivocally declared that "civil rights, such as are guaranteed by the Constitution against state aggression, cannot be impaired by the wrongful acts of individuals, unsupported by state authority in the shape of laws, customs or judicial or executive proceedings."[25] Also, it was intimated that mere "social rights"[26] were involved in the cases under consideration. Justice Harlan countered with an emphatic denial that only *individual* action was involved:

> In every material sense applicable to the practical enforcement of the Fourteenth Amendment, railroad corporations, keepers of inns and managers of places of public amusement are agents or instrumentalities of the state, because they are charged with duties to the public, and are amenable in respect of their duties and functions, to governmental regulation. . . . I agree that government has nothing to do with social, as distinguished from technically legal, rights of individuals. . . . The rights which Congress, by the Act of 1875, endeavored to secure and protect, are legal, not social rights.[27]

Justice Harlan's dissent opened with the words: "The opinion in these cases proceeds, it seems to me, upon grounds entirely too narrow and artificial. I cannot resist the conclusion that the substance and spirit of the recent amendments of the Constitution have been sacrificed by a subtle and ingenious verbal criticism."[28] The interpretation adopted by the Supreme Court was by no means inevitable. It was rather the outcome of a judicial will to legislate, as in the Dred Scott case of a generation earlier. In the Reconstruc-

[23] *Ibid.*, 51 (L. Ed. at 853).
[24] *Ibid.*, 15 (L. Ed. at 840–841).
[25] *Ibid.*, 17 (L. Ed. at 841).
[26] "Congress did not assume, under the authority given by the Thirteenth Amendment, to adjust what may be called the social rights of men and races in the community." *Ibid.*, 22 (L. Ed. at 843).
[27] *Ibid.*, 58–59 (L. Ed. at 855–856).
[28] *Ibid.*, 26 (L. Ed. at 844).

tion era, Congress had been motivated as much by the desire for revenge on the conquered foe as by any benevolence toward the Negro. By 1883, the Court thought that it was time to stop legislating for the blacks in order to humiliate their former masters. At least this seems to be the thought behind the declaration,

> When a man has emerged from slavery, and by the aid of beneficent legislation has shaken off the inseparable concomitants of that state, there must be some stage in the progress of his elevation when he takes the rank of a mere citizen, and ceases to be the special favorite of the laws, and when his rights, as a citizen or a man, are to be protected in the ordinary modes by which other men's rights are protected.[29]

Since Congress was not ready to repeal or modify the probably premature Civil Rights Act, the Supreme Court declared such legislation unauthorized by the Constitution. It was thus put beyond the power of Congress to enact such a law at any future time when conditions might be ripe for it. To the distress of many laymen, the accommodations section of the civil rights bill of 1963 is based on the interstate-commerce power of Congress rather than on the Fourteenth Amendment.

About a dozen years later, in 1896, Negro hopes for equal status under the Fourteenth Amendment received a further setback in the decision of *Plessy* v. *Ferguson*.[30] A Louisiana statute required railroads to provide separate but equal accommodations for the white and colored races and made it a misdemeanor for a passenger of one race to enter a car set aside for members of the other. Plessy, of mixed Caucasian and Negro blood, had deliberately taken a seat in a coach reserved for whites and now sought a writ of prohibition against the state judge by whom he was to be tried. Although the plaintiff had been arrested under a state law and his case thus involved far more than the individual action of a railroad corporation, his Constitutional claims were rejected by the Supreme Court in an almost unanimous decision.

Of course, the opinion in *Plessy* v. *Ferguson* reviewed the leading cases on the interpretation of the post–Civil War amendments, but these cast little or no light on the present problem. No citation accompanied the conclusion reached by the Plessy Court as to the intent of the Fourteenth Amendment:

[29] *Ibid.*, 25 (L. Ed. at 844).
[30] 163 U.S. 537 (1896).

The object of the amendment was undoubtedly to enforce the absolute equality of the two races before the law, but in the nature of things it could not have been intended to abolish distinctions based on color, or to enforce social, as distinguished from political equality, or a commingling of the two races upon terms unsatisfactory to either.[31]

The Supreme Court sought precedents in a considerable number of state cases that had held that the establishment of separate schools for colored children was a valid exercise of legislative power, even in "states where the political rights of the colored race had been longest and most earnestly enforced."[32] Particular stress was laid on the Massachusetts case of *Roberts* v. *Boston,* decided in 1850.[33] As properly noted in Justice Harlan's solitary dissent, decisions reached before the adoption of the recent amendments were entirely irrelevant on the issue of validity under the Constitution as amended.[34]

Both opinions in *Plessy* v. *Ferguson* were concerned primarily with questions of psychology and policy. To the plaintiff's assumption "that the enforced separation of the two races stamps the colored race with a badge of inferiority," the Court replied, "If this is so, it is . . . solely because the colored race chooses to put that construction upon it"; to the assumption "that social prejudice may be overcome by legislation," the rejoinder was:

Legislation is powerless to eradicate racial instincts or to abolish distinctions based upon physical differences, and the attempt to do so can only result in accentuating the difficulties of the present situation. . . . If one race be inferior to the other socially, the Constitution of the United States cannot put them upon the same plane.[35]

Justice Harlan was equally vehement in voicing his dissenting views:

What can more certainly arouse race hate, what more certainly create and perpetuate a feeling of distrust between the races, than state enactments which in fact proceed upon the ground that colored citizens are so inferior and degraded that they cannot be allowed to

[31] *Ibid.,* 544.

[32] *Ibid.,* 544–545.

[33] 5 Cush. 198.

[34] "I do not deem it necessary to review the decisions of state courts to which reference was made in argument. Some, and the most important, of them are wholly inapplicable, because rendered prior to the adoption of the last amendments to the Constitution, when colored people had very few rights which the dominant race felt obliged to respect." 163 U.S. 537, 563.

[35] *Ibid.,* 551–552.

> sit in public coaches occupied by white citizens? That, as all will admit, is the real meaning of such legislation as was enacted in Louisiana.[36]

Again:

> State enactments, regulating the enjoyment of civil rights, upon the basis of race, and cunningly devised to defeat legitimate results of the war, under the pretense of recognizing equality of rights, can have no other result than to render permanent peace impossible and to keep alive a conflict of races, the continuance of which must do harm to all concerned.[37]

Not the reasoned analysis of text, but rather a weighing of policies in judicial legislation, introduced the separate but equal doctrine into the Constitutional law of the equal-protection clause of the Fourteenth Amendment.

In the half-century following *Plessy* v. *Ferguson,* the separate but equal pattern became universal and unquestioned in the former slave states. The constitutionality of racially segregated public schools was taken for granted by the Supreme Court in the first school cases presented to it for decision.[38] Until the very eve of World War II, no inquiry seems to have been made as to whether the separate accommodations for Negroes were actually equal to those furnished the white race.[39] In 1939, however, the decision of *Missouri ex rel. Gaines* v. *Canada* opened a new era.[40] The Court here held that, since there was a law school for whites at the state university, Missouri could not deny to a Negro a tax-supported legal education in the state; an offer of funds to enable Gaines to study at the law school of an adjacent state was insufficient. A decade later, in

[36] *Ibid.,* 560.

[37] *Ibid.,* 560–561.

[38] In *Cumming* v. *County Board of Education,* 175 U.S. 528 (1899) it was held that a county might spend tax money for a high school for white girls while leaving secondary education for white boys and for Negroes of both sexes to private schools that charged fees no higher than those at the girls' high school. In *Gong Lum* v. *Rice,* 275 U.S. 78 (1927), it was ruled that a child of unmixed Chinese ancestry might be excluded from a white school in Mississippi and assigned to a school for children of the colored race.

[39] The Mississippi statute involved in *Gong Lum* v. *Rice* made inequality of schooling practically inevitable. Each county was divided into white school districts and also independently divided into colored districts that were not coterminous with the white districts; four months of school a year were required by law in every district, but any district was permitted to levy an additional tax for the purpose of maintaining a longer school term (275 U.S. 78, 80). Of course only white school districts ever levied the additional tax.

[40] 305 U.S. 337 (1938).

1950, *Sweatt* v. *Painter* decided that a small new law school for Negroes in Texas was unequal to the long-established and highly respected law school at the University of Texas and that a qualified Negro must therefore be admitted to that previously white law school.[41] Although the Supreme Court was steadily raising the level of the Negro's Constitutional rights, it continued to apply a time-honored formula, and its decisions were accepted as the outcome of an appropriate exercise of the judicial power. A progressive intensification of insistence on *equality* in separate schools might perhaps have led to a gradual diminution of color prejudice even in the Deep South and to a step-by-step integration of public education at one educational level after another down to the primary schools.

Unfortunately the Supreme Court abandoned the separate but equal doctrine in the school segregation cases decided in 1954 under the title of *Brown* v. *Board of Education of Topeka*.[42] At the time I accepted with jubilation the unanimous decision that racially separate schools cannot be equal, but I now regard it as essentially nonjudicial. The Court voiced the judges' preference as to policy rather than the requirements of any Constitutional text, and I believe that judges should not legislate beyond the bounds of necessity.

My concurrence with the vehement critics of the decision is only partial. It extends neither to the implication that the Court had never before legislated nor to the charge that the 1954 decision was unprecedented in its reliance on psychological principles. Chief Justice Warren certainly employed nonlegal language in asserting in the Brown case: "To separate them [colored children in grade and high schools] from others of similar age and qualifications solely because of their race generates a feeling of inferiority as to their status in the community that may affect their hearts and minds in a way unlikely ever to be undone."[43] But, as already pointed out, *Plessy* v. *Ferguson* had used nonlegal, emotion-tinged phrases in establishing the separate but equal doctrine. Referring to the psychological factor in the earlier decision, the 1954 Court asserted:

> Whatever may have been the extent of psychological knowledge at the time of *Plessy* v. *Ferguson,* [the] finding is amply supported by modern authority . . . [that] "Segregation of white and colored

[41] 339 U.S. 629 (1950).
[42] 347 U.S. 483.
[43] *Ibid.,* 494.

children in public schools has a detrimental effect upon the colored children. . . . A sense of inferiority affects the motivation of a child to learn. Segregation with the sanction of law, therefore, has a tendency to [retard] the educational and mental development of Negro children and to deprive them of some of the benefits they would receive in a racial[ly] integrated school system."[44]

The Court avoided a direct overruling of the decision in the Plessy case that separate cars on railroads were permissible; it held merely: "We conclude that in the field of public education the doctrine of 'separate but equal' has no place. Separate educational facilities are inherently unequal."[45] In the years since the Brown decision, the doctrine has been declared inapplicable in one field after another until it is now of little more than historical interest.[46]

The abolition of the separate but equal doctrine has brought many undoubted gains which it would be tragic to attempt to destroy either by judicial reversal or by Constitutional amendment. At least in the border states, the Negro is probably far closer to first-class citizenship today than he would be if the doctrine were still recognized, no matter how stringent the Supreme Court demand that *actually* equal facilities be provided him. It is, nevertheless, highly questionable whether the gains are worth the cost. The separate but equal doctrine had been a bulwark of Constitutional law for almost sixty years when it was abandoned. It had originated in judicial legislation in 1896, but in 1954 it was too late to obliterate it under the guise of rendering a merely judicial decision. The shock to Southern opinion was as convulsive as that suffered by Northern opinion in 1857, when the Missouri Compromise Act was declared void almost forty years after its enactment. The Dred Scott decision led to the Civil War and to an almost complete collapse of the prestige of the Supreme Court. There is no danger of war today, but Southern sectionalism has been intensified, and there is talk of impeaching the chief justice of the United States. Perhaps the Court

[44] *Ibid.,* 495, 494. The Supreme Court quoted with approval the words of a Kansas court, as shown by the inner quotation marks, but did not identify the court or the case in which it spoke.

[45] *Ibid.,* 495.

[46] Most of the Supreme Court decisions are mere memoranda, affirming or vacating judgments of lower federal courts. The earliest are *Baltimore City* v. *Dawson,* 350 U.S. 877 (1955), on the subject of a municipal bathing beach and bathhouses, and *Holmes* v. *City of Atlanta,* 350 U.S. 879 (1955), on the subject of a municipal golf course.

will never again enjoy its one-time reputation as the oracle of the Constitution.

The modification of law in the interest of greater justice is the appropriate function of the legislature. When it is a question of modifying the fundamental law of the Constitution, all but infinitesimal changes should be left to the process of Constitutional amendment. It is contrary to the principles of representative government for policies of the highest moment to be determined by the fluctuating preferences of nine elderly men enjoying life tenure in appointive office. However desirable the policies favored by the Supreme Court, judicial legislation should be kept to a minimum. At the least, let the Court imply by its language that it is exercising "neither force nor will but merely judgment" (to use the words of *The Federalist*). That the judiciary is reason incarnate is a myth, but perhaps it is also an ideal.

HISTORICAL REFLECTIONS

12

ON REREADING MACHIAVELLI
AND ALTHUSIUS:
REASON, RATIONALITY, AND RELIGION[1]

CARL J. FRIEDRICH

Decisionism is a modern stance. The increasing sophistication about man and his environment, the technical complication of
life in all its reaches, and the resulting need for continuous adaptation have multiplied the number of alternative courses of action.
The digital computer is the symbol of this state. To a degree un-
dreamt of in traditional societies, modern man must choose. The
choice of a school, the choice of a car, the choice of a place of resi-
dence—not to speak of the more intimate choices—stand at the
gateway to adult life, as does the choice of one's rulers. Universal
suffrage may be only a façade, a thinly disguised pretense, hiding

[1] This paper is an extension of what is said on the subject in my *Man
and His Government* (*1963*), *Constitutional Reason of State* (1957), and
Politica Methodice Digesta of Johannes Althusius (1932).

the rule of party bosses and pressure groups, but it demands a choice between candidates, perhaps equally undesirable, certainly often shadowy figures to most of their electorate. Who would be able to demonstrate that these choices are wholly rational, no matter how rationality be defined?

It is therefore understandable enough that, to an increasing degree, philosophers and other truth-seekers should have asked questions about how men go about making choices, about deciding what is to be done or left undone.[2] Politics and law provide, of course, some of the most promising fields of inquiry into what mental processes may be involved in decision-making, since they are more public than other areas of human activity. Because of the urgency of such decision-making, some thinkers have, in fact, made an absolute out of the decision. The existentialist school of philosophy has developed a set of concepts which seek to adumbrate this aspect of the human condition.[3] In conclusion, I expect to return to some general comments on these views.

It is a striking fact that the great writers on politics and law, from Aristotle to Kant, did not give focal attention to decision-making. Even philosophers so centrally concerned with politics as Hobbes and Spinoza were preoccupied with the question of the content or substance of political decisions rather than with their mode and process of actualization. In this perspective, decisionism appears a late sequel to the Cartesian challenge. The process of truth-finding which Locke, and more especially Kant, developed into an epistemology or critique of reasoning becomes the focal point of philosophy rather than the truth to be found. In a sense, it was the next step in the direction of radical skepticism: to inquire merely into how men decide rather than how they reason upon the grounds for their decisions. In this connection, the problem of reason and rationality appears in a new and operational light. Are decisions rational in the sense of being directed toward the choice of means

---

[2] Note, for example, *Toward a General Theory of Action,* ed. Talcott Parsons and Edward A. Shils (1951).

[3] Christian Graf von Krockow, *Die Entscheidung—eine Untersuchung über Ernst Jünger, Carl Schmitt, Martin Heidegger* (1958), has interestingly and critically examined three leading thinkers of the decisionist propensity in Germany. See also the paper by Judith N. Shklar in this volume. Reference to these and other decisionist writers is found in later footnotes. In the U.S., decisionism has primarily appeared in scientist form, as well as in the realist school of jurisprudence and international relations.

calculated to achieve the desired end? Or are they habitual or traditional in the sense of following established routines of behavior? Or are they perhaps adventurous and even playful, stimulated by the charm of novelty? Some of the more radical studies in decision-making proceed on the premise of an affirmative answer to the first alternative. Indeed one writer has gone so far as to assert that one need not regard the description of human rationality as hypothetical, but as "having been verified in its main features."[4] If rationality is interpreted purely in terms of relating means to ends, which is of course the meaning this writer gives to it, the proposition is arguable though, I believe, erroneous. If the meaning of rationality involves the "higher" reason of discourse on the ends and the values they involve, it reduces to the ancient fallacy, already discussed at length in antiquity, that a man needs only to "know" in order to act "rightly." The notion of rationality may, however, in the sense of reasonableness, be made to cover the other two alternatives; for habit and tradition involve implicit reasoning (in past situations), while adventure and play have their place in many human situations, where they may be defended as entirely "within reason."

These brief reflections suggest that the problem of rational decision-making is as much in need of inquiring into the empirical ground for speaking of it as rational as it is of inquiring into the making of the decision. It is by no means self-evident what constitutes rationality in general, nor what is the distinguishing characteristic of political rationality. If one abandons the idea that means and ends, as well as facts and values, ought to be treated as existentially separate and apart,[5] rationality in general and more particularly political rationality may be understood as the activity of the mind which reasons upon the "seamless web" of what happens by distinguishing means from ends, as well as facts from values, in short, by tearing the seamless web apart. Rational decisions then become those decisions in which such reasoning has been involved to a greater or lesser extent. This statement about the extent of rationality, though highly tentative at this state in the analysis, suggests that decisions are not to be distinguished and separated into rational and nonrational ones. Rather, they are to be seen on a

---

[4] Herbert Simon, *Models of Man* (1957). See also his *Administrative Behavior* (1947, 1957).

[5] For this see *Man and His Government* (1963), chaps. i and ii, where the position is argued at greater length.

continuum of degrees of rationality—both the completely rational and the wholly nonrational being "unreal" limits.

In the history of political thought, the notion of a simple alternative between the rational and the nonrational decision has played a decisive role in a number of connections, none more important than the extended controversy over "reason of state." In the heyday of reason-of-state theorizing, such overconfidence about knowing what the truly rational conduct was produced the doctrine of the secrets of empire, governance, and rule. This doctrine basically argued that only those "in the know" could cope with the problems of public policy, especially foreign policy, but it implicitly also assumed that, once they were "in the know," they would be capable of acting rationally. Many experts even today lean toward such a view. Overlooking their disagreements, they fail to appreciate the degree of contingency and hence the limitation upon rationality of all action involving an infinitely complex reality.[6]

In the light of this ever-present contingency, one might argue that a rational decision is one which most nearly can be defended in reasoning upon all the facts and values involved in a given situation. But if this is done, the decision-maker is cast in the mould of a Hamlet-like worrier who postpones action in waiting for the on-going search of additional "data." (The need of deciding in time, the deadline, the *kairos,* are aspects of all decision-making which, although themselves part of the rationality of the process, are in turn contingent and do not permit of reasoned elaboration beyond a certain point.) The tremendous role of authority in all political decision-making comes into play at this point. When understood as the capacity for reasoned elaboration,[7] it can be understood as an integer by which a great deal of potential rationality is introduced into the equation of the decision in condensed form, as it were. The much criticized doctrine of the secrets of empire, the *arcana imperii,* is thereby revealed to be no more (nor less) than the recognition of the role of authority in political decision-making—not as an alternative to rationality, but as an integral part of such rationality.

Reason of state is often interpreted as merely the rationality of politics. One of the first theorizers, and in some sense the founder of reason-of-state theorizing, Giovanni Botero, started the confusion by defining it as the knowledge of the means which are suited to

---

[6] For further elaboration, see *ibid.,* chap. vii.

[7] *Ibid.,* chap. xii.

found a state, to maintain it, and to enlarge it. In such a statement, the state appears as the end for the realization of which the means are provided by reason of state. A detailed study of Botero and the many writers who followed his lead discloses, however, that they were as much or even more concerned with *justifying* these means within the context of Christian ethics. The reasoning extends, in other words, into the range of the "higher reason" of religion and its revealed tenets. As Cardinal de Luca was to write: *"Questa parola Politica è sinonima, e dinota l'istesso che la Ragione di Stato, posiachè la parola 'ragione' abbraccia tutto quello che di giusto e di ragionevole dalle leggi Divina, naturale, delle genti, positiva e di convenienza si dispone ovvero si richiede anche tra privati. . . ."*[8] In spite of its confusing comprehensiveness, this statement reveals the difficulty of escaping from the range of considerations involved in justification once reasoning is made the focal point of decision-making.[9] This difficulty is at the very core of the problem of political rationality and reason of state. Nor is it limited to Christianity. Any set of ethical rules or norms of conduct for individual men, notably all the codes evolved by the great world religions, is confronted with how to argue the possible conflict between what the security and survival of the political order appear to require and what the norms call for. Only when political order is posited as the penultimate value possessing an absolute claim of priority does the need for justifying such violations of individual conduct disappear. It is possible to call only this radical outlook "reason of state." It has often been done. "Considerations of reason of state" or in contemporary phraseology "security considerations" would then be those reasons for action which pure expediency calls for. The difficulty of staying away from justificatory arguments is, however, very great; even in Machiavelli justifactory reasonings appear, because of his insistence upon the vital role of religion and *virtù* in the maintenance of a sound body politic. In a famous passage where he discusses the murder of Remus by Romulus, Machia-

[8] Giovanni Battista de Luca, *Il Principe Cristiano Practico* (1680), pp. 66–67, as cited in R. de Mattei, "Il Problema della 'Ragion di Stato' nel Seicento" *Rivista Internazionale di Filosofia del Diritto* (1949–1953).

[9] Botero's *Della Ragion di Stato* (1589) provides ample illustration for this difficulty. The large number of writers who were dealing with reason of state in ever repetitive fashion was reviewed by B. Croce and S. Caramella, *Politici e Moralisti del Seicento—Strada, Zuccolo, Settala, Accetto, Brignole Sale, Malvezzi* (1930). See also the several studies by R. de Mattei, cited in fn. 26, p. 33 of my *Constitutional Reason of State* (1957).

velli points out that this admittedly immoral act could be excused
by the paramount achievement of founding the Roman state. He
had pointed out in another famous passage that next to the founders
of religion those of states are most praised.[10] It is highly significant
that Machiavelli speaks of "excusing" rather than justifying. He has
generally been erroneously considered the expounder of the doctrine
that the end justifies the means. In support of this contention, the
passage usually cited is one in the *Prince*[11] where Machiavelli merely
says that the actions of men regard the end—a rather obvious remark which he qualifies by saying that this is so when there is no
"judgment to claim." This would seem to be an open recognition of
the intrusion of justification into the reasoning about actions, especially in politics. One must consider this view (as contrasted with
the erroneous view that the end justifies the means) within the
framework of Machiavelli's more general conception of the state
as a work of art and the source of all moral values and therefore of
all virtue. Hence Machiavelli's insistent stress upon the importance
for any ruler to *appear* pious, faithful, sincere, and religious.

The apparent cynicism of this view must, however, not be over-
emphasized. Machiavelli was fully aware of the political superiority
of rulers who are good in the moral sense. Nothing shows this more
clearly than his discussion of the Roman emperors and their republican antecedents. Machiavelli is inclined to look upon the
Roman Republic as the best state, the model to be imitated by any
founder. In this respect he is fully the man of the Renaissance idoliz-
ing antiquity. This admiration for the Roman Republic and its *virtù*
causes him considerable difficulty when it comes to political rationality. For the *virtù* of the Romans, and more especially the Stoic
version of it, may come into conflict with security and survival considerations as do other kinds of individual ethic. His perplexity and
his ultimate resolution are nowhere more succinctly expressed than
in the discussion of Caesar and of his efforts at rescuing the Roman
state by founding an autocratic regime;[12] Machiavelli has no "excuse" at all to offer; instead, and in challenging a good deal of
traditional lore, he writes:

---

[10] *Discorsi* i. 10; the previous discussion, i.9.
[11] The phrase occurs toward the end of chap. xviii of *Il Principe* and
reads ". . . *e nelle azioni di tutti li unomini . . . si guarda al fine.*"
[12] *Discorsi* i. 10.

Let no one be deceived by the glory of Caesar feeling that he has been so much celebrated by writers [in the past]. For those who thus praised him were seduced by his good fortune and frightened by the duration of the empire which was maintained under his name and hence did not permit writers to speak freely about him. But he who wants to know what free writers might have said, only needs to consult what they said about Catilina. For Caesar is the more detestable since he who commits an evil deed is more to be blamed than he who only wanted to commit it. . . .

Clearly Machiavelli recognizes the possibility of wrongdoing in politics here. But if it were objected (and it has been done) that after all the standard of good and evil is essentially derived from his *political* preference for the republican order, the answer is that Machiavelli carries the analysis over into the imperial order and suggests that one should consider "how much more praise those emperors deserved who lived under the law and as good rulers" than those who did the opposite, and he then contrasts Titus, Nerva, and the Antonine emperors with Nero, Caligula, and Vitellius whom he calls criminal (*scellerati*) emperors. To be sure, he reinforces his moral judgment by an argument derived from political rationality: The good emperors did not need Praetorian Guards and other such military protection, but were defended by the love of the people and the respect of the Senate. By contrast, he observes that the bad emperors were usually murdered, whereas none of the good emperors was. In short, Machiavelli recognizes that actual goodness, not only its appearance, is the "best policy." Indeed, he bursts forth into a veritable paean in describing such a rule.[13] This strong praise for the rule of a good emperor helps one to understand better the values which Machiavelli cherished in speaking of a ruler as good; it also indicates the limits of his republican conviction. Obviously it is more important that these values be realized than that the rule be republican. Even so he returns to the original theme by contrast-

---

[13] *"Perchè in quelli governati da' buoni, verrà un principe securo in mezzo de' suoi sicuri cittadini; ripieno di pace e di giustizia il mondo; vedrà il Senato con la sua autorità, i magistrati con i suoi onori; godersi i cittadini ricchi le loro ricchezze; la nobiltà e la virtù esaltata; vedrà ogni quiete ed ogni bene; e dall'altra parte, ogni rancore, ogni licenza, corruzione e ambizione spenta; vedrà i tempi aurei, dove ciascuno può tenere e difendere quella opinione che vuole; vedrà in fine trionfare il mondo; pieno di riverenza e di gloria il principe, d'amore e di sicurità i popoli."* Discorsi i. 10. Leo Strauss, in his interesting revival of the moral condemnation of Machiavelli, does not give sufficient attention to passages such as these.

ing the rule of bad emperors in equally moving terms, and then concluding with the bitterly sarcastic remark: "and thus one will recognize best how much Rome, Italy, and the world owes to Caesar."[14] In short, Machiavelli sees moral goodness and survival as two sides of the same coin of political rationality. On the one hand, virtue must not be allowed to interfere with the task of statecraft, but, on the other, sound statecraft calls for superior virtue. To put it another way, and in terms of ends, the state exists for the sake of the virtue of its rulers and citizens, but the virtue at the same time exists for the sake of the state. There is no way of distinguishing means and ends in the operations of political rationality, except ad hoc and for limited undertakings. The normativity of the moral norms is circumscribed by the requirements of what the artist builder or rebuilder of the state needs for his undertaking. Yet what he needs above all is *virtù*—the excellence of ruler and citizens in the strictest sense of civic duty as conceived by a Cato. Looked at from the standpoint of the state as a work of art, the statesman, as founder and lawgiver, will handle his human material with strict regard to the success of his enterprise: man's greatest, most noble, most magnificent creation. But such is the nature of man, weak and corruptible, that he must be inspired, must be given a faith, and therefore "the founders of religions are most praised."[15] There can be little doubt, in the perspective of history, that religion has indeed such a vital relation to political order. The role of religion in implanting convictions about right and wrong, thereby creating consensus in the community and character in the individual, is generally recognized. The spread of certain religious beliefs is intimately linked to the political order of the community professing the particular faith and practicing the cult which flows from it.[16] Because Machiavelli noted these forms

[14] As a further illustration of this dimension of Machiavelli's conception of political rationality, the passage on the bad ruler deserves to be quoted in extenso: "*gli vedrà atroci per le guerre, discordi per le sedizioni, nella pace e nella guerra crudeli; tanti principi morti col ferro, tante guerre civili tante esterne . . . vedrà premiare li accusatori, essere corrotti i servi contro al signore, i liberti contro al padrone; e quelli a chi fussero mancati i nemici, essere oppressi dagli amici. E conoscerà allora benissimo quanti obblighi Roma, Italia e il mondo abbia con Caesare.*" The passage resembles in some striking respects Hobbes's famous description of the state of nature, *Leviathan* i. 13.

[15] For the way in which this approach is utilized to develop the notion of constitutional dictatorship, see my *Constitutional Reason of State* (1957), pp. 27 ff.

[16] See what is said in my *Man and His Government,* chap. vi

of interplay between religion and politics, and indeed stressed the vital role of religion for politics, he has been misinterpreted as believing that this political function was the only value of religion. There are, however, a number of passages in Machiavelli which attest to his response to religious feelings; like others before him and since, he detested the direct interference of ecclesiastical organizations in politics precisely because of the vital function of religion for a sound political order. Marsilius of Padua, Hobbes, and Rousseau share with Machiavelli this intense enmity to the ecclesiastic in politics because of their political religion.

In a famous chapter of the *Discorsi*, Machiavelli discusses the matter explicitly and begins by insisting upon the functional value of religion. "Those princes and republics who want to remain uncorrupted have above all to maintain religious ceremonies uncorrupted and to uphold their veneration," the reason being that "there can be had no greater sign of the ruin of a land than to see the cult of God disparaged."[17] Machiavelli states this view positively in the sequel and asserts that a republic is good and united when it is religious (*repubblica religioso, e per conseguento buona e unita*). He describes this cult of religion as a *natural* thing which requires, however, that the prince or ruler see to it that its fundamentals be maintained. And the misfortune of Italy he believes to be due to this failure to stick to fundamentals as found in the New Testament. Machiavelli's indignation about the guilty of the Roman court parallels that of Luther and other contemporaries; that is well known. What is often overlooked is that Machiavelli, like Luther again, pleads with many humanists for a return to the original fountain, in order to escape from the "infinite disorders" which the establishment of a political authority in ecclesiastical hands has produced. For this means division, and only a land which obeys one prince or one republic can be united and happy. The church, on the other hand, has neither been strong enough to provide this single ruler, nor has it been weak enough to abandon its claims to secular power,[18] and so it has prevented Italy from having "a single head" (*Capo*). The invasion of foreigners is the direct consequence of this,

---

[17] *Discorsi* i. 12.

[18] Machiavelli's analysis here clearly anticipates that of the French *Politiques* and more especially Bodin, whose concept of sovereignty constitutes a fully developed juristic category in response to the problem of unity.

and the papacy has had a hand in their coming.[19] All this, then, Italians owe to the church, and he who does not believe it need only to imagine the papacy to be transferred to Switzerland, which now lives most nearly like the ancients both as concerns religion and defense; the Swiss would soon be as corrupt as the Italians! A strange and certainly not a very convincing argument. But its emotional quality serves to reinforce the conclusion about Machiavelli's specific source of indignation, not religion, nor more particularly the Christian religion, but the church and more especially the papacy, through its participation in secular politics, is the enemy. It is a position which Hobbes and Rousseau were to radicalize, Hobbes by speaking of the church as the "kingdom of darkness" and Rousseau by developing the notion of a "civic religion." All these views rest upon a sharp separation of faith from reason, following the lead of the medieval nominalists. It is a trend which eventually leads to Hobbes's formula "that reason is but reckoning." The calculation which is epitomized in the activities of capitalist enterprise becomes the prototype of rationality. Reflection let alone contemplation is excluded from such a notion of reason.

The Age of Reason, of enlightenment and benevolent despotism, did not remain content with so narrow a concept. On the basis of the striking insights which the "reckoning" of natural science had produced—highlighted by the work of Newton—reason was gradually broadened and expected to provide a rational foundation for everything, including religion. From the later seventeenth century onward, rational foundations were constructed for everything, but especially for religion and law. Rational religion and rational (natural) law were confidently expected to provide for the spiritual and political needs of men everywhere. Such shallow misreading of the holy and the just reigned supreme and culminated in the Great Revolution which erected altars to the goddess Reason, though Hume and Kant had shattered such ready confidence and demonstrated the "limits" of reason in a devastating critique of its facile premises. Curiously enough, some of their penetrating analysis of the limits of "reason as reckoning" seems still to be unknown to some of the more ardent advocates of scientistic rationalism in contemporary social science. Their "Machiavellian" realism rests upon the simple premises concerning the calculability of the ingredients of political

---

[19] *". . . tanta disunione e tanta debolezza . . . [Italia] . . . preda, no solamente de'barbari potenti, ma di qualunque l'assalta."*

decisions (and other aspects of political behavior), which the Age of Reason had once before assumed to be "self-evident."

Actually, decisions (and other actions) always are compounded of elements which may be calculated and subjected to rational manipulation and elements which may not. Projected into the future, which is to some considerable extent unknown (and in any absolute sense completely so), the lacunae left by the incalculable risks will be filled by beliefs and convictions or plainly neglected. Religion has always played a very important role in supplying men with grounds for social and cosmic beliefs and ethical convictions. Such beliefs and convictions frequently outweigh the reason that is "reckoning." One instance may be retold: One of the officer conspirators against Hitler, after explaining to his wife in a goodbye letter that in his opinion the plot was almost certain to fail, added that this prospect did not matter. "Because of it, we must do it," he added.[20] Martyrdom is, of course, an extreme case, but it dramatizes the everyday role of the victory of belief and conviction over the chasm of the contingent which confronts man, and more particularly political man, at every turn. Decisions such as Truman's to come to the assistance of Korea or Kennedy's to challenge the deployment of Soviet soldiers and arms in Cuba are unthinkable as purely calculatory "reckonings."

Since these considerations have brought us back to the role of religion as a companion to reason and as a particular form of rationality or reasoning, it would seem appropriate to turn to a thinker, close to the time of Machiavelli, in whose theorizing on politics the role of religion was recognized as paramount. It could be a Jesuit, since a form of political rationality, "reason of church," was at the very core of their discipline. Mariana or Bellarmine might do. But their work lacks the systematic unity which Johannes Althusius' *Politica* displays. Johannes Althusius was an orthodox Calvinist— the only one among them who theorized systematically on politics. And the politically (and economically) most calculating men among the ardently Protestant were the Calvinists. Political rationality had, with them, a religious base. It was intimately linked to their view of nature and the natural group,[21] the understanding of which was of

---

[20] Treskow in a letter reprinted in Annedore Leber, *Das Gewissen steht auf* (1954). See for this general problem the interesting study by W. A. R. Leys, *Ethics for Policy Decisions* (1952).

[21] For the problem of nature in Althusius and the Calvinists, see my *Politica Methodice Digesta of Johannes Althusius* (1932), pp. lxvii ff. The

188

vital importance for effective action which in turn was related to predestination.[22] Predestination apart, Calvin and his followers were humanists and aware of the naturalist focus of much secular knowledge. This was as important an ingredient of their approach to politics as Calvin's juristic bent. The combination provides the framework within which Althusius' analyses are presented. Nature and reason are therefore not necessarily antithetical, though the Puritan's "disparagement of reason" which Richard Hooker disputed might suggest it. To look upon nature and reason as mutually exclusive is a recurrent line of thought. It dominates much medieval thinking, and not only on society and politics. Modern natural science rests upon the contrary belief that nature is structured rationally and that the scientist discovers this built-in rationality. To be sure, a countertrend prefers to consider this rationality as superimposed by the human mind seeking to "order nature." Kant, of course, was one of the originators of the notion that the human mind is "legislating" for nature. Althusius, however, shared the view of the inherent rationality of nature and a corresponding scientific concept of reason. Throughout his work we find reason and nature as concomitant explanatory principles. Thus in speaking of the functions of officials, he adds, "as the nature and reason of such calling and function requires."[23] The question must be raised, however, what the precise meaning of *ratio* in such propositions is. In a number of contexts it is clear in earlier and contemporary writing that *ratio* or reason refers not only to general principles, but to the specific requirements of an individual being or particular situation as well. When referring to situations, *ratio* would then be the rational response to its requirements, as, for example, when a threat to a man's existence is met by self-defense—a situation which became paradigmatic in rational natural law. When referring to individual

considerable and valuable literature on Althusius published since then has confirmed these views. What follows is based upon the earlier study.

[22] See for this Max Weber's controversial *Protestant Ethic and the Spirit of Capitalism*, trans. Parsons (1930) and the commentaries by R. H. Tawney, *Religion and the Rise of Capitalism* (1926); J. B. Kraus, *Scholastik, Puritanismus und Kapitalismus* (1930); H. M. Robertson, *The Rise of Economic Individualism* (1933), and A. Fanfani, *Catholicism, Protestantism and Capitalism* (1935). Weber's original study appeared in 1904–1905 in the *Archiv für Sozialwissenschaft und Sozialphilosophie*.

[23] *Politica* 8. 56: *"Prout vocationis et functionis suae naturae et ratio postulat."*

beings, it must be remembered that not only persons, but also collectivities such as families, guilds, churches, cities, and states constitute such individuals, such living entities whose *ratio* may come into play. All these entities have their own *ratio* which embodies rules of action adapted to meeting the requirements of their being. *Ratio status* or reason of state is only the most exalted of these different collective rationalities. Like all the *rationes,* it embodies those general principles which the foundation and survival of any such state depend upon, as well as the specific rational responses to the needs of each particular state. The linking of both these aspects of *ratio status* is not only characteristic for Althusius, but is found in other writers of the time; it actually goes back to the Middle Ages.[24] Later, in Pufendorf, Montesquieu, and Hegel, the individualizing of reason of state became so pronounced as to lead to the notion of an "esprit" or "spirit" peculiar to particular states or forms of government.

It is interesting and significant, in light of contemporary discussions, that, in an antiauthoritarian writer and theorist of the cooperative political order, such as Althusius, the *ratio status* is linked to and often substituted by a *ratio administrationis*. Again it is compounded of the general principles of good administration and an understanding of the particular needs of a specific government. It consists in either case of rational knowledge or, if you please, scientific insight. Political and administrative prudence is at the heart of it. Such prudence is not, however, seen in any "value-free" operational code, but embraces an understanding of the ends of politics and administration.[25] Reason, rule, and norm (*ratio, regula,* and *norma*) are involved here, and the *ratio administrationis* is more particularly political prudence. He, Althusius, distinguishes between two aspects of such political prudence, namely, the *intellec-*

[24] Friedrich Meinecke, in his well-known *Die Idee der Staatsräson in der Neueren Geschichte* (1924) (Eng. tr. by D. Scott, published under the misleading title of *Machiavellism* [1957]), suggested that a generalizing *ratio status* of the sixteenth century may be juxtaposed to an individualizing one in the seventeenth; no such sharp cleavage existed.

[25] See *Politica* 21. 2; "*Ejusmodi igitur Reip. seu regni administratio a populo comissa, et a magistratu suscepta, est jurium majestatis, hoc est, negotiorum et bonorum regni et subditorum, secundum naturam conditionemque eorundem, prudens, diligens et just cura, tractatio, dispensatio et defensio, ad gloriam Dei, et regni atque subditorum salutem directa.*" The stress on public interest or welfare as the ultimate reference point of all rational conduct of public affairs raises, of course, a host of questions. See *Nomos V: The Public Interest* (1962), *passim.*

tus and the *delectus*. The *intellectus* consists in the faculty by which a magistrate understands and knows what is to be done or left undone, in light of the rational notion of the office (*rationis officii*). It is essentially compounded of doctrine and practice, and Althusius therefore stresses the importance of experience and what may be learned from "explorers, merchants, soldiers, travellers, diplomats and others which travel abroad. . . ." We cannot here follow the elaboration of his discussion of all the elements of rationality; suffice it to say that he includes the "nature of the people" and the "nature of the kingdom" along with the *regula vivendi et administrandi* which is *Dei voluntas*. And since God's will is embodied in the laws, the administration and government of a *respublica* (state) is nothing else but the execution of these laws.[26] This clear recognition of the transcendent, religious basis of political and administrative rationality we shall return to presently. It is interesting, however, to explore how far Althusius might be prepared to go in the direction of the kind of political rationality which Machiavelli stressed.

The policy of alliances which he outlines—and the obligation of treaties is a fertile field of Machiavellian statecraft—varies little from that which a follower of Machiavelli might maintain, except that Althusius would exclude a *foedus* with infidels (*implii*). Characteristically, Botero appears as authority for such Christian statecraft.[27] It is linked to a discussion of war which does not recoil from advocating various violations of the moral code which are the more significant when it is recalled that Althusius' concept of war covers the civil war that might have to be waged to suppress a rebellion. Various stratagems, including deception and fraud, are permitted during war.[28] Even the instruments of radical absolutism for the maintenance of public order and security, such as the use of spies and torture for the discovery of sedition, are approved, as well as the employment of vague promises to the rebels, followed by ruthless suppression. His ideas are not novel, but they are significant because of their inclusion in a system of politics based upon Christian foundations. Their justification and rationalization is provided by

[26] *Politica* xxi. 16. An interesting recent contribution to the growing literature on Althusius rightly stresses this point; see Peter Jochen Winters, *Die "Politik" des Althusius und ihre zeitgenösischen Quellen* (1963).

[27] *Politica* 34. 49–51.

[28] "*Insidiae, igitur, strategemata, astutia, solertia et dolus in bello contra hostem sunt licita,*" *ibid.* 35. 57. Althusius here refers to Machiavelli's *Discorsi* iii.14, as well as to Botero and Lipsius.

citing instances from Old Testament history, more especially the rebellion of Absolom.[29]

By transforming the *ratio status* into the *ratio administrationis,* Althusius not only adjusts the familiar doctrine of rising absolutism to his constitutionalist outlook, but he also returns to the earlier medieval doctrine of a generalized *ratio* of all human collectivities. Human beings, acting on behalf of groups or organizations in an effort to realize the group's or organization's goals or ends, have a fairly general inclination to accept these ends as "absolutes" and to subordinate personal preferences to them. Groups and organizations are apt to prefer men who will behave in this way, and thus reinforce the inclination. However, the error of Machiavelli of seeing the ensuing tasks as technical problems is avoided by Althusius, largely because of his stress on the symbiotic nature of communities, including the state. The naturally cooperative human community organizes its effective living together by drawing upon the general human inclination to act rationally up to a point. Indeed, this natural rationality is the condition of its communal life. Hence we find the extention of this rationiity to all the different functions, and more particularly the functions of public servants which Althusius' concept of the *ratio officii* embodies.[30]

In various places, but more especially in discussions about the function of public officials, it is clear that the *ratio officii* and the *ratio administrationis,* although not devoid of a link to higher values, are inspired by knowledge which is strictly pragmatic. Such knowledge is valuable, because it facilitates successful cooperation among men. Therefore, "the man who knows what is fruitful and useful for the state, not the one who knows much, is rightly to be praised."[31] Such pragmatism has, of course, ancient roots and constitutes more particularly a Stoic heritage. Thus Cicero goes so far as to insist that knowledge is valuable only when it is useful to the community.[32] That such an activist approach to knowledge is short-sighted and stands in the way of fundamental research this tradition did not appreciate, and Althusius is no exception.

[29] II Sam. 15:34ff.; 2:6–7; 3:7–13; 15:31–32.

[30] For the *functio publica,* see *Politica* vii. 29ff. Although the term *ratio officii* does not appear in this particular discussion, it is animated by a thoroughly rationalist conception. The public function is described as a rational pursuit of rational ends.

[31] *Ibid.* 21. 12.

[32] Cicero *De Officiis* i.157–8; see also, i.19.

In keeping with these ideas, we find Althusius strongly in favor of the active life. As a good Protestant, and more particularly Calvinist, he cannot see any value in the contemplative life.[33] Monks and hermits are worthless. They are miserable and of no use to themselves or others. The love of one's neighbor, a fundamental tenet of the Christian faith, cannot be practiced by them.

Althusius' arguments, which are in line with much Calvinist thought, illustrate impressively an implication of Calvinist doctrine: it provided a rationalization for a predominant impulse of the growing urban and commercial class.[34] It is easy to underestimate the importance of this worldliness which provided the threshold for a more secular utilitarianism. Max Weber, with whom I agree when he says that Calvinism was the precursor to utilitarianism, that indeed utilitarianism is the secular form of Calvinism, was inclined to think that this turn occurred toward the end of the seventeenth century.[35] The work of Althusius shows that the force of this trend produces already toward the end of the sixteenth century and in the writings of an orthodox Calvinist some of the sociological and utilitarian implications. This force is the force of rationalism. The urge toward sanctifying the life of man was given a secular twist by looking upon worldly success as a test of sanctity. The field of success in which this inherent trend first appeared was politics, not economics. Service to God consists in fulfilling one's function or office, success means that one "fits" into the divinely ordained

[33] *Politica* i. 24–25: *Itaque eremitae* μισάνθρωποι ἀπόλιδες, *sine certo lare, foco, vel domicilio et sede viventes, plane per se miseri, neque sibi neque aliis utiles sunt. Nam quomodo proximi sui commoda promovere hi possunt, nisi societati humanae se insinuent? . . . ideo Deus voluit, ut alter alterius opera et auxilio egeret. . . . Si enim alius auxilio alterius non indigeret, quae societas, quae reverentia, quis ordo, quae ratio, quae humanitas esset?* It is noteworthy that *ratio,* reason, appears at this crucial point along with *humanitas* as the ultimate focus of value.

[34] C. B. McPherson, in an interesting recent study, has stressed the aspect of "posessive individualism" in Hobbes and Locke; see *The Political Theory of Possessive Individualism—Hobbes and Locke* (1962). Such possessive individualism is already markedly present in Calvinist Protestantism, and more especially in Althusius, but subject to utilitarian collectivism which, I believe, also animates Hobbes and Locke.

[35] See Max Weber, *op. cit.,* fn. 22 above, pp. 259–260, where Weber cites Richard Baxter's *Christian Directory:* "It is for action that God maintaineth us and our activities; work is the moral as well as the natural end of power. . . . It is action that God is most served and honored by. . . . The public welfare or the good of many is to be valued above our own." Commenting on these sentences, Weber remarks: "We see here the starting point for the turning of God's will into the pure utilitarianism of liberal theorists."

scheme of things. Such rationalized conduct is provided with a transcendent religious sanction. This is undoubtedly the reason orthodox Calvinists attached such a high value to the political order.[36] Calvin himself placed the organizer and maintainer of the political community very high among men. While not himself a major officeholder in his Geneva, he played a continuing and decisive role in Genevan politics to such an extent that some commentators have spoken of "theocracy" in describing it.[37] But this is a misnomer or at least an oversimplification. To be sure, each social and political function has a religious significance, so that each function is inspired by an intensely religious spirit. The thoroughly rational fulfillment of the duties of one's office and the surrendering of personal preferences to the impersonal requirements of the office—these are the real bases for the intensely practical emphasis of Calvinism. It also motivates the Calvinist appreciation of the value and importance of the political order, of the state.[38] For the state provides an appropriate function for everybody. This does, of course, include the protective role of the state which Christian orthodoxy had recognized since St. Augustine, but which Calvin stated with all due precision: "It is the purpose of temporal rule, so long as we live among men, to foster and support the external worship of God, and to defend pure doctrine and the standing of the church." But he did not say who was to decide which doctrine was pure, or which church was the right one. The answer to such a question appeared to Calvin self-evident, as it had to Luther, St. Augustine, and many others.[39]

In short, for Calvin and his followers, rationality was as much intertwined with religion as it had been for medieval thinkers, and

[36] Max Weber, *op. cit.*, has shown convincingly how this development of thought was linked to the doctrine of predestination. See especially pp. 109 ff. and 129 ff. For critical commentaries, see fn. 22 above.

[37] J. W. Allen's interesting analysis in *Political Thought of the Sixteenth Century*, chap. iv, overemphasizes the theocratic aspect. See Hans Baron, *Calvin's Staatsanschauung* (1924), for a more balanced view. See also J. Bohateč, *Calvin und die Lehre von Staat und Kirche* (1937).

[38] See, for a further elaboration, my introduction to Althusius' *Politica*, as cited above fn. 21, lxxix–lxxx. See also *Politica* 8. 56, "*Tunc perfecta est civium congregatio, quando quilibet in suo statu debitam habet dispositionem et operationem prout vocationis et functionis suae natura et ratio postulat.*" Note his combining of all the key terms: *operatio, vocatio, functio, natura,* and *ratio.*

[39] See Jean Calvin, *Institutes of the Christian Religion* 14.20. 2. Translation my own.

indeed for Machiavelli. Right conduct and behavior could only be determined by considering the transcendent determinants of motivations which religion alone could provide. Hence it would seem desirable to analyze what Althusius has to say on religion in order to compare it with the Machiavellian position. What place has it in human society, and what is its relation to state and government? Althusius, it appears, tends to interpret religion politically and to subordinate ecclesiastical to governmental considerations. Not only the highest sovereign, but also his provincial governors have the function of supervising the ecclesiastics in the exercise of their functions, to make sure that they fulfill their office in good faith and with diligence. In support of these propositions, he refers to passages in the Old Testament.[40] But this does not mean that a magistrate is to use his office for the forcing of conscience. Instead Althusius espouses a measure of toleration and declares that a magistrate who would undertake to use the sword to secure religious conformity exceeds the limits of his jurisdiction and becomes a malefactor. In this connection he advocates general moderation, rebuking sharply all dogmatism and fanaticism and emphasizing the weakness of human reason and the frequency of disagreement among the learned.[41] He suggests, in the German tradition, that universities may be called upon to resolve such doubts. And he firmly contests the Jesuit contention which maintains that a government could not tolerate diverse religions. "For the question is not whether there can be two religions, which we deny with them. Nor is the question whether the governor can embrace two religions which we deny. Nor is the question whether the government can dispose of a religious controversy which we deny as contrary to the word of God. The real question only arises when a state comprises cities or estates which embrace conflicting confessions for the defense of which each adduces the word of God. Then in that case may the

---

[40] *Politica* 8. 58: *"In sacris functionibus, providebit, ut ordo sacer et collegium ecclesiasticorum cum fide et diligentia officium faciant, atque ad explicationem et expeditionem muneris ipsorum nihil desit, aut obstet. Nam suprema inspectio, cura et auctoritas in personas et officium ecclesiasticorum pertinet ad magistratum, seu praesidem provinciae. . . ."* It is evident that this position is in keeping with the formula, *cujus regio, ejus religio,* and that it protected the Protestant believers in Nassau whose *praeses provinciae* was one of them. See also *ibid.* 9. 49 ff.; 28. 61 ff. In these last paragraphs Althusius supports what follows in the text.

[41] *Politica* 9. 43: *"Nam nullum unquam ingenium tam eliminatum emersit, cujus judicio omnium doctorum sententiae subscribentur."* See also 39.

governor of such a state who himself accepts one of these confessions persecute those who embrace another with force of arms? In this case we say that a governor who cannot alter the discrepancy without danger and disturbance to the State should tolerate the dissenters, until God illuminates them."[42] Like Bodin, Althusius points to the experience of the free city of Frankfurt, which permitted four religions until 1561. Althusius' outspoken plea for toleration does not extend, of course, to admitting atheists and others whose belief is wholly contrary to the Christian faith to public office, except for Jews, whom Althusius with other Calvinists would tolerate, perhaps out of respect for the Old Testament.[43] Atheists, on the other hand, are anarchists and endanger the political order—a sentiment which political thinkers from Machiavelli to Rousseau shared.

This notion is rooted, of course, in the conviction discussed before that religion is vitally important for the political order. To return to it once more: After a long recital, mostly from the Old Testament, of evils which have befallen the state when religion was neglected, Althusius declares that the care for religion is both necessary and useful for the sovereign.[44] Discussions such as these, which stress the utilitarian implication, show that the emphases on utility and the instrumental rationality of religion are quite compatible with deep religious sentiment and indeed with orthodoxy. Protestant ascetic ethics, when applied to the political order and its government, comes close to the *virtù* idea of Machiavelli with which it shares its Roman origin. And beyond government service and the duties of office the maintenance of a vigorous citizenship, able to participate in and defend the order, are concomitants of religion. This decisive role of religion in politics is as relevant to a theory of rational decision as it is to a theory of rational action or rational law. It would be worthwhile to trace the unfolding of the interaction of reason, rationality, and religion through succeeding political thinkers from Hooker and Hobbes to Rousseau and Kant. For the interrelation is a recurrent theme which would enable us to show that religion, by providing transcendent grounds for value

[42] *Politica* 9. 35 ff. The view is similar to that of James I as expounded in *Apologia pro juramento fidelitatis*, 16, and approved of by S. Lubbertus. See fn. 5, p. lxxxii, introduction. The key passage reads: *"Supremus magistratus . . . non habet potestatem cogendi subditos suos ad hanc vel illam opinionem, quam ipse sequitur, amplectandam."*

[43] *Politica* 28. 69–71.

[44] *Politica* 28. 11. See also chap. 30.

judgments, enables political man to choose and hence to decide. Such a review would, however, merely reinforce what the paradigmatic study of the two early political theorists we have examined has already made abundantly clear, namely, that a concern with the substantive goals of human and more especially political action leads to the religious or pseudoreligious sources of human reasoning. These sources are understood as the basis of human existence, rather than any mere decisionism for the sake of deciding. The ever more numerous choices which modern man is confronted by and to which we alluded at the outset of this paper become the occasion of psychoses and other mental disorders, when the deeper layers of consciousness from which decision-making needs to be fed are dried up in a purely operational rationalistic scientism. The existentionalist school, by making a virtue of this human tragedy, has provided no more than an activist escapism. It is basically a matter of indifference whether we are "thrown" or in some other involuntary way placed into a situation which we cannot master, but from which we merely escape by a "decision" which lacks any conviction as to what is right. The inevitable consequence is a surrender to some "decision-maker," whether man or movement, who claims legitimacy on the ground of some species of inevitability. It is well worth remembering that the great tradition of political theory has, by contrast, always recognized the role of religion in reasoning about the rationality of the political order and of its agents and participants.

13

RATIONALITY AND REPRESENTATION IN BURKE'S "BRISTOL SPEECH"

HARVEY C. MANSFIELD, JR.

How can government be both rational and representative? It is notorious that what is rational is not necessarily representative of the people and is unlikely to be so. Having the capacity for speech, man uses or implies reasoning when he communicates with other men; man is a rational being. When he is "irrational," he compounds the bestiality of animals without the capacity for speech; and he shows his peculiar capacity as much in the misuse as in the proper use of reason. Every speech contains a reasoning, an opinion, but not necessarily a true reasoning. In a multitude men seldom achieve a true reasoning, though they may be able to come to a reasonable compromise of opinions. But the search for such a compromise indicates what prevents the dominance of a true reasoning. This search for compromise means recognizing that the opinions of most men are supported by their power as well as by their reason. It presupposes that most men are stubborn with their opinions and that they could not be ruled on the basis of a true reasoning. The sense in which all men are rational prevents the success of the true reason which only a few men come to.[1] Thus a government which represents a multitude seems to be in one sense rational, because it is based on opinions, and in a partly unopposed sense, irrational, because it compromises the true reasoning. "Representative government" at first seems to mean compromise between the few true reasoners and the many inexact reasoners.

But this meaning of representative government is too general, as it would apply to all actual governments. In modern times, since the seventeenth century, representative government has meant the making of decisions by the government on the basis of the opinions or the feelings or the will of the people. In the political science of Hobbes, for example, the sovereign makes decisions for the people which the people could not make themselves. "The people" are a mere number of private individuals until they authorize a sovereign with power to enforce his decisions. But the sovereign makes decisions for the sake of the end authorized by the people, their self-preservation. The sovereign makes decisions on that basis if it obeys the law of nature, which is to say, if it follows its own true self-interest. For Hobbes, sovereignty is absolute and unchecked in its decision-making, so that even the most irrational decision should be obeyed. Yet irrational, unnecessarily oppressive decisions will be few; for the sovereign has neither to think wisely nor to sacrifice its own interest in order to make a rational decision in accord with the law of nature. It is easy for the sovereign to see its own interest and then to follow it; so there is a kind of guarantee that its decisions will be rational. The reason why the worst decisions will be rare shows why the worst decisions should be obeyed. They should be obeyed because the sovereign must never receive the impression that its self-interest diverges from rational decisions to protect the people. Thus, for Hobbes, the sovereign is absolute in its decisions, but it does not *rule* the people. It is authorized by the people to make decisions for the people for the sake of the natural end of every one of the people. It does not rule the people by fixing an end for them which they would not have authorized on their own.[2]

---

[1] Spinoza, *Tractatus Theologico-Politicus*, chap. 4, beginning.

[2] Hobbes, *Leviathan*, chaps. 5, 6, 15–18; *Of the Citizen*, Part II, chap. 5,

Representative government in the narrow, specific sense is a special case of representative government in the broad sense of all government. In the broad sense, representative government is a compromise of true and inexact reasoning. In the specific sense, representative government is that compromise which assumes that the inexact reasoning of the people is true enough to form the basis for the decisions of the government. Just as for Hobbes, the people are assumed to know the end of government well enough.

Thus representative government in the specific sense permits a shift in emphasis from rationality to decision-making. Since the end of government is a natural law simple enough for the people to understand, the government needs only enough reason to find means to this end. It may have to search and scramble to protect the security of its citizens; but having this standard, it will have fewer hard choices and use less deliberation than a government which rules. Under this relatively clear and simple standard of security, more choices will seem indifferent to the government. Often a mere choice will serve as well as a wise choice; or perhaps a choice may be entirely avoided, as, for example, in matters of religious doctrine. Decisiveness in government may be sufficient wisdom, as a counterpart to the steadiness of the people in their desire for security, which is also sufficient wisdom. Representative government in the specific sense has less need to be rational than government which rules the people. The people need it only to make decisions.

Yet the shift from rationality to decision-making is only a shift in emphasis. We have already noted the ambiguity of the rationality of man: All men, or at least all normal men, are rational because they speak, giving reasons. But only a few men know true reasons, and only to a limited degree. Yet a reason is in the highest sense not a reason unless it is a true reason. All men are rational, and few men are rational. There is a similar ambiguity in decision-making. All normal men make decisions because all normal men are in some degree free to choose. But again, in the highest sense, only a correct decision is truly a decision. If a man has decided foolishly, he was not in control of the situation in the way that he believed. Something unknown to him affected the situation and obstructed his intention; something unknown to him controlled him and made him

sect. 6; chap. 6, sect. 11; chap. 12, sect. 8; *Elements of Law*, Part II, chap. 2, sect. 11; chap. 9, sect. 9.

unfree to make his decision.[3] He did not really decide; he only seemed to decide. The meaning of "decision" tends in the direction of "correct decision," just as the meaning of "rational" tends in the direction of "true." The popular meaning of "decision" is closer to any decision than to "correct decision," whereas the popular meaning of "rational" is closer to "true" than to "arguable." The shift from rationality to decision-making which is characteristic of representative government in the modern specific sense can be seen in the opposite emphasis of the popular meaning of these ambiguous terms. But this shift does not seem to remove the ambiguity of rationality, which is the problem of all governments.

Can this ambiguity be removed? Is there an understanding of decision-making which resolves the ordinary meaning of decision as any choice and the refined meaning of decision as rational decision? One could seek a philosophical or theoretical resolution of the problem by attempting an analysis of the word "decision" or by working out a typology of decision-making. It is at least possible, however, that there is no theoretical resolution of the problem. There may be only a practical or political resolution. The ambiguity of "decision" may be resolved only in the principles and practice of representative government. In Hobbes's thought, there is a shift from rationality to decision-making or acts of the will by the sovereign; and there is a shift from the rational intelligibility of the universe to the naming constructs of the scientist. If these two shifts are connected, it may be that the former controlled the latter. It may be that Hobbes's political science controlled his philosophy, rather than the reverse.[4]

But if a practical understanding of rational decision-making should be sought, there is reason for seeking it closer to the practice of representative government than is Hobbes's thought. There is reason for a fresh consideraion of Burke's famous "Bristol Speech," in which he laid down principles to guide the judgment of the people's representatives. This speech may be taken as a practical reflection on the problem of rationality and representation both in the narrow and in the broad sense of representative government. Many say today that the scope of rational judgment claimed for the

---

[3] See Felix E. Oppenheim, *Dimensions of Freedom* (1961), pp. 17–18.
[4] Compare Leo Strauss, *The Political Philosophy of Hobbes* (1936) with Michael Oakeshott, *Introduction* to *Hobbes's Leviathan* (1957), pp. xxvii-xxviii.

representative by Burke is unreasonably broad, for his time as well as for ours. His synthesis of rationality and representation may seem too good to be true. If that is so, then one would have to consider whether to move toward more representation or toward more rationality. Burke's "Bristol Speech" is a practical speech, and, therefore, it takes Britain's eighteenth-century representative government for granted. But a careful analysis of the speech can reveal implications for modern representative government, for all government, and for human rationality.

The common impression of the "Bristol Speech" is that it asserts the independence of the representative from his constituents in terms so decisive and in style so disdainful as to make it now obsolete. This speech was suitable to an aristocratic age, it is thought, but not applicable to the present. Representative government has been perfected, which is to say democratized. For democracy is now taken to be not the rule of the people, but the expression of the people's will through the competition of parties.[5] In most popular thinking now, there is no distinction between representative government and democracy. Burke's speech would stand as an early effort to defend aristocracy against the advance of representative government. It would have merely historical importance in this age of representative government perfected.

But in addition to this disparagement of the present importance of the "Bristol Speech," some have doubted its historical importance and its sincerity. Burke spoke "at the conclusion of the poll," so that there was prudence in his brave words.[6] He spoke as the political dependent of men who furnished him with an uncontested seat in Parliament both before his victory at Bristol in 1774 and after his defeat at Bristol in 1780. However little such men controlled Burke's politics, he spoke from a situation of security. Moreover, there has been considerable recent research into Burke's activities in behalf of his Bristol constituents. He was not so aloof as a quick reading of the "Bristol Speech" from the standpoint of current opinion might suggest. He acted almost as ship broker for merchants and watched over the passage of private bills to secure their particular interests. As an agent for such interests, he seems to have been as busy as a

[5] Carl B. Cone, *Burke and the Nature of Politics* (1957), pp. 195–196, 276; Philip A. Gibbons, *Ideas of Political Representation in Parliament, 1660–1832* (1914), p. 38.
[6] Ross J. S. Hoffman, *Edmund Burke, New York Agent* (1956), p. 165.

Congressman and much busier than a contemporary M.P.—perhaps because the party government which he struggled to establish was not yet established. Against the demands of his constituents he could plead the overriding importance of a party program and his own inability as an opposition M.P. to influence the Civil Service; but his pleas were unconvincing in the infancy of party government.[7]

All this criticism is offered from the standpoint of current opinion on representative government, by which representative government is seen as the expression of the people's will through the competition of parties. The doctrine of the "Bristol Speech" is regarded as inapplicable in our day because representative party government offers a more realistic way of ensuring that representatives act on principles; and it is regarded as grandiose in its own day because it suggested a reliance on the disinterestedness of representatives. We have then three kinds of representative government: first, in the broad sense, a compromise between the few true reasoners and the many inexact reasoners; second and more specifically, decision-making by the government on the basis of the will of the people; third, substantial decision-making by the people through parties. Burke seems to have defended the middle position, somewhere between the sovereignty of rationality and of decision-making. We hope to show that it is more correct, and more revealing, to see his speech as a defense of this middle than to consider it as a clumsy early effort to define a relation now adequately understood. Burke himself did not regard this speech as a piece for this occasion only, although it occupies only seven pages in his *Works*. In a later defense of his consistency, he wrote of himself:

> He was the first man who, on the hustings, at a popular election, rejected the authority of instructions from constituents; or who, in any place, has argued so fully against it. Perhaps the discredit into which that doctrine of compulsive instructions under our constitution is since fallen, may be due, in a great degree, to his opposing himself to it in that manner, and on that occasion.[8]

[7] P. T. Underdown, "Edmund Burke, the Commissary of his Bristol Constituents, 1774–1780," *English Historical Review*, LXXIII (1958), 252–269; George H. Guttridge, *Introduction* to *The Correspondence of Edmund Burke*, ed. Thomas H. Copeland (4 vols. to date, 1958–63), III, viii–xiv.

[8] Burke, *Works* ("Bohn Library," 8 vols., 1854), III, 26; See P. T. Underdown, "Henry Cruger and Edmund Burke: Colleagues and Rivals

One should test the merit of this speech on the level of the high claim made for it.

The full difficulty of the occasion may not be quite apparent from these words. We must first understand that the "Bristol Speech" is an embarrassed speech. Burke is an outsider. He cannot feel the same emotion as his colleague in success (Bristol was a two-member constituency),

> who through the easy gradations of acquaintance, friendship, and esteem, has obtained the honour, which seems of itself, naturally and almost insensibly, to meet with those, who, by the even tenor of pleasing manners and social virtues, slide into the love and confidence of their fellow-citizens.[9]

This man has a connection with the opinions and interest of the people; his emotion is therefore proper, and Burke is embarrassed because he cannot share it. Even more embarrassing, this man has delivered an opinion which Burke finds necessary to oppose; and that opinion refers to the relation between the representative and his constituents! Thus it rests with an outsider, newly favored, to tell his benefactors, excited with the flushed pride of recent purchasers, that they must not issue authoritative instructions to him, contrary to the opinion of the man with whom he was equally favored, whom they know.

Burke presents two separable arguments against authoritative instructions from the people to their representatives. The first is that "government and legislation are matters of reason and judgment, and not of inclination"; the second is that the representative must deliberate on the interest of the whole people, not only of one locality. Burke finds the relation between these two arguments in a way which constitutes his special conception of representative government.

. Burke allows that, if government were a matter of will, "yours, without question, ought to be superior." But government is a matter of reason:

> and what sort of reason is that, in which the determination precedes the discussion; in which one set of men deliberate, and another

---

at the Bristol Election of 1774," *The William and Mary Quarterly*, 3rd Series, IV (1958), 31; *Letters of Lord Acton to Mary Gladstone*, ed. Herbert Paul (1904), p. 97.

　[9] Burke, *Works*, I, 442.

decide; and where those who form the conclusion are perhaps three
hundred miles distant from those who hear the arguments?[10]

This argument is Aristotelian. If government were a matter of will,
those with the most power, the many, should rule, and would rule
willy-nilly. But all government is a matter of reason, in the minimal
sense that power is always exerted in accordance with an opinion,
a reasoning. Every act of power, every decision, is preceded by an
act of deliberation, however inadequate or habitual. If this deliberation were in fact as well directed as it always claims to be, it would
provide the basis for a distinction between those who can truly
deliberate and those who deliberate inadequately and habitually.
The former would rule and the latter would be ruled. In every
regime, those who truly deliberate would be sovereign. Aristotle
says that the sovereign part of a regime is the deliberative part.[11] The
minimal sense of human rationality thus points to the sovereignty
of the wise, to the maximal sense of human rationality. Men, being
men, are incapable of brute power with its innocence; they must
give a reason. When they do, they admit by implication the principle of the sovereignty of the wise, of the most prudent. Yet it is
realistic and empirical to assert that deliberation is the sovereign
part of every regime, even the most "irrational"; for there is no
decision without *some kind* of deliberation. When Burke says that
government is a matter of reason, not will, he seems to mean that
government is representative government in the broad sense we
have used. It is a compromise between the few exact and the many
inexact reasoners, favoring either the few or the many.

Burke emphasizes, however, not the distinction between exact
and inexact reasoning, but the *situation* which exact reasoning requires. Reason in government requires an acquaintance with all the
circumstances, and they can be known only where they can be
gathered together, in Parliament. Reason in government requires
an attention to circumstances, in contrast to theoretical reason.
Burke implies that the distinction between theoretical and practical
reason is of more importance for representative government than
the distinction, within practical reason, between the few exact and
the many inexact reasoners. Hobbes's argument for representative
government had emphasized a simple reasoning from the obvious

10 *Ibid.*, I, 447.
11 Aristotle, *Politics* 1275^{b}6–7. 1277^{b}25–31. 1298^{a}4–9.

situation of man in the state of nature to the necessity of a unity of will in the sovereign. The people, following the natural law of reason to seek peace, could easily reason out the necessity for a sovereign; they authorized his use of prudent deliberation in the circumstances of each situation. The separation of decision-making from deliberation of which Burke complains in the "Bristol Speech" began with Hobbes's separation of the natural law of reason, to be exercised by any man, from prudent deliberation in the circumstances, confined in political matters to the sovereign. The deliberative part of government is sovereign, as with Aristotle; but the deliberative part is first authorized by a quasi-theoretical use of the natural law of reason.[12] Hobbes's argument opened up the possibility of a similarly simple or theoretical reasoning (not adopted by Hobbes) in which the people could instruct the sovereign, instead of authorizing his decisions. Under this assumption the people could deliberate as effectively and as easily on the acts of the sovereign as on the authorization of the sovereign. Burke's first argument against authoritative instructions is antidemocratic, but is not a straightforward defense of the sovereignty of the wise. It is affected by the argument for representative government in the specific sense which Hobbes had advanced. Burke does not say that the people are weak reasoners, though he would not deny it. He says that the people are prevented from a suitable exercise of reason because they are poorly placed; they cannot hear the discussion nor weigh the arguments. It may be that, having put so much unpalatable truth in this speech, Burke did not wish to tell the people they were weak reasoners. But his first, Aristotelian argument against authoritative instructions points in the direction of his second, non-Aristotelian argument.

This second argument is the most famous passage of the speech:

> Parliament is not a *congress* of ambassadors from different and hostile interests; which interests each must maintain, as an agent and advocate, against other agents and advocates; but parliament is a *deliberative* assembly of *one* nation, with *one* interest, that of the whole; where, not local purposes, not local prejudices, ought to guide, but the general good resulting from the general reason of the whole.[13]

[12] Hobbes, *Leviathan*, chaps. 6, 15; *Of the Citizen*, Part I, chap. 3, sects. 13, 26; *Of Human Nature*, chap. 12; *Elements of Law*, Part I, chap. 4, sect. 9.

[13] Burke, *Works*, I, 447; emphasis in original. See Algernon Sidney, *Discourses Concerning Government* (2 vols., 1750), chap. 3, sect. 44, p.

Parliament is a deliberative assembly rather than a congress because it represents one national interest. The nation is a whole having a general reason which produces a general good or national
interest; Parliament must deliberate upon this national interest.
This emphasis on an overriding national interest may seem no different from Aristotle's view that the good regimes aim at the common good. But there is a fundamental difference caused by Burke's
adherence to the Hobbesian argument for representative government.

In Aristotle's political science, the national interest cannot be
represented by the government because the government is the chief
cause of the community. More precisely, the regime (*politeia*) is the
chief cause of the community (*polis*), being the form of the community; and the government (*politeuma*), being those who rule, is
the regime.[14] Britain is Britain chiefly insofar as it continues to be
ruled by the same men: When ruled by an aristocracy, it has one
national interest; when ruled by the people, it has another national
interest. In this view there is no national interest considered apart
from the government. One could say that it is equally the interest of
an aristocratic and a democratic Britain to prevent France from
controlling the mouth of the Scheldt, as Pitt supposed when he went
to war against revolutionary France. But it is not an *overriding*
interest of an aristocratic Britain to prevent this. It is an interest
instrumental to the security of an *aristocratic* Britain. The overriding
interest of an aristocratic Britain is to remain an aristocratic Britain.
To say that there is no national interest considered apart from the
government means that there is no impartial national interest which
a government can merely represent. The government chiefly constitutes the national interest.

This difference is too much to infer from the quotation given,
but it becomes clearer when we see what *is* the one national interest,
on which Parliament deliberates. According to Burke, it has three
aspects: commerce, a free constitution, and monarchy. Regarding
commerce, the oneness of the national interest is not evident. The
interests of a rich commercial nation are "various, multiform, and
intricate," all the more when the nation has a widespread empire.

370; and William Blackstone, *Commentaries on the Laws of England*
(4 vols., 5th ed.; 1773), I, 159.

[14] Aristotle *Politics* 1276^{b}1–13; 1278^{b}9–15; See Burke, *Works*, III, 302–
303.

Further, "the machine of a free constitution is no simple thing; but it is as intricate and delicate as it is valuable." The source of oneness seems to be the "great and ancient monarchy": "We must preserve religiously the true legal rights of the sovereign, which form the keystone that binds together the noble and well-constructed arch of our empire and our constitution."[15]

Despite the difference (to be noted) between the Hobbesian and the Burkean conceptions of sovereignty. Burke seems to follow Hobbes's view that the sovereign is an impartial, common power, elevated above his subjects. Hobbes thought that a multitude became a people or achieved a single, national interest by virtue of the authorized elevation of a common power. Aristotle thought that a multitude became a community chiefly by virtue of a certain form imposed by the regime; the regime molds a people according to a certain way of life. For Hobbes, the sovereign is simply power; for Aristotle, the sovereign is power directed to a characteristic end. Thus, for Hobbes, Britain is a nation whose sovereign is called monarchical because it is one in number, whereas, for Aristotle, Britain would be a limited monarchy whose regime makes it a partly monarchical, partly aristocratic nation.

Burke seems to agree with Hobbes that a multitude has one national interest because of a common power above it, not because of a certain form given it by the regime. That is why Britain has a free constitution. When the sovereign is merely elevated power, then those under the sovereign are free to live as they please, providing that they do not dispute the power of the sovereign. As simple power, the sovereign is impartial, and leaves subjects as free as possible. But as the form which molds a multitude into a community, the regime cannot be impartial; it recommends and requires a certain way of life. An aristocratic regime produces an aristocratic way of life. How can this result be avoided? How can the British limited monarchy be a free constitution? How can the British sovereign remain impartial?

Burke's solution is a commercial way of life. If the way of life of a community is chiefly virtue or religion, then some conception of virtue or some religion must be chosen. There are different conceptions of virtue and different religions, and they are mutually exclusive. The sovereign could not make a multitude into a people without choosing one and rejecting the others; he could not be im-

[15] Burke, *Works,* I, 440–441, 448.

partial. But if the sovereign presides over a commercial nation, he can allow a variety of interests to exist; indeed, he must allow them to exist, so that commerce may flourish. The necessity of a free constitution is commerce, and the practical result is the freedom to be acquisitive. Commerce splits the people into interests, so that a free constitution can avoid the unsteady, tyrannical majorities of ancient democracies. Yet the policy of commerce achieves the unity of a people because it turns their attention from questions of virtue and religion which could divide them. The oneness of the national interest is preserved in and by the variety of commercial interests. Our search for the one national interest on which Parliament deliberates ends in the solution of variety. It is a homogeneous variety, in which everyone is acquisitive for himself, and in his own way.[16]

Commerce has the essential nonpartisan excellence of unity in variety, but it must be protected as a unity. Although commerce makes a free constitution viable by dividing the massed irrationality of the people, it must still be protected as the one national interest. Burke therefore distinguished between agents and representatives: agents work within the commercial machine as advocates of interests before the government; representatives consider, compare, and reconcile these interests. Agents work under authoritative instructions and mandates; representatives deliberate upon the management of interests to secure commerce as a whole. Agents are natural factors in a commercial society, and Burke had no objection in principle either to their task or to their manner of operation.[17] While a Member of Parliament, he accepted a salary as agent for the New York assembly, and, while he represented Bristol, he performed many services for its merchants. In arguing for the special status of representatives to protect the national interest, Burke was not denying the need for advocacy of local and private interests. His own activity as an agent was not inconsistent with his loftier conception of the representative.[18]

The danger of authoritative instructions can be understood as the

[16] *Ibid.*, V, 89, 100, 124.

[17] See his defense against the charge of neglecting his constituents, *Ibid.*, II, 131–134; and Underdown, *op. cit.*, 269.

[18] See Samuel H. Beer, "Representation of Interests in British Government: Historical Background," *American Political Science Review,* LI (1957), 614–628, to which this essay is greatly indebted; Hoffman, *op. cit.*, pp. 104–106, 181, 189–193; Burke, *Correspondence,* II, 303, 522; III, 81, 135, 167, 197, 307–308, 356; IV, 274.

confusion of the work of the agent and the representative. Burke believed, with Adam Smith, that merchants need to be protected from the consequences of their abuse of economic freedom. They need to be restrained from securing their interests through monopolies guaranteed by the government. In acting as agent for Bristol merchants, Burke also acted as their representative in order to protect commerce as a whole; for Bristol as a so-called outport suffered from privileges granted to the port of London by the government.[19] In this example Burke acted consistently, that is, separately, as agent and representative. In another example Burke displeased his Bristol constituents by supporting Irish free trade.[20] When the advocacy of commercial interests is encouraged, the familiar danger is that the public power will be used to support an advocate and the public authority depressed to the level of the advocates. In a society of interested partiality, it is especially difficult and absolutely essential to keep the sovereign power impartial. The force of Burke's argument in support of the representative is necessary to counteract the importance of the agent in a commercial society. The distinction between the agent and the representative is in part explained by the necessities of laissez-faire economics.

But the immediate need of this distinction is more directly political. The "Bristol Speech" is directed against Bristol Radicals, not against London merchants. Henry Cruger, Burke's successful colleague at the election of 1774, had accepted his own victory with a speech in support of authoritative instructions, to which Burke's speech was a reply. Cruger had been a leader of the Radical Independent Society in Bristol, whose program comprised remedies for aristocratic corruption. These remedies were to be enforced by mandates from the people to their representatives, or from organizations of the people such as the Independent Society. Since the remedies were designed to prevent the corruption of representatives, they could not be effected through the unmandated judgment of representatives. Consistently with this program, Cruger promised before the election to support shorter Parliaments and a Place Bill. In his acceptance speech he asserted:

> I shall always think it my duty in Parliament to be guided by your counsels and instructions. I shall consider myself the servant of my

[19] Underdown, *op. cit.*, 261.
[20] Burke, *Correspondence*, IV, 222–225; Alfred DeGrazia, *Public and Republic* (1951), p. 37.

constituents, not their master. Subservient to their will, not superior
to it.[21]

Burke opposed the bill for shorter (triennial) Parliaments as
leading to one of two consequences, each very dangerous: an increase in the power of the crown or "a violent and furious popular
spirit." More frequent elections would increase the expense of elections and serve the interests of those who have great resources for
elections, the ministers; and they would work against those whose
property is landed and encumbered, the great families and the
country gentlemen. By a spirit of emulation, each election could
become more expensive, as the ministry redoubled its efforts to
secure a Parliamentary majority; the number of contested elections
would rise, and the payment of bribery would become more frequent
and flagrant.[22]

But perhaps the electorate would not remain as corrupt as it has
been; perhaps "the inflammation of liquor" would no longer aggra-
vate the disorders of modern elections, compared to those of Rome.
In that case the people might become inflamed in their imaginations.
Organizations formed to secure constitutional reforms by issuing
mandates to representatives might arouse the people from their
amiable and well-paid deference to local notables. The proposal of
more frequent Parliaments was designed to improve the enforcement
of authoritative instructions. But suppose that representatives were
instructed not merely in measures for local monopolies, but in anti-
Catholic legislation? This was no imaginary danger, for the Protestant Association under the leadership of Lord George Gordon
inspired fierce anti-Catholic riots in London in June, 1780. The
riots began after Gordon, in the company of a crowd of sixty
thousand, presented a petition to Parliament urging repeal of the
Catholic Relief Act of 1778. The petition was in fact a mandate.
During the election battle in Bristol in 1780, as I. R. Christie has
shown, Henry Cruger assiduously stirred up every latent discontent
against Burke, especially against his policy of toleration to Cath-
olics.[23]

[21] Quoted in G. E. Weare, *Edmund Burke's Connection with Bristol,
From 1774 till 1780* (1894), pp. 30, 79.
[22] Burke, *Works,* I, 366; VI, 133–141.
[23] I. R. Christie, "Henry Cruger and the End of Edmund Burke's Connection with Bristol," *Transactions of the Bristol and Gloucestershire Archeological Society,* LXXIV (1955), 153–170. Christie blames Cruger for

Authoritative instructions are the result of the spirit of partiality misapplied. The people can be partial to their commercial interests without producing civil discord, but they cannot be partial to their opinions in the same way without danger of civil discord. Commerce is the policy which keeps the people peaceable while free and, in that sense, rational. It is that public policy which recommends attention to one's private concerns. To extend the principles and means of commercial advocacy to constitutional questions is to have forgotten the problem of popular irrationality for which commerce was a solution. The Radicals forget the necessity of that public policy and the experience of ancient democracies in supposing that public, constitutional questions can safely be raised by the people. The reforms they regard as imperative cannot be discussed, much less undertaken, with safety. Burke began his 1780 speech against a bill for more frequent Parliaments in this way: "It is always to be lamented when men are driven to search into the foundations of the commonwealth."[24]

Thus Burke's thought on authoritative instructions leads to his thought on prescription and presumptive virtue. It is no accident that his defense in 1782 of the existing system of representation called forth one of his fullest statements on prescription. Prescription is so clearly the center of Burke's thought that we can give only the briefest summary in this space. Prescription is the policy which protects commerce. The policy of prescription keeps the self-interest of the people from invading those political or constitutional matters where partiality is dangerous. "Prescription is the most solid of all

---

Burke's defeat at Bristol in 1780, showing that Cruger deliberately undermined Burke's position with demagogic arguments and disingenuous maneuvers. Underdown refuses to censure the Radicals, and seems to blame Burke for not seeking a rapprochement with Cruger to secure one of Bristol's two seats for the opposition ("Burke's Bristol Friends," *Transactions of the Bristol and Gloucestershire Archeological Society,* LXXVII [1959], 128, and "Henry Cruger and Edmund Burke," *op. cit.,* 22–23, 28, 34; cf. Burke, *Correspondence,* IV, 266n.). But as the opposition could hope to hold only one seat in 1780, Burke would have had to withdraw in favor of Cruger. This he would not do because of the serious issue between them. Whether Cruger was sincere or not, there was a serious issue, the issue of this essay; and it was as well understood by the Bristol voters then as such issues are ever understood at large. Personal accusations and confusion of opinions are typical of representative government not only in its primitive age. In general, the more passion, the more serious the issue.

[24] *Works,* VI, 132. This searching was the cause of the troubles in America, Burke believed; *ibid.,* I, 270

titles, not only to property, but, which is to secure that property, to government."[25] Prescription is no casual discovery of the Roman law; it is a "great fundamental part of natural law."[26] It is the law of nature by which human things are made to last. Things made to last must be made gradually by shrewd adaptations, leaving tested principles and institutions untouched. Since prescription is part of the law of *nature*, and not merely a legal convention, it is the rule for public authority as well as for private property. The civilization which perfects human nature is a delicate accretion, so delicate that it can be destroyed by a public examination of what it is fundamentally. "No man examines into the defects of his title to his paternal estate, or to his established government."[27] Prescription is the most solid title for public authority because it is the principle which wards off all public inquiries into that title. It permits the representatives of the people to deliberate reasonably on the one national interest because it denies the right of the people to raise doubts of what that one national interest is. Since government has its authority from the principle that protects property from doubt and inquiry, it is assumed that government will protect property and the acquisition of property. By prescription, the one national interest is assumed.

Prescription is therefore accompanied by presumption.[28] Since property is constituted by a presumption, men of property can be presumed steady and honest; having property, and especially settled, landed property, they are most aware of the continuity which preserves, or rather *is*, property. And since the rule for property is the rule for public authority, men of property have a natural inclination to wisdom in politics. Such men as representatives are not, as a rule, corrupt, but comfortably correct. They should be preferred over ambitious men of talents, and even protected from them. Men of talents seek a quick reward and easy rank from the crown, or the people, or both, endangering the delicate balance of society by the force and example of their rise. Men of talents should be forced to make their way through "the establishments" (Burke used the plural)[29]—the army, the law, the church, the government departments. In Parliament their ambition should be disciplined and made

25 *Ibid.*, VI, 146.
26 *Ibid.*, II, 422.
27 *Ibid.*, II, 26.
28 *Ibid.*, II, 323–325; III, 86; VI, 146.
29 *Ibid.*, II, 360, 363 ff.

respectable; to secure office, they should be driven to enlist in a party under the leadership of a member of one of the great political families. Prescription and presumptive virtue are instituted in the establishments. It is contrary to sound policy, it is contrary even to natural law, to support a Place Bill forbidding representation in Parliament to the establishments. Independent establishments are (contrary to Hobbes) necessary to the maintenance of the common power of the sovereign.[30]

Burke's argument against authoritative instructions is involved in his deepest thought on natural law. We can suggest that it presents his solution to the problem of human rationality. Rationality is the capacity in all men which makes a few of them wise and most of them stubborn. Burke's solution turns the stubbornness of most men to account. Natural law is for him chiefly the rule of reason by which men get and keep property. Progress and order are both ensured, and stagnation and anarchy both avoided; for the dynamism of commerce is matched with the traditionalism of prescription. Men can be sufficiently rational and remain stubborn in the getting and keeping of property.[31] In their activity and in the society which centers on this activity, men do not need the few exact reasoners in their government. They do not need to make special allowance for the inequality of reasoners, which we have seen to be the ambiguity of rationality. The inequality of reasoners is provided for in the inequality of property. Where men are free to acquire wealth, it can be presumed that the more rational will rise; and where they are free to keep property, it can be presumed that the more rational will be educated in the needs of property and of society.

This solution to the problem of rationality is representative government in the specific sense: decision-making by the sovereign representatives for the people. Representatives use their reason to further the one national interest accepted by them as the interest of the people. Burke, we recall, had two arguments against authoritative instructions: that government is a matter of reason, not will, and that Parliament represents one national interest. These two arguments are kept separate. Government is a matter of reason; but public reason cannot inspect the one national interest, which is inherited. Parliament cannot accept authoritative instructions from the people, but it must accept the *general* instructions of the people.

[30] *Leviathan*, chaps. 21, 26.
[31] Burke, *Works*, II, 410.

"It is very rare indeed for men to be wrong in their feelings concerning public misconduct; as rare to be right in their speculation
upon the cause of it."[32] General instructions from the people take
the form of feelings or grievances; it is for their representatives to
find the cause and remedy.

It follows that virtual and actual representation cannot exist
without each other. Virtual representation is a communion of
interests between the people or some part of the people and the
representative when the people do not actually vote for the representative. But when they do vote for him, he is not bound by their
particular instructions. So all representation is virtual representation; the status of voter is not especially important. Yet all virtual
representation, Burke says, has a substratum in actual representation.[33] It is sometimes forgotten that Burke gave his famous explanation of virtual representation when he denied that Ireland had
even virtual representation. Ireland had no virtual because it had
no actual representation. The representative must have a sympathetic interest in the people, which he can have only by contact with
their feelings. An intellectual regard for the good of the people is
not enough, or it is too much. It may be an excuse for subservience
to the court, or it may be a scheme for inflaming the passions of the
people. We conclude that for Burke, government is reason, yet
never transcends the feelings of the people.

And yet it is evident that Burke did not fully accept this solution. His dissatisfaction can be seen in his embarrassment in the
"Bristol Speech." In this speech Burke, as an outsider, has to tell
insiders to behave as insiders, and how to behave as insiders. The
insider is his worthy colleague, who, unlike himself, was able to slide
into the love and confidence of his fellow citizens. What this insider
should know is that having a natural, almost insensible, connection
to the people, he does not *need* authoritative instructions from
them. Burke cannot say this outright, first because the subtle difference between a natural connection to the people and authoritative
instructions from the people could not be appreciated by his worthy
colleague, much less by the people; and secondly, because the insider who is told that he has a natural connection to the people will
naturally suppose that he knows what the natural connection is.

[32] *Ibid.*, I, 311; cf. II, 66.
[33] *Ibid.*, III, 334–335.

Thus Burke's expressed embarrassment in the "Bristol Speech" is truly rhetorical; it is essential to the communication of his meaning. He must appear to offer advice as from a faltering and hesitant outsider. This necessity is compatible with a very confident statement of the advice itself, as Burke presumed; it is enough that the advice be surrounded, as it is, by expressions of embarrassment, at the beginning and end of the speech.

Of course, it is at least partly irony that Henry Cruger is said to have slid into the love and confidence of his fellow citizens. In a letter Burke credited him only with an instinctive sympathy for the body of "low voters."[34] The true insiders are the great political families, to whom also Burke finds it necessary to teach their duty in other writings. In the *Thoughts on the Cause of the Present Discontents* Burke presented the first argument in Britain that party was a necessary and respectable part of a free constitution. Faithful to the antipartisan *opinions* of the old Whigs of 1688, the great political families had refrained from imitating their partisan *deeds*.[35] Burke tried to teach them that representatives need an institution to ensure consistency and principle in politics. In this general principle he agreed with the Radicals. He disagreed that the proper institution was authoritative instructions. He thought that the judgment of representatives should be free of ignorant interference from the people, but subject to the discipline of the virtue presumed in the established political elite.

But who is he who teaches? This man who managed his betters by a shrewd compliance and a proud deference, just as a statesman governs a nation, had nothing "of what is called a natural interest" in Bristol and only a new estate at Beaconsfield.[36] He stood "merely upon publick ground," which is to say merely upon his capacity for exact reasoning. The exercise of his own higher prudence casts doubt upon the sufficiency of prescription and presumptive virtue. For it seems that steadiness and honesty are not enough to alert the great political families to the danger of authoritative instructions. Being aware of the need for his interventions, Burke realized that representative government in the specific sense was not a certain solution. The defense of his own career turned his thoughts back to the

[34] Burke, *Correspondence*, IV, 268–269.
[35] Burke, *Works*, I, 374–375.
[36] *Ibid.*, I, 307; *Correspondence*, IV, 221.

problems of rationality and to the problematic solution of representative government in the first, broad sense.[37] At the same time, his defense of the respectability of party soon developed beyond his intent towards modern, representative party government. His doctrine of representative government stands between his own doubts of that doctrine and its later development.

---

[37] Burke, *Works,* II, 518; III, 113–114.

14

RATIONAL DECISIONS
AND INTRINSIC VALUATIONS

FELIX E. OPPENHEIM

I am an advocate of birth control. Moreover, I maintain that, in view of certain further goals, it is *rational* for people in overpopulated countries to practice contraception and for government to encourage the practice. I have then the burden of proving that birth control is *desirable* under those conditions. I may justify contraception by pointing out that such a policy is required to reduce the population to the point where the necessities of life become available to all and that this condition is in turn a necessary means to "the greatest happiness of the greatest number." Now, means-end statements can be translated without loss of meaning into cause-effect statements which can, in principle, be empirically tested. Accordingly, if my prediction of the causal chain (contraception—decrease of population—increase of the average living

standard—general well-being and happiness)[1] is empirically warranted and if I am committed to the principle of utility, then my
advocacy of contraception is rational, and it will be rational for
any government which aims at maximizing the general welfare and
happiness to adopt a policy of contraception in case of actual or
threatened overpopulation.

Now, suppose someone disagrees with me. Suppose, however, he
does not challenge my factual allegations. He concedes that failure
to check the threatened population explosion will with practical
certainty lead to the greatest unhappiness of the greatest number.
He realizes the ineffectiveness of the rhythm method and the
futility of preaching continence. He nevertheless opposes contraception, and his sole argument is that such practices are contrary
to God's will. Our disagreement then boils down to the question:
Should everyone (including every government) aim at maximizing
the general welfare, or at complying with allegedly divine commands, even if in conflict with the principle of utility?

Professor Kaplan points out the unsatisfactory state of the theory
of rational choice even for the purpose "of acting so as to secure
the values pursued." But, on the other hand, he is convinced "that
rationality is not limited to the choice among means" but applies
also to the determination of "the relative worth of disparate and
perhaps conflicting values" in the sense of ultimate goals. He would
presumably claim that it is either rational or irrational to adopt the
principle of utility as an aim in itself. He thereby espouses the meta-
ethical theory of value cognitivism, according to which not only
extrinsic, but also intrinsic value judgments have cognitive status.
Accordingly, the intrinsic value judgment that the greatest happiness principle is worth implementing for its own sake would be
either demonstrably true or demonstrably false. If true, it would
follow that it is rational to pursue this goal and irrational to be
guided by any conflicting value, for example, my opponent's.

I cannot think of any scientific argument by which either my
opponent or I could justify our respective intrinsic valuations. He
might contend that an action is demonstrably rational if and only
if it does not deviate from the moral law ordained by God and that
the practice of contraception violates this principle and is therefore irrational as well as immoral. This argument may be *persuasive,*

---

[1] Here, each of the causes constitutes a necessary, but, of course, not a
sufficient condition for each of the effects.

but only to those who happen to believe in an anthropomorphic God issuing commands—commands incompatible with birth control. However, an argument which is in principle acceptable only to some is not *valid* in the intersubjective, scientific sense. But I deny just as categorically the possibility of validating the greatest happiness principle or any other intrinsic value judgment. I agree with the meta-ethical position of value noncognitivism. Intrinsic valuations are a matter of subjective commitment, not of objective truth. Neither my adoption of the utilitarian standard nor my opponent's adherence to a particular religious faith can be called *either* rational *or* irrational. Both are commitments and, as such, non-rational.

I nevertheless agree with Professor Kaplan that rationality is not limited to the choice of means, and value noncognitivism does not entail that it is. To arrive at a rational decision, one does not start with the arbitrary selection of some ultimate end and then proceed to the choice of whatever means are most conducive to its realization. Means have consequences other than the goal, and the negative utility of the former may outweigh the positive utility of the latter. A rational actor must therefore predict (with as high a degree of probability as possible) the *total* outcome of each alternative action open to him in the given situation. Then he must establish a preference rank order among these total outcomes.[2] The preferred outcome may include elements which the actor would disvalue if he considered them in isolation, and it need not include his original, but tentative, ultimate goal. Intrinsic valuations in connection with rational choice do not pertain to separate goals but to total outcomes. I have thus oversimplified the previous example. I must ask the following, more complicated question. What do I prefer on the whole: government-sponsored birth control *and* a higher living standard *and* increased promiscuity *and* a disregarding of certain religious beliefs and so on; or the outlawing of information about contraception *and* increased misery *and* the upholding of a particular faith and the like? This is the type of question which the theory of rational choice cannot answer; it does cover all other steps of the decision-making process.

[2] In the case of decision-making under risk, he must assign utilities to the alternative outcomes, and the correct combination of probabilities and utilities will yield the net expectable utility of each outcome. The choice of a course of action will be rational provided the net expectable utility of its whole outcome is maximal.

The tools of rationality can thus be applied for better and for worse, or rather, for purposes of which we may approve or disapprove. "But that Satan has a fine mind and is lacking only in heart" is more than Professor Kaplan is willing to admit; he believes "he is a fool from beginning to end." If Satan has a fine mind, he is no fool, but a rational actor, however diabolic his goals may appear to us. This is precisely why he is so dangerous, as are those wielders of absolute power who incarnate him. Their scale of values may be abhorrent to us, but reason is of no avail to prove that they should act otherwise.

Unlike Satan, many of us are fools not lacking in heart. We base our decisions on predictions which fall short of even our limited capacity for estimating probabilities, compute our utilities on the basis of isolated goals rather than of total outcomes, and cling to incompatible goals. The area in which we may profitably be guided by criteria of rationality is large indeed.

RATIONALITY OF VALUE JUDGMENTS

SIR ISAIAH BERLIN

Professor Oppenheim draws the distinction usually attributed to Hume between descriptive and value judgments and points to the existence of a chasm across which no logical bridge can be thrown. He maintains, if I understand him rightly, that the predicate "rational" may legitimately be used only to describe judgments or beliefs about matters of fact or logical relations—for example, about facts or events, including such issues as whether a given means is adequate for the fulfillment of a given end or whether a particular policy is compatible with some other policy pursued by the same agent, and the like. But the term "rational" cannot, I gather, be applied to ends themselves; those are neither rational nor irrational, since values are not the kind of entity to which the conception of rationality is applicable. I have much sympathy with this view, which I myself once used to hold. But it seems to me that negative instances can be produced which falsify the proposition

221

that this gap between means and ends is logically unbridgeable. Let me suggest one. Suppose I meet a man who is in the habit of pushing pins into other people. I ask him why he does this. He says that it gives him pleasure. I ask him whether it is the fact that he causes pain that gives him pleasure. He replies that he does not mind whether he causes pain or not, since what gives him pleasure is the physical sensation of driving a pin into human bodies. I ask him whether he is aware that his actions cause pain. He says that he is. I ask him whether he would not feel pain if others did this to him. He agrees that he would. I ask him whether he would allow this to happen; he says that he would seek to prevent it by every means that he could command. I ask him whether he does not think that others must feel pain when he drives pins into them, and whether he should do to others what he would try to prevent them from doing to him. He says that he does not understand: Pins driven into him cause him pain and he wishes to prevent this; pins driven by him into others do not cause him pain, but on the contrary, positive pleasure, and he therefore wishes to continue to do it. I ask him whether the fact that he causes pain to other people does not seem to him to be relevant to the question of whether it is desirable to drive pins into people or not. He says he cannot see what I am driving at—what possible difference can pain caused to others or the absence of it make to the desirability of obtaining pleasure in the way that he seeks to obtain it? I ask him what it is that gives him pleasure in this particular activity. He replies that he likes driving pins into resilient bodies. I ask whether he would derive equal pleasure from driving pins into, say, tennis balls. He says that he would, that what he drives his pins into, human beings or tennis balls, makes little difference to him—the pleasure is similar, and he is quite prepared to have tennis balls substituted, if that is what I want; he cannot understand my strange concern—what possible difference can it make whether his pins perforate living men or tennis balls? At this point, I begin to suspect that he is in some way deranged. I do not say (with Hume), "Here is a man with a very different scale of moral values from my own. Values are not susceptible to argument. I can disagree but not reason with him," as I should be inclined to say of a man who believes in hara-kiri or genocide. I rather incline to the belief that the pin-pusher who is puzzled by my questions is to be classified with homicidal lunatics and should be confined in an asylum and not in an ordinary prison.

I do this because a man who cannot see that the suffering of pain is an issue of major importance in human life—that it matters at all—who cannot see why anyone should wish to know—still less mind—whether pain is caused or not, provided he does not suffer it himself, is virtually beyond the reach of communication from the world occupied by me and my fellow men. His whole pattern of experience is remote from mine; communication is as unattainable as it is with a man who thinks that he is Julius Caesar or that he is dead or that he is a doorknob, like the characters in the stories of E. T. A. Hoffman. This seems to me to show that recognition of some values—however general and however few—enter into the normal definition of what constitutes a sane human being. We may find that these ends do not remain constant if we look far enough in time and space; yet this does not alter the fact that beings totally lacking such ends can scarcely be described as human; still less as rational. In this sense, then, pursuit of, or failure to pursue, certain ends can be regarded as evidence of—and in extreme cases part of the definition of—irrationality. Although in general I agree with Professor Oppenheim, if my example is valid, it is incompatible with the general proposition which I take to be the basis of his view of the relation of facts to ends, descriptive judgments to those of values; it would demand a radical modification of this view. I do not, of course, wish to claim any originality for my position (which owes as much to Aristotle as to Kant), only validity.

16

SOME LIMITATIONS ON RATIONALITY:
A COMMENT

CHARLES E. LINDBLOM

Suppose we take very seriously Mr. Kaplan's belief that in political affairs we are not rational if we pursue values not worth pursuing. To be rational we must judge not only means but the relative worth of ends. (Note that he does not say "postulate" or "assume" the relative worth of values; he says "judge.") Although we will disagree among ourselves on how ends can be judged, will we not agree that, if they can be judged or evaluated at all, it will not be in isolation from each other? And whether the relations among values are hierarchical or not, they are exceedingly complex, so much so that the pursuit of judgments on values will, many would argue, require a thoroughgoing, comprehensive attempt at comprehension of the social or political world as a whole and of the relations among its parts. One's judgment of the worth relative to other values, say, of more equality in income distribution would depend on a searching and complex investigation of how this end relates to a multitude of other ends and means.

If such an examination of social interrelations, especially the relations among possible ends, is required for rationality in political life, then Mr. Kaplan's paper might be regarded as having misjudged the character of a successful attack on the limitations on rationality against which we contend. For political rationality requires, by the line of argument just taken, and by his excerpt from Mill, not so much an extension of the brave new techniques that Mr. Kaplan applauds but a comprehensive political philosophy no less daring in scope than that of Plato or Hobbes. Without employing such a philosophy, one cannot judge any *political* decision to be rational. Moreover, some would be driven to conclude, by the line of argument taken, that we would also need a comprehensively competent social science in order to establish the empirical relations among parts of the political or social whole.

I do not assert that anything I have said is true; I am merely examining the implications of Mr. Kaplan's assertion of the need to evaluate ends if we are to achieve rationality.

By the line of argument taken, Mr. Kaplan would also appear to have overestimated the significance of what he calls contemporary "advances in the exact formulation and analysis of what constitutes rational behavior," which, he ventures to say, are greater in our lifetimes than in the whole of history. For if rationality requires that we evaluate ends and not merely means, where can one find in contemporary philosophy and social science an insight so rich in implication for the evaluation of ends as the Greek distinction between natural and conventional man or any formulation or analysis of relations among ends as rigorous as Hobbes's? The contemporary "advances" of which Professor Kaplan speaks are small innovations in the study of rationality made by scholars who have largely turned their backs on the problem of evaluating ends. He identifies many of the problems they leave untouched; I would go even further.

In contemporary work that commands Mr. Kaplan's enthusiasm, for example, values have become preferences or utilities, as though the problem of evaluation of ends that Kaplan himself identifies could be washed away by taking degree of want satisfaction in some superficial sense as an index of the relative value of alternative ends. To be sure, the preferences or utilities that figure in much contemporary analysis can be—it is logically possible—the preferences or utilities of thoughtful persons who have undertaken the comprehensive social analysis that I have argued is called for by Kaplan's assertion that values need evaluating. But contemporary analysis says nothing about how such a thoughtful person might work his way to a preference scale. Thus the introduction of preference scales, utility functions, pay-off matrixes, and social-welfare functions into the analysis of rational behavior constitutes methodological innovations that only tidy up otherwise often less precise discussion (though even on this score they are not more precise than the best of earlier work); their introduction has not been the engine of any new fundamental insight into the problem of evaluating ends.

The style and thrust of the kind of contemporary analysis that Kaplan praises is perhaps worth illustrating by a specific example of it from economics, to which he refers: Arrow's excellent analysis of the difficulties of aggregating individual preferences into a collective preference. Arrow showed with admirable rigor that some of the simplest, most plausible conditions we might agree to impose with respect to how individual preferences are to be aggregated into a collective preference turn out to contradict each other. I have heard a social scientist at a professional meeting say that if we could solve the Arrow problem—specifically, that is, find a way to reconcile the five conflicting Arrow conditions—we would have solved the aggregation problem! What in fact would be the consequence of overcoming or bypassing the problem that Arrow identified? It would be a return to all the problems of aggregation of individual values that have always been on the agenda of social science and philosophy. For to solve Arrow's problem is merely to resolve certain elementary conflicts in value whose resolution leaves untouched all the traditional conflicts.

I can elaborate the point—and perhaps clarify it—by calling attention to the relation between the "aggregation problem" and the problem of distributive ethics. Contemporary analysis appears to strip the age-old problem of distributive ethics of its most troublesome aspects by reducing it to what, under the name of the "aggregation problem," appears to be a clean scientific problem of somehow adding things together. But the new name works no magic. To aggregate individual values, whether considered to be preferences or not, into a collective value or choice is to attack all the old problems of distributive ethics, to which the contributions of contemporary analysis are, though not trivial, minor. (Arrow's conditions, he himself well knows, are ethical propositions.) Moreover, because values are in fact culturally aggregated, the problem of "aggregation" is in fact a "formation" problem to which contemporary analysis is insensitive.

I have been arguing that Mr. Kaplan's own position on the need to evaluate ends calls for a political philosophy in which all important ends are related to all other important ends with which they interact significantly, rather than for an extension of the techniques he praises. What if such a political philosophy is beyond our capacities to construct? Or if constructed by any one man remains unhappily idiosyncratic? Are political decisions then to be surrendered to the irrational? Or to old-fashioned and conventional commonsense rationality? Is there no alternative?

I think there is. There are substantial possibilities for raising the level of rationality in political systems that depend neither on new advances in political philosophy nor on the new techniques for calculation and simple decision-making. They take the form of specific calculated adaptations to the enormous discrepancy between man's cognitive faculties, even when extended by electronic computation and other helpful devices, and the complexity of the problems that he must attack. They do not promise rationality, but they raise its level.

Faced with a problem in evaluation that exceeds his capacities, a would-be rational decision-maker can go in either of two ways: He can, like Major, the horse in Orwell's *Animal Farm*, resolve to work harder. Or he can try to develop strategies that adapt to his difficulties and make the most of his capacities by respecting limits on rationality. In its conventional endorsement of clarification of values when they will nevertheless remain obscure, of systematic canvassing of alternative means, when alternatives are countless, and of exhaustive tracking of consequences, when consequences go on forever, conventional decision theory displays the mentality of Orwell's horse.

Some obvious strategic adaptations are these, especially interesting because they violate the canons of most contemporary theory of rational choice: In collective decision-making, do not try to clarify values if the parties concerned can agree on policies, as they often can, despite their disagreement on values. Or: Neglect those consequences of possible decisions for which there exist watchdogs elsewhere in the society who will probably attend to the neglect. Or: Cut off the analysis of consequences at any point at which you yourself can probably at a next step in a sequence of decisions attend to them if unfavorable.

It is in the extension of such a list to include less obvious and more complicated adaptations that we can perhaps best push back limits on political rationality. And there will be at least two noteworthy features of such a list already apparent from the preceding. The first is—and here I pick up a point from Mr. Kaplan's paper— that what can be listed as a rational adaptation to difficulties of complex decision-making will depend on the social context of decisions. Theories of decision-making that continue, as most do, to examine the rationality of forms of decision-making without regard for the relation of one decision-maker to another (except for the obvious case of the superior-subordinate relationship in a hierarchy) are impoverished. The second is that what can be listed as a rational adaptation depends on the position of a decision in a sequence. To move the preoccupation of decision theorists from the decision to the sequence of decisions, as it has been moved in statistical decision theory but not generally, is to enrich theory and to discover new possibilities for rationality.

I have been doing some work to extend such a list of strategies, and there is scattered interest in it in the social sciences. The work has at least the merit of restoring distinctly political elements to the study of rationality.